POLICING INDIGENOUS MOVEMENTS

POLICING INDIGENOUS MOVEMENTS

DISSENT AND THE SECURITY STATE

**ANDREW CROSBY
AND JEFFREY MONAGHAN**

FERNWOOD PUBLISHING
HALIFAX & WINNIPEG

Editing: Fazeela Jiwa
Cover design: Tania Craan
Printed and bound in Canada

Published by Fernwood Publishing
32 Oceanvista Lane, Black Point, Nova Scotia, B0J 1B0
and 748 Broadway Avenue, Winnipeg, Manitoba, R3G 0X3
www.fernwoodpublishing.ca

Fernwood Publishing Company Limited gratefully acknowledges the
financial support of the Government of Canada, the Manitoba Department
of Culture, Heritage and Tourism under the Manitoba Publishers Marketing
Assistance Program and the Province of Manitoba, through the Book
Publishing Tax Credit, for our publishing program. We are pleased to work
in partnership with the Province of Nova Scotia to develop and promote
our creative industries for the benefit of all Nova Scotians. We acknowledge
the support of the Canada Council for the Arts, which last year invested
$153 million to bring the arts to Canadians throughout the country.

Library and Archives Canada Cataloguing in Publication

Crosby, Andrew, author
Policing indigenous movements : dissent and the security state / Andrew
Crosby and Jeffrey Monaghan.

Includes bibliographical references and index.
Issued in print and electronic formats.
ISBN 978-1-77363-012-0 (softcover).—ISBN 978-1-77363-045-8 (EPUB).—
ISBN 978-1-77363-046-5 (Kindle)

1. Social movements—Canada—Case studies. 2. Native peoples—Canada—
Politics and government—Case studies. 3. Police—Canada—Case studies.
I. Monaghan, Jeffrey, 1980-, author II. Title.

HN110.S62C76 2018   303.48'40971   C2017-907869-0

CONTENTS

ACRONYMS

ABL	Algonquins of Barriere Lake
ADM NSOPS	Assistant Deputy Ministers' National Security Operations Committee
ADM	Assistant Deputy Minister
AFN	Assembly of First Nations
AFNCNB	Assembly of First Nations Chiefs in New Brunswick
AIG	Aboriginal Intelligence Group
AIM	American Indian Movement
ALEA	Assistance to Law Enforcement Agencies
APTN	Aboriginal Peoples Television Network
ATA	*Anti-terrorism Act*
ATIA	*Access to Information Act*
BCCLA	British Columbia Civil Liberties Association
CAF	Canadian Armed Forces
CAPP	Canadian Association of Petroleum Producers
CBSA	Canadian Border Services Agency
CSC	Correctional Services Canada
CSEC	Communications Security Establishment Canada
CFNCIU	Canadian Forces National Counter-Intelligence Unit
CI	Critical Infrastructure
CICI	Critical Infrastructure Criminal Intelligence
CIIT	Critical Infrastructure Intelligence Team
CJOC	Canadian Joint Operations Command
CN	Canadian National Railroad
CSIS	Canadian Security Intelligence Service
CTIO	Counter Terrorism Information Officer
DFO	Department of Fisheries and Oceans
DND	Department of National Defence
EFI	Energy Framework Initiative

FOI	Freedom of Information
FN	First Nations
FNCFCS	First Nations Child and Family Caring Society of Canada
FNSB	First Nations Strategic Bulletin
FNFTA	*First Nations Financial Transparency Act*
GC	Government of Canada
GOC	Government Operations Centre
INAC	Indigenous and Northern Affairs Canada (formerly Indian Affairs)
INSET	Integrated National Security Enforcement Team
INM	Idle No More
ISL	Industrial Security Ltd.
ITAC	Integrated Terrorism Assessment Centre
JIG	Joint Intelligence Group
JRP	Joint Review Panel
NEB	National Energy Board
NDA	National Day of Action
NICC	National Intelligence Coordination Centre
NRCan	Natural Resources Canada
NSES	National Security Enforcement Section
NWMP	North West Mounted Police
OPP	Ontario Provincial Police
OSINT	Open-source Intelligence
RCMP	Royal Canadian Mounted Police
OPIRG	Ontario Public Interest Research Group
PCO	Privy Council Office
PMO	Prime Minister's Office
PROS	Police Reporting and Occurrence System
PSC	Public Safety Canada
RCAP	Royal Commission on Aboriginal Peoples
SIR	Suspicious Incident Report
SOI	Suspect of Interest
SCISA	*Security of Canada Information Sharing Act*
SPROS	Secure Police Reporting and Occurrence System
SQ	Sûreté du Québec
SWN	Southwestern Energy Company
UNDRIP	United Nations Declaration on the Rights of Indigenous Peoples
VPIRG	Vancouver Public Interest Research Group

ACKNOWLEDGMENTS

Writing this book came at a time of widespread Indigenous resurgence against settler colonialism in Canada. We are deeply indebted to the communities and movements subjected to the pervasive surveillance and violent policing that we detail in this book. Your determination inspires this project and our desire to challenge the injustices of settler colonialism.

We have many individuals to thank for their support and contributions to the work we do. We relied on a lot of previous research for this book, and we would like to thank the many other researchers and activists who have been uncovering and challenging various aspects of settler colonialism and its various tentacles of policing. Our book would not be possible without the tireless and determined work of others. Thank you to all of those that have contributed to these important efforts and those whose work we've used to educate ourselves and further our analysis. In preparing this book, a number of people have assisted — both directly and indirectly — in the final outcome. In no particular order, we'd like to thank Kevin Walby, Ajay Parasram, Shiri Pasternak, Miles Howe, Tia Dafnos, Martin Lukacs, Tim Groves, Tim McSorley, and Jorge Barrera.

This book came about through work with different projects, our respective engagements, and years of talking shit during band practice. We have lots of people who have provided encouragement and support. You, of course, know who you are — thank you very much!

Andy: Thank you to all who have remained close, offered advice, and showed support over the years, including Ajay, Fuz, Eddy, Adam, Jen, Guillaume, Birch, and Steve, among many others. I would also like to thank the numerous independent journalists and editors, especially at the *Leveller* newspaper and the *Media Co-op*, who have helped shape me as a writer and thinker. In particular, I would like to acknowledge the late and very much missed Mat Nelson. I would also like to acknowledge the tireless efforts of those at OPIRG who have never ceased to inspire and amaze me. I would further like to acknowledge those in the local social justice–oriented punk rock scene. I would also like to thank certain teachers over the years who helped shape my politics and focus into where it lies today — Marc Doucet, Labeeb Bsoul, Simon Dalby, William Walters, Abdulghany Mohamed, and Jai Sen, to name a few. Finally, I would like to acknowledge the support of my loving family and the inspiration of my adoring children.

Jeff: Thank you to many of my friends and colleagues at Carleton/ UOttawa who have contributed in various ways to this work, including Nic Carrier, Evelyn Maeder, Lara Karaian, Maddy Santos, Dale Spencer, Justin Piché, Dawn Moore, Aaron Doyle, Kelly Fritsch, Valerie Steeves, David Moffette, and Mike Mopas. I would also like to thank David Murakami Wood, Jennifer Matsunaga, Kevin Walby, David Lyon, Adam Molnar, Lucas Melgaço, Özgün Topak, Emily Van der Meulen, Fahad Ahmad, Abigail Curlew, Etienne Turpin, DT Cochrane, Gordie and Karen, Pete V, Yavar Hameed, and the many others who have provided inspiration and support along the way. Special thanks to my family/ies, especially Ange and the kiddos.

Thank you to Fernwood Publishing and its dedicated staff for believing in this project, for giving us the opportunity to present this research. In particular, Candida Hadley for her guidance and wisdom throughout the editing phases, as well as Fazeela Jiwa for her keen-eyed copy editing and indexing. The support of other staff during this project has been invaluable and we are very grateful to the entire Fernwood team for believing in this project, including Beverley Rach and Curran Faris, among others who we might not have dealt with directly but whose work is very much appreciated. We would like to extend our appreciation to the two anonymous reviewers who provided thoughtful and thorough comments and suggested revisions. Through the editorial direction from Candida and the encouragements from reviewers, the book has been significantly improved. Thanks to Neal Shannacappo for his artwork for the website and Abigail Curlew for helping with organizing our ATI data on the website.

We hope the book is something that is both educational and provocative. Many of us engaged in social justice movements have long been accustomed to the proliferation of everyday surveillance practices, as well as the more covert and insidious surveillance that has targeted movements in Canada. This book details the driving forces, many of the mechanics, and some specific cases with the aim of shedding light on these contemporary practices, the implications of which have yet to be fully revealed. While we provide many specifics through the documents of police and government agencies, what we narrate here is only a small window into the police's current efforts to demobilize movements that challenge settler colonialism and extractive capitalism. The expansion of surveillance against social movements has progressed in highly opaque and secretive ways. We hope our efforts to empiricize these developments contributes toward broader (and necessary) efforts that challenge policing and security powers.

PROJECT SITKA, POLICING, AND THE SETTLER COLONIAL PRESENT

"Serious criminality associated to large public order events with national implications was designated a RCMP National Tactical Intelligence Priority in January 2014," reads the introductory sentence of a secret Royal Canadian Mounted Police (RCMP) report on Indigenous activism (CSIS 2016-47: 16).[1] Uncovered in the process of researching this book, the report was the final product of an extensive, quasi-criminal investigation known as Project SITKA. SITKA demonstrates the extensive policing and surveillance powers — or as the RCMP say, the "national tactical intelligence priority" — directed toward a "small 'core' group of subjects" associated with "Aboriginal public order events" who oppose extractive capitalism or assert a politics of self-determination (ibid.: 15–16). According to the RCMP report, the investigation was launched as a response to a resurgence in Indigenous activism around prominent issues including "the 'Idle No More' movement, land claims settlements, missing and murdered Aboriginal women, and natural resource development" (ibid.: 14). "Overall, 313 individuals were identified and reviewed within the scope of the project" reads the executive summary, and "of these, 89 were found to meet the criteria for criminality associated to public order events" (ibid.: 15). From January 2014 to January 2015, the RCMP's National Intelligence Coordination Centre (NICC) gathered intelligence on these 313 prominent Indigenous rights activists, creating profiles and assessments about their associations and their participation in various protests, as well as an evaluation criteria that assessed the level of threat associated with each individual on the watchlist.

Somewhat reminiscent of PROFUNC surveillance programs during the Cold War that aimed to weed out the prominent functionaries of the Communist Party, the RCMP's year-long secret investigation has been assisted by the rise of databanks and contemporary surveillance capacities that allowed police to compile vast amounts of intelligence on activists who challenge settler colonialism. To assemble a list of prominent Indigenous functionaries, the RCMP made a "request for assistance" to other RCMP divisions and "law enforcement partners." At a minimum, this included consultations with "all" RCMP divisions, provincial police in Ontario and Quebec, as well as unidentified "law enforcement databank holdings" (ibid.). SITKA officers received an array of information regarding Indigenous-related events and activities from various partner agencies. The investigation went far beyond issues of crime and explicitly requested surveillance data on "protest event types" related to "land claims issues," Idle No More, "anti-capitalist protest" such as those against the G8 and G20 meetings, and the Occupy movement "particularly in British Columbia, Ontario and Halifax" (ibid.: 20). Other activities under surveillance included "Demands for Missing and Murdered Women Inquiry — particularly [in] Saskatchewan, Manitoba, and Ontario" and events "such as speaking tours, disruption of political proceedings, and direct action training camps" (ibid.). With an ability to access surveillance intelligence in police databanks on a wide number of issues, the report says that SITKA gathered information from as far back as 2010. This staggering affront to activities protected by the *Canadian Charter of Rights and Freedoms* is eclipsed by Project SITKA's final report that claims to have evaluated people based on "their *background, motivation and rhetoric*" (ibid.: 15, emphasis added). With near-absolute impunity, the RCMP engaged in these investigative activities with no notification to those under investigation, no venue to cross-examine or challenge the intelligence being used against these individuals, and no indication of when a "suspect" would cease to be under this quasi-criminal investigation.

To predict whether these individuals presented future threats of "serious criminality," Project SITKA created protester profiles for 313 individuals and then evaluated them based on a methodology of "volatile, disruptive, or passive" developed by RCMP psychologist Dr. Eli Sopow (ibid.: 17). Based on these secret investigations, the RCMP officers involved with Project SITKA claimed that 89 of the 313 individuals investigated were considered threats that "meet the criteria for criminality associated to public order events" while simultaneously claiming that they found "no intentional criminal nexus" and "no known evidence that these individuals pose a direct threat to critical infrastructure" (ibid.: 15). Despite these confounding and contradictory claims, eighty-nine individuals were classified as high-risk potential threats. Those deemed as high-risk threats were identified as "core subjects" whose "primary common interest ... was natural resource development — particularly pipelines, shale gas, and mining" (ibid.: 22). Over half were associated with the Mi'kmaw[2] resistance at Elsipogtog — thirty-five from New Brunswick and ten from Nova Scotia. SITKA documents reveal that the "protester profiles" for the eighty-nine were subsequently "made available to front-line officers, divisional analysts and law enforcement partners through the Automated Criminal Intelligence Information System" and the Police Reporting and Occurrence System (PROS) database (ibid.: 17–18). It remains unclear how widely available these profiles are across police agencies or how long these "investigations" remain open. From the SITKA files, it appears that police and security agencies will retain these surveillance catalogues to share among a number of agencies, departments, and industry "partners," circulating volumes of personal information in police databanks *indefinitely*.

SITKA illustrates a new dynamic of policing that we call "the security state": a sprawling array of national security and policing agencies, industry and corporate partners, and public bureaucracies that are increasingly integrated through surveillance, intelligence databanks and institutional partnerships in efforts to pre-empt or disrupt potential threats in the "war on terror." Practices of the security state demonstrate how the "war on terror" has expanded the focus of policing efforts beyond any clear definition of terrorist groups or activities that aim to inflict violence against unknowing civilian populations. Instead, national security policing — and the expanding domain of the security state — harness their resources and capacities toward domestic groups. While a number of groups are targeted in a discriminatory way by the security state, the extensive policing of Indigenous Peoples or groups in the "war on terror" has been rationalized by the development of categories and labels such as "Aboriginal extremism" and "critical infrastructure" specifically to criminalize Indigenous movements that challenge extractive capitalism, demand self-determination, or contest federal and provincial claims to Indigenous lands.

While it is not new that security agencies would classify people involved in these Indigenous movements as criminals, extremists, or troublemakers, the context of the "war on terror" has given national security, policing, and social control agencies a host of resources and powers to intensify their efforts against Indigenous communities. Policing efforts like SITKA are illustrative of a global trend toward data-driven security and surveillance, but the practices that we detail in this book are less about a "new profiling" based on algorithms and new calculations of risk (Leese 2014; see also Amoore 2011) and more about the ability to more effectively catalogue Indigenous activists that threaten Canadian material and immaterial interests. As an extension of settler colonialism, these practices use the labels and powers of national security to suppress efforts that challenge colonial control of land and resources. In doing so, the security state is not merely an objective or neutral policing entity but an active supporter of extractive capitalism and settler colonialism.

This book provides extensive, first-hand accounts of how the security state has developed a prolific surveillance regime that targets Indigenous Peoples as national security threats. We use first-hand accounts because we refer extensively to the records of police and security agencies to narrate this book. Compiled using thousands of declassified documents from dozens of government departments and hundreds of *Access to Information Act* (ATIA) requests, we believe this book is one of the most comprehensive accounts of contemporary government surveillance. Moreover, our aim is to report on these widespread and dubious surveillance practices as a vivid demonstration of how the security state actively delegitimizes and suppresses Indigenous movements that challenge settler colonialism. We examine four prominent case studies: the long-standing conflict involving the Algonquins of Barriere Lake, the struggle against the Northern Gateway Pipelines, the Idle No More movement, and the anti-fracking protests surrounding the Elsipogtog First Nation. Other researchers have shown how Indigenous movements have been policed through the discourses and resources of the "war on terror" (Dafnos et al. 2016; Monaghan and Walby 2017; Proulx 2014), and we extend this analysis by showing how the security state has monitored and aimed to suppress the Indigenous movements we have chosen for our illustrative case studies.

While the security state's frames of national security or critical infrastructure are new discursive tactics of criminalizing Indigenous movements, we stress that these contemporary practices are part of a continuum of long-standing settler colonial efforts to target Indigenous movements. We view the security state as an extension or a new iteration of ways in which policing and social control practices have disrupted Indigenous activism, specifically types of activism that challenge Canadian sovereignty over land and resources. Acts that assert self-determination and the treaty rights of Indigenous communities to control land and resources have always threatened settler colonialism and solicited violent reactions from Canadian authorities. This is particularly true when self-determination is used to disrupt the extraction of resources and wealth from Indigenous lands.

SITKA itself emerged explicitly as an effort to prepare a response to another set of mobilizations such as protests against tar sands pipelines, the resistance to shale gas exploration around Elsipogtog, or the Idle No More movement. These policing efforts are a response to growing momentum in the politics of Indigenous self-determination, meaningful efforts at settler solidarities, and the abilities to disrupt the status quo. As agencies that serve to protect the status quo of settler colonialism, they are also responding to the need to protect the wealth accumulated through the exploitation of Indigenous lands. Speaking to how Idle No More represents both a link to histories of Indigenous resistance and possibilities of future collective action, the Kino-nda-niimi Collective (2014: 21) have suggested that the Native Winter of 2012–13

> will be remembered — alongside the maelstrom of treaty-making, political waves like the Red Power Movement and the 1969–70 mobilization against the White Paper, and resistance movements at Oka, Gustefson's Lake, Ipperwash, Burnt Church, Goose Bay, Kanonhstaton, and so on — as one of the most important moments in our collective history.

Momentum from these Indigenous movements have presented important opportunities to advance a politics of decolonization, yet these impressive movements have also provoked a counter-movement of the security state and extractive corporations that aim to disrupt our collective abilities to challenge settler colonialism. In the past, assertions of Indigenous sovereignty and efforts to disrupt settler colonialism have also been treated as criminal threats (A. Simpson 2014: 115–46). This book provides a contemporary account of how an extensive apparatus of settler colonial actors, from police to bureaucrats to the forestry and pipeline companies extracting from Indigenous land, engage in processes of surveillance and social control with the aim of safeguarding the settler colonial present.[3]

THE SETTLER COLONIAL PRESENT

To properly contextualize the policing of Indigenous movements, our analysis starts with an emphasis that Canada has never decolonized, and it cannot be regarded as a post-colonial society. In Canada, the notion that 1867 marks a new national beginning of a post-colonial society following quasi-independence from British rule serves as the source of a deeply held belief that Canada is free from the "burden" of colonial history. Evoking what Sunera Thobani (2007) calls "exaltations" of Canadian values, Prime Minister Justin Trudeau echoed this belief when he told a New York audience that Canada was "without some of the baggage ... [of] colonial pasts or perceptions of American imperialism" (Fountain 2016). Similarly, former prime minister Stephen Harper claimed — again to an international audience — that Canada had "no history of colonialism" (Ljunggren 2009). These exaltations recirculate the notion that Canada is a post-colonial society by reaffirming the commonplace belief that colonialism is a thing of the past. There is a strong repertoire of Indigenous histories, scholars, and activist interventions that confront these popular myths of Canadian post-coloniality.[4] Our work is indebted to these efforts at confronting Canadian expressions of post-colonialism, and we focus on how contemporary policing and surveillance are integral components in the maintenance of settler colonialism.

A critique of the security state is especially relevant on two accounts. First, because of the popular historical imaginary of what Constance Backhouse (1999) has called Canada's "mythology of racelessness" or what Eva Mackey (2002) calls the "benevolent Mountie myth" or what Jeff Benvenuto, Andrew Woolford, and Alexander Laban Hinton (2015) refer to as the "Canadian myth of peaceful colonization." Popularized mythologies of Canadian colonialism and especially the role of the North West Mounted Police (NWMP) have generally relied upon smug contrasting with the brutalities of U.S. Indian policies to valourize a more humane history of colonialism.[5] These hagiographies are especially potent in the histories of the NWMP (later the RCMP), as well as the Indian Affairs bureaucracies that aimed to civilize Indigenous populations. Critical retellings of these dominant histories have been recently popularized thanks to the activism surrounding residential school practices, yet historical beliefs that Canadian Indian policy was one of benevolence and assistance still persist.[6] Claiming to assist with crime, poverty, or development remain dominant techniques used by contemporary colonial agencies to justify targeting Indigenous movements. We highlight continuities in these logics that animate police activities against Indigenous Peoples, a key aspect of our settler colonial present.

The second aspect of our research's contemporary relevance relates to the powers of Canada's security state. The policing and surveillance practices that we detail are pervasive and have become highly normalized. Mass accumulation of intelligence and cataloguing of data within police and security databanks, and the sharing of this information with policing agencies and industry, has become an integral yet routine and mundane function of the daily work of the security state. These practices are highly acute when directed against Indigenous movements, and little — if any — oversight exists. Meanwhile, complaint systems are virtually non-existent (or ineffective). As an aggregate, the security state has become a large network of bureaucracies, with vast mandates and resources, who engage in the widespread monitoring and policing of Indigenous populations — as settler colonial an enterprise as there has ever been.

Our book is a critical illustration of these settler colonial security practices. As settlers supportive of decolonization struggles, we do not comment on tactics or strategies of Indigenous movements. Our attention is directed toward the institutions of settler colonialism, specifically the policing and security apparatus that remains so integral to maintaining these systems of exploitation. We do offer some comments in the book's conclusion regarding the challenges of confronting settler colonialism; however, our primary objective is to provide a detailed illustration of how agencies of the security state has normalized these pervasive practices of policing Indigenous movements. We also provide a critical framework for interpreting these contemporary illustrations of colonial rule in a broader context of land theft, economic development, and post-colonial imaginaries that consolidate and manage the social privileges of our settler colonial society.

In using the term settler colonialism to position our analysis and argumentation, we borrow from recent conceptualizations that highlight distinctions between colonialism and settler colonialism.[7] This distinction rests on how colonial powers approach the management of Indigenous Others, with an emphasis on how colonial regimes extract wealth and manage majority populations while settler colonialism is more focused on settlement and the creation of a new settler-majoritarian polity. Glen Coulthard (2014a: 7) has argued that the settler colonial relationship is a relationship of domination maintained to "facilitate dispossession of Indigenous peoples of the lands *and* self-determining authority" (emphasis added). Canadian settler colonialism has employed tactics of reform and management, but this happens within an unconditional assertion of Canadian sovereignty and the production of a Canadian post-colonial social imaginary that buries the lifeworlds of Indigenous self-determination and freedom under Canadian laws, customs, and identities.

In underlining how Canada is better understood as a settler colonial regime, we stress a distinction where modes of colonial domination are primarily structured around two intertwined rationalities: 1) the theft and acquisition of land (as opposed to reforming Indigenous Peoples as labourers); and 2) the production of a new, post-colonial subjectivity of Canadians (as opposed to reforming Indigenous subjectivities within a hierarchy of empire). In combining the theft of land with the production of a collective post-colonial identity among the non-Indigenous majority population, land theft and assimilation policies are rationalized through layered appeals to democratic rights, law and order, the assistance of undeveloped or uncivilized non-capitalistic Natives, as well as more explicit tenets of white supremacy. We have elsewhere focused on the liberal ideas of "assistance" and crime control in developing the concept of settler governmentality (see Crosby and Monaghan 2016, 2012; Monaghan 2013b), yet the key component for understanding the functioning of settler colonial regimes of governance is that they do not require Indigenous co-operation. In fact, the opposite is true: settler colonialism uses a diversity of mechanisms that aim to fully replace Indigenous societies with a new post-colonial order.

By using mechanisms of violence as well as reward systems of less-violent coercion, settler colonial practices operate according to rationalities that seek to eliminate self-determining Indigenous lifeworlds upon which Canada is built. In what Derek Gregory (2004: 7) has called the "elusive fiction" of post-colonialism, the logic of settler colonialism produces a post-colonial society (Canada) through the settlement of land and the displacement of Indigenous Peoples, the subsequent management of Indigenous populations, the fortification of legal regimes of sovereignty on top of Indigenous societies, and the myriad techniques that fall under what Patrick Wolfe (2006, 1999) has characterized as a "logic of elimination." Wolfe's notion of the logic of elimination has been highly influential, marking a point of departure in contrasting colonialism and settler colonialism as well as in discussions about the distinct possibilities for the politics of decolonization in settler colonial societies like Canada (Park 2015). Centrally, Wolfe argues that settler colonialism possesses an eliminatory logic that can be characterized as genocide. A conclusion taken up recently by the Truth and Reconciliation Commission and a number of scholarly texts (Patzer 2014; Sinclair 2017; Woolford 2015), the genocidal rationality of settler colonialism is, according to Wolfe, based on a desire to accumulate territory. Wolfe (2006: 388) writes that "territoriality is settler colonialism's specific, irreducible element," where settler societies "[erect] a new colonial society on the expropriated land base — as I put it, settler colonizers come to stay: invasion is a structure not an event." Challenging the notion of genocidal practices as events, which can be narrated in the grammar of criminal law, Wolfe has emphasized how settler colonialism reshapes structural relations to make elimination normal, benign, and largely uncontroversial in the eyes of the majority population. Even if well meaning, as the residential schools have been described, eliminatory practices are embedded into social logics of settler society.

Focusing on the role of the security state in the broader regime of settler colonialism, we demonstrate how policing practices treat assertions of traditional Indigeneity as *abnormal*. Framed this way, any challenge to settler colonial authority is marked as potential violence against the post-colonial order. The result is that these expressions of Indigenous autonomy and self-determination are coded as threats to be neutralized and eliminated from the space of Canadian post-colonial society. As a rationality of majoritarian rule, policing practices that target potential insecurity seek to eliminate these Indigenous expressions of autonomy, independence, or collective identity that are at odds with the Canadian post-colonial imaginary. Elimination thus serves a dual purpose: to suppress challenges to Canadian sovereignty and to facilitate access to the tremendous wealth and prosperity that can be accumulated through the theft of land.

Indigenous politics that confront the vision and practices of the Crown's assertion of sovereignty are translated by agencies of the security state as indications of non-acquiescence to the values of prosperity inherent in the settler colonial project. Indigenous assertions of autonomy are then interpreted as a challenge to the authority of the Canadian government. In addition to challenging the imagined post-colonial society, these expressions of Indigeneity disrupt Canadian political-economic dependenc the exploitation of Indigenous lands and resources. Craig Proulx (2014: 83) has noted that Canadian police have a long tradition of targeting movements that challenge settler colonial control over land, capitalism, and governance because "non-indigenous peoples fear the economic and political costs of activism, protests and blockades," which then lends to the representation of people involved in Indigenous movements as "potential insurgents, terrorists and criminals threatening the security of the Canadian state." Canada's history as a settler colonial society is founded on rationalizations that translate these expressions of Indigeneity into forms of "crime" in an effort to make an Indigenous politics of self-determination unspeakable. In casting Indigenous autonomy as an abnormal politics, a criminal politics, a politics that threatens the Canadian extractive economy, and as a politics that presents an existential threat to Canada as a post-colonial "home and Native land," policing institutions have served as the ground-level enforcement of settler colonialism's project of eliminating Indigenous sovereignties.

In the efforts to police and eliminate Indigenous self-determination, settler society often fixates on the notions of "tradition" or "culture" that demarcate aspects of Indigenous freedom from the imposition of settler sovereignty. In some instances during our discussions of police and security efforts against Indigenous movements, we are reporting on how settler society represents these notions of Indigeneity. We do not want to suggest that a specific Indigenous culture exists, that it is homogenous, or that particular cultures do not change over time. We aim to underline that what is most commonly narrated as "traditional Indigenous culture" is itself a knowledge production of settler society — often a marker of danger, crime, or threat to settler order. These notions of culture or tradition are not "real" in the sense of reflecting the lived experiences of Indigenous communities, but they are real in the sense that they inform a cultural imaginary of settler society. In other words, we are not speaking about Indigenous societies — we are speaking about realities within settler society that view Indigeneity and assertions of Indigenous freedom as a threat to post-colonial authorities. Moreover, our effort is to underline how perceptions of Indigeneity are often framed through a primary mechanism of colonial power: the police.

THE SECURITY STATE AND THE "WAR ON TERROR"

Contemporary policing institutions have extended the history of settler colonial law enforcement within the context of the "war on terror." To illustrate the scope of contemporary policing, we use the term security state to capture the broad array of institutions engaged in settler colonial policing. Illustrating the integrated character of settler colonial governance, we show how many non-policing entities are engaged to maintain and do the work of security governance. While the convergence of multiple agencies under the banner of "security" does not exclusively impact Indigenous communities, there is a long history of controlling Indigenous communities through multiple arms of state agencies — often grounded in efforts to provide security, development, rights, or other impositions of colonial authority (Razack 2015; Shewell 2004; Woolford 2015). Given the history of settler assertions of security, the contemporary politics of the "war on terror" presents another layer in the use of security as a mechanism for policing Indigenous communities.

What is novel in the current policing of Indigenous movements is the infusion of national security resources and the dramatic extension of intelligence-led surveillance practices. We use the term security state to capture the current character of policing, which is comprised of what police agencies call "integrated" approaches that institutionalize the ways in which multiple agencies work collaboratively to pre-empt security threats. Called the "fusion centre" approach to security (Monahan 2010; Monaghan and Walby 2012), this includes public agencies as well as private corporations, and also refers to traditional policing and security agencies as well as social control agencies like Indian Affairs. Given the emphasis on pre-emptive policing, the security state is also networked through surveillance. As SITKA shows, surveillance information on activists can be stored in a myriad of databanks, which can be shared, recontextualized, and recirculated by numerous actors within the security state. These practices of widespread surveillance on social movements have been completely normalized among actors of the security state because of the centrality of protecting economic interests against supposed national security threats.

A number of other jurisdictions have moved toward "fusion centre" models of policing, and our examination of the Canadian security state shows how integrated practices of information sharing and surveillance have become a central organizing principle within the "war on terror." Our efforts are to show the Canadian character of this trend. In using the term security state, we do not refer to a singular entity but the fusion of varied governance entities that, despite the broad heterogeneity and competing interests of agents and institutions that comprise it, nonetheless operate in a unified and coordinated manner. Over the course of the case studies detailed in this book, readers will get a sense of the vastness of the Canadian security state. We suggest that the security state is best characterized as a top-loaded entity, where federal authorities have strong direction over its construction and management while provincial, territorial, and municipal agencies fit into lower (though also powerful) places in the hierarchy.

Our research deals primarily with the top elements of this hierarchy, beginning with the host of federal departments and agencies that have been fused through the growing network of security, surveillance, and information sharing. Central to this network are policing and security agencies like the RCMP, Canadian Security Intelligence Service (CSIS), and supporting bureaucracies like Justice Canada. We also highlight the role of Public Safety Canada (PSC) and their fusion centre known as the Government Operations Centre (GOC), which has emerged as a central hub for information sharing on social movements. Other policing agencies with important roles in the network are the Department of National Defence (DND) — who also operate an intelligence arm known as Communications Security Establishment Canada (CSEC) — and departments like Correctional Services Canada (CSC) and the Canadian Border Services Agency (CBSA), who have particularly active surveillance practices targeting Indigenous threats. Other departments and agencies detailed in this book include Transport Canada, who are fused through various "critical infrastructure" hubs, Natural Resources Canada (NRCan), the Privy Council Office (PCO), the Department of Fisheries and Oceans (DFO), as well as a litany of sub-agencies that have a high degree of autonomy under the larger departments. In total, a recent report from the Auditor General (2013) listed thirty-five departments and agencies that fund activities related to public security and anti-terrorism.

An additional and fundamental component of the security state's policing and surveillance of Indigenous Peoples is the Indian Affairs bureaucracy. Now broken into two departments of Indigenous Affairs (one called the Department of Crown–Indigenous Relations and Northern Affairs, and the other Indigenous Services), we continue to use the term Indian Affairs (or INAC) in this book to link its current iteration with the long history of the department that, until very recently, had maintained that name. As Indian Affairs features prominently in our narrative, it is worth noting how contemporary policing is shaped through its historical antecedents.

Scholars have detailed the exceptionalism that has characterized the surveillance of Indigenous Peoples in Canada (Comack 2012). Keith Smith (2009) has argued how Indian reserves have represented a system of segregation and surveillance that is unparalleled in the British Empire, with the possible exception of South Africa. Focusing on the settlement of the Prairies, he details the expansive network of surveillance coordinated by Indian Affairs and the NWMP. These settler colonists engaged in systematic observation, measurement, classification, and judgment of every aspect of Indigenous life. Far exceeding any aggregate of information in publicized census data, Smith (2009: 93–130) details the massive "tabular reports" created through this surveillance and how these practices produced representations of Indigeneity and post-colonial whiteness, ensuring that "the slightest deficiency, aberration, or stubborn endurance of 'Indianness' was singled out for further corrective action." Smith (2009: 20) writes,

> What appeared as the "Indian" was a collage of images that were often contradictory, but always inferior to Anglo-Canadians. The "Indian" was not mere fantasy, though, but an enduring political, economic, and social instrument. It was a device that bolstered the colonizers' images of themselves as benevolently superior while at the same time ensuring the advancement of their material interests.

INAC's historical framing of Indigenous inferiority juxtaposed with white settler superiority justified ongoing regimes of intervention and corrective measures under liberal notions of development. As a technology of rule, liberalism promotes notions of equality and inclusion, yet practices of settler colonialism have mobilized liberalism as an exclusionary force based on racialized hierarchies of progress and civilization. The extensiveness of the surveillance projects targeting Indigenous populations has served as the primary means of detecting and intervening in expressions of Indigenous autonomy or non-conformity with the settler colonial project.

An impressive repertoire of scholarship has detailed the magnitude of surveillance and policing of Indigenous populations as an aspect of settler colonialism. Our efforts are to detail contemporary surveillance practices that are entwined with these histories, specifically the ways in which the

"war on terror" has been mobilized to advance and further legitimize the
scope of policing Indigenous Peoples. Not only has the "war on terror"
produced a new lexicon of "extremism" for the security state to further
entrench the targeting of Indigenous Peoples, but it has also flooded these
security and policing agencies with new authorities and resources. Given
the proliferation of security-related resources, it is illustrative how little
public accounting has been published on the spending practices associated
with this securitarian turn. In fact, our research has found only two detailed
analyses of post-9/11 security spending: one from the non-profit Rideau
Institute (MacDonald 2011) and the other from the federal Auditor General
(2013). The Rideau Institute report, *Costs of 9/11*, is particularly instructive.
Providing inflation-adjusted figures, they calculate the increase in spending within security-related departments. Their analysis from 2000 to 2011
shows that spending on security increased by $92 billion (or $69 billion
when inflation is adjusted to 2011 values) based on spending projections
had budgets remained in line with pre-2001 patterns. Though the figures
compiled by the Rideau Institute include military spending — which
dramatically inflate the overall figures — they detail how bureaucracies
of the security state (our term) have tripled their budgets in a ten-year
period. This burgeoning of the security bureaucracy creates conditions
where security bureaucrats (or what Patryk Pawlak [2009] calls "securo-
crats") justify their funding by finding newer and newer sources of threat.

Major beneficiaries of the security funding bonanza have been public
police forces in Canada. By 2015, the total costs of policing in Canada have
approached $14 billion, up from less than $7 billion in 2000 (Mazowita and
Greenland 2015) and are likely to continue growing due to the entrenched
powers of police unions and the political officials who do little to confront
these interests. Meanwhile, the trend of accelerated police spending at the
federal level will continue, as the Liberal government announced $439
million in new security spending in their first budget (2015), which followed the passage of Bill C-51 in 2014 (the amended *Anti-terrorism Act*) by
the Harper Conservatives immediately before the 2015 election. Moreover,
despite making election promises to reduce powers given to security and
policing agencies and curtail Bill C-51 (as lacklustre as the promises were),
the Liberals are likely to follow the trend of granting more powers to
policing and security agencies while pursuing modest reforms that allow
a completely underfunded and under-mandated system of accountability
and oversight to continue.

As the "war on terror" has gradually extended over the past decade, a spatial shift in its operations has gradually redirected the primary focus of its operations, resources, and attention from overseas (Afghanistan, Iraq, Libya, Syria) to domestic populations. While Muslim residents are the primary targets of this surveillance, the discursive expansion of "extremism" and "radicalization" has also been directed toward non-Muslim groups and actors as a means of rationalizing increased domestic surveillance.[8] Given that we are living in what is increasingly a "surveillance society" that comprises layers of indiscriminate and systematic observation and classification practices (Bennett et al. 2014), the security state has expanded its practices of discriminate surveillance against those who are deemed suspicious. Much of this regularized surveillance takes place with no oversight or means of appeal. As we detail in this book, Indigenous movements are among the primary identities associated with "extremism"—although we also address how environmental groups have been lumped into the categories of extremism to rationalize routine surveillance.

Indigenous communities who challenge settler colonialism have always been labelled as treasonous outsiders, and the recent iterations of the "war on terror" have accelerated the practices of targeting Indigenous movements. In fact, the first known targets of a policing operation under the *Anti-terrorism Act* of 2001 was a joint RCMP–CSIS police raid against the British Columbia West Coast Warrior Society (Moore et al. 2015). Ostensibly the police were searching for weapons, and while no unauthorized weapons were found and no charges were laid, the two individuals targeted had participated in many years of Indigenous activism for organizations such as the Union of B.C. Indian Chiefs, United Native Nations, Native Youth Movement, Indigenous Sovereignty Network, and the West Coast Warrior Society (ibid.). Efforts to police Indigenous groups have intensified with the expansion of the "war on terror," particularly as a result of the now widely invoked notion of "Aboriginal extremism." As a concept, the notion of "Aboriginal extremism" was created by the national security agencies in an effort to expand their domain of surveillance and policing by using the language of the "war on terror." Referred to as "mission creep" within criminological studies (Monahan and Palmer 2009: 624–28), the concept itself is a by-product of the "extremism" vernacular that has been invoked to rationalize the broader expansion of national security policing.

A key component of the category of "Aboriginal extremism" rests on its racialized character, itself a product of settler colonialism. As we detail in our case studies, the category of "Aboriginal extremism" has been deployed against Indigenous movements that assert self-determination and challenge settler sovereignty as a delegitimizing tactic that has resulted in criminalization and systems of intensified policing. With an emphasis on intelligence collection and surveillance, Adam Barker (2009: 342) describes how "every [Indigenous] challenge [to settler authority] is met with increasing levels of control to the point that control becomes preemptive." Surveillance practices like Project SITKA are undertaken by policing agencies with the unstated objective of mapping Indigenous activism, which allows for targeted police interventions to disrupt and/or criminalize prominent activists.

Scholarship on the policing of social movements has stressed how surveillance practices are often integral components of larger efforts at criminalization and movement suppression (Boykoff 2007; Earl 2011; Kinsman and Gentile 2010). Surveillance itself can promote a dangerous culture of suspicion and paranoia, producing cyclical patterns of (in)security. A consequence of these accelerators is that police use insecurity to rationalize increased "national security" resources; yet, we would stress that these policing practices have an additional productive impact in building closer relationships between the police and business community. By constructing the figure of a criminal and terrorist threat that is hedged against "Canadian interests," the police reproduce their own image as the virtuous agents of control and position corporations as victims (and partners) who need protecting. These caricatures are amplified when the subjects of police scrutiny are racialized, particularly when police construct these protesters as unreasonable Natives or, as members of the RCMP have described them, members of Indigenous "sovereignty" movements or "Aboriginal extremists."

In this book, we stress how policing entities have construed Indigenous movements as irrational, violent, and extremist threats, while simultaneously exalting themselves as reasonable and objective. Anchored in long-standing cultural repertoires of settler society, these processes code Indigenous claims as unreasonable and produce a common, shared attitude within the security state that perceives the unrelenting scrutiny of these movements as justified. Moreover, the inclusion of corporate partnerships within the security state under the rubric of "critical infrastructure protection" allows for the widespread surveillance against, and interventions in, Indigenous communities to become normalized as national security practices aiming to protect economic interests and resource development. Through these relationships of the security state, policing and social control agencies have extended their roles as the protective arm of extractive capitalism.

EXTRACTIVE CAPITALISM, CRITICAL INFRASTRUCTURE, AND THE REPRODUCTION OF ORDER

Extractivism refers to a specific model of economic growth that prioritizes the extraction of resources to sell on international markets (Veltmeyer and Petras 2014). As a contemporary iteration of capitalism, an embrace of extractivism has particularly devastating consequences for the environment and the world's Indigenous Peoples who are being violently displaced in the drive to accumulate wealth from their lands. Canada has a long history of resource extraction and land theft, and the turn toward making Canada an "energy superpower" — as Harper put it — has intensified settler colonial efforts to control the land and resources of Indigenous communities. A push toward developing the tar sands and building pipelines to ship bitumen to foreign markets is a major element within this trend, and the security state has been an active player in advancing the development agenda of extractive capitalism through the widening domain of critical infrastructure protection.

As we detail throughout the case studies in this book, the umbrella of critical infrastructure has become a prominent element in the surveillance of social movements. Developed in the mid-2000s after the release of the National Security Strategy, the category of critical infrastructure expanded over the course of a decade to include numerous entities from railways and pipelines to nuclear factories (Monaghan and Walby 2017). Though critical infrastructure includes a wide array of sites, as well as natural disasters and "human induced" emergencies (Canada 2009a, 2009b), we document how security agencies and extractive corporations have used the umbrella to direct substantive resources toward issues of civil unrest — in other words, protest movements. As Tia Dafnos et al. (2016: 327) have noted, critical infrastructure has been invoked to pit "acts of indigenous sovereignty ... against acts of national security."

Prioritizing protest movements as national security threats under the umbrella of critical infrastructure is a product of integrating corporations into the expanded arena of the security state. Declassified notes from a "security briefing forum" between CSIS and the Canadian Association of

Petroleum Producers (CAPP) in 2007 detail how an unidentified CSIS agent told the group of corporate representatives that the changing domains of the "war on terror" meant "a transformed national security environment" that was moving "from national security to critical infrastructure protection" (CSIS 2012-27: 15). The CSIS presentation emphasized the move away from "national security" as military operations abroad toward the centrality of protecting domestic critical infrastructure through "enhanced information and intelligence sharing" between corporations and the security state (ibid.). Moreover, it is expressed as a means of establishing "partnerships" to integrate corporations into the security state. With a growing number of police–corporate collaborations, extractive corporations have the ability to supply intelligence to other partners of the security state, as well as a privileged position within the security state to influence the perception and labelling of certain threats. Given that 90 percent of what is considered critical infrastructure (pipelines, nuclear stations, hydro dams, airports, etc.) is owned by private corporations, our research shows how these corporations have become more than merely stakeholders — they are active policing partners.

Throughout our case studies, we highlight how an expanded security state actively delegitimizes Indigenous groups while also explicitly privileging the corporations and economic interests that profit from extractive capitalism. Although the police claim to be neutral and independent, we show how they actively support processes of Indigenous dispossession through the surveillance and criminalization of movements that assert Indigenous rights and claims to land. In many respects, the "war on terror" has further advanced a number of collaborative engagements between extractive capitalism and the security state, yet we also stress that policing and surveillance practices are constituted from their institutional histories and cultural repertoires. The current iterations of the security state are rooted in longer trajectories of policing, representing a current character of settler colonialism in a time that is increasingly defined by extractive capitalism and security governance.

Policing has long functioned "as a technology to morally patrol these systems of values, particularly through the profiling of those "symbolic assailants" (Skolnick 1966) who do not fit the stereotypes of good citizenship. As a mechanism that has the ability to impose non-negotiated solutions backed by violence, policing is not only about the enforcement of criminal law but also the protection of a particular vision of Canadian identities and values. This includes the promotion of capitalist development, the guardianship of moral notions of good and bad behaviour, the circulation of stereotypical images of enterprising youth versus troublesome youth, the perception of racialized gang or group behaviours, the monitoring of attitudes toward political or governmental authorities, and the ensemble of valourizations that are packaged into the stereotypes and expectations of being a "good Canadian."

Building on critical accounts of policing, Elizabeth Comack (2012: 57–65) has borrowed from Richard Ericson's (1982) work on police patrols to argue that the policing of Indigenous Peoples is a deeply racialized practice aimed at the "reproduction of order." Comack (2012: 57) writes that, given the context of settler colonialism, the order that the police reproduce "is decidedly raced (as well as gendered and classed)." She explains this as a process of "surveilling the social spaces that they [police] are assigned to govern" and notes that "race and racialization are put into everyday policing practices as officers bring to bear the cultural frames of reference or stocks of knowledge that inform their work" (ibid.). In demonstrating that policing is about the reproduction of a settler colonial order (our term), Comack's work borrows from Ericson's insistence that police do not produce a "new" order. Rather, the order they are charged with reproducing is that of the status quo, and that status quo is fundamentally threatened by expressions of Indigenous autonomy that disrupt the settler colonial present.

Our aim in this book is to provide a detailed, empirical narrative of how the security state is a contemporary configuration that engages in the reproduction of settler colonial order. Animated by increasing practices at intelligence collection and pre-emption, pervasive efforts to control Indigenous populations are rationalized by notions of "law and order" but remain implicitly grounded in an eliminatory logic that desires to consolidate a post-colonial society without Indigenous counter-authorities. Particularly under the new discourse of "Aboriginal extremism," we contend that the policing of these "extremisms" are far more illustrative of settler colonialism — and the anxieties of settler colonial authorities — than the groups and movements that the security state seeks to control. In fact, the Indigenous movements that are categorized as "extremists" have maintained a remarkable consistency in their politics and demands over the past five hundred years. These political demands are straightforward: self-determination, autonomy, nation-to-nation relations, and an end to the violent interventions from settler colonial authorities and most importantly the institutions of the security state and the criminal injustice system. Those demands continue today, yet are met with the vilification and repression we document throughout this book. Instead of continued surveillance and additional funding for the security state, we suggest that there is only one pathway toward resolving the conflict between settler colonialism and Indigenous Peoples: decolonization.

DECOLONIZING THE CANADIAN (SECURITY) STATE

Decolonization in the context of a deeply rooted society of settler colonialism is a daunting challenge. As we demonstrate in this book, any movements that challenge the norms of settler colonialism will have to contend with the extensive powers of policing and surveillance from the security state, which is charged with the reproduction of settler colonial order. A transformative politics of settler decolonization has to contend with a consensus among Canadian political parties where Indigenous politics attain legitimacy only when they surrender claims of autonomy to the overarching authority of Canadian sovereignty. Moreover, the politics of settler decolonization will have to contend with pervasive racism in settler society that has long stigmatized Indigeneity as backwards, criminal, and a threat to the post-colonial fictions of progress and development.

Decolonization efforts are challenging because they must contend with the power of settler colonialism, which stems from its ability to translate unrelenting and uncategorically violent practices of governance into everyday, commonplace activities. In many ways, decolonization efforts remain politically diverse, located at multiple local sites of struggle, and indelibly impacted by colonial powers (Sium, Desai and Ritskes 2012). Likewise, settler colonialism is not a strategy of elite rule or a centralized mode of domination but a heterogenous form of domination. It draws its strength and continuation specifically from widespread and normalized feelings of what Mark Rifkin (2013) calls "settler common sense," often producing mixed (sometimes contradictory) attitudes toward Indigenous Peoples and widespread complicity and complacency toward colonial systems of oppression. Often, the conflicting feelings can include empathy and a desire to assist as well as strongly ingrained notions of fairness and equality before the law, alongside cultural stereotypes of substance abuse, corruption, or dangerousness. An animating factor through these emotive dimensions of settler society is to regard Canadian governance as a self-evident authority. Indigenous communities, laws, customs, and political and social aspirations, are always assumed — in whatever circumstance — to be subordinate to the authorities and best intentions of settler society.

Central to the "common sense" of settler beliefs is the decentring and erasure of Indigenous sovereignties and authority to self-determination, which allows the assertion of Canadian sovereignty to remake the violence of colonization into benign and everyday questions of governance. Writing about the deeply engrained "settler expectations" that are particularly explicit during conflicts over land, Eva Mackey (2016: 8) has described the strong entitlements held by non-Indigenous populations and how these powerful feelings of entitlement "almost always supersede the just desires of Indigenous nations for recognition of their historic rights to their land." She writes, "The long history of the construction of supposedly authoritative knowledge about Indigenous peoples provides settlers with what has become a self-evident right to assess, control and manage Indigenous lives and sovereignties, thus bolstering the fantasy of uncontestable settler sovereignty" (ibid.: 13). As many other Indigenous and non-Indigenous writers have detailed, Canadian society has — and continues to — rationalize a form of systematic control over every aspect of Indigenous life.[9]

Manifestations of settler domination are maintained by social processes that produce images of Indigenous and non-Indigenous life, and our focus is to show how policing and surveillance practices are central in suppressing Indigenous movements that demand self-determination. We provide a detailed empirical account of how the security state operates against Indigenous movements. However, we want to underline that despite these machinic efforts to suppress movements that assert Indigenous sovereignty, we do not contend that settler colonialism has been successful in its quest to eliminate Indigeneity. We underline that the project of settler colonization has been disrupted, disturbed, and continues to be undone by the resistance it engenders (Alfred 2005; Coulthard 2007; Manuel 2015; Palmater 2015; Smith 2009). Our aim is not to suggest that settler colonialism is a completed project; instead, we see it as a logic of domination that continues in contemporary social relations but remains continuously ruptured by the strength and perseverance of Indigenous communities. We are conscious that our research does not fully appreciate or account for the resistance, nuance, and survivity[10] of Indigenous communities.

Our focus, however, are the practices of the security state. Our contention is that the security state is one of the principal avenues through which settler society maintains vigilance against Indigenous assertions of sovereignty; it acts as an instrument to safeguard and protect the settler status quo. Numerous scholars and activists have presented visions of decolonization, as well as ways to conceptualize settler solidarity, however this book does not engage with these important questions in large part because we, as authors, are still learning from these conversations. We contend that contesting the powers of settler colonialism starts with a centring of Indigenous sovereignty and self-determination. It requires actively working against the rationalizing forces that normalize the everyday interference, governance, ordering, and policing of Indigenous communities and Indigenous lifeworlds. It also involves working against practices in settler society that contribute to these normalized interventions.

Moreover, challenging settler society requires that the notion of nation-to-nation relations be taken seriously. Hollow declarations of nation-to-nation relations are epitomized by Prime Minister Trudeau and others who repeat the mantra without acknowledging that authentic nation-to-nation relations require a retraction of Canadian sovereignty. These relations require Indigenous freedom and self-determination, not lip service under the sovereign authority of the Canadian government. Michael Asch (2014) has underlined the importance and legal possibilities of building authentic treaty relationships as they are understood by Indigenous Peoples, as has John Borrows (2016). Our contention is that the legacy and contemporary practices of settler colonialism demonstrate how settler society can co-opt Indigenous demands, and we suggest that efforts to claim one-way "treaty relationships" under the sovereignty of Canada are unacceptable.

Although we do not present a means of decolonizing the spectrum of settler colonial relations, we do underline that the process of decolonization must begin by dramatically reining in the security state. The breadth of policing efforts against Indigenous movements calling for self-determination cannot be understated, and we provide an illustrative — although still only cursory — account of these practices. Importantly, the dramatic growth of the security state is a fundamental threat to all denizens and, more broadly, to principles of democracy that policing entities claim to uphold. Indigenous movements are a particular, high-profile focus of the security state, yet other groups are also profiled and over-policed — particularly racialized peoples, those with mental health struggles, LGBTQ+ communities, and the poor. We underline the importance of an intersectional critique of policing and security practices and, in our conclusions, we demonstrate a fundamental need for the dismantling of the sprawling, opaque, and completely unaccountable security state.

ACCESS TO INFORMATION AND THEMES OF THE BOOK

In this book, we detail how national security powers and resources have created an expansive policing infrastructure that targets Indigenous movements. Though a number of activists, scholars, researchers, and journalists, among others, have done excellent work reporting on these practices,[11] we offer a comprehensive account of how policing agencies target Indigenous movements. We do so exclusively using documents from policing and security agencies to narrate these developments. We have accessed these documents through extensive use of Access to Information (ATI) requests at the federal level and various Freedom of Information (FOI) requests at provincial and municipal levels. Our research project has involved hundreds of unique ATI/FOI requests, as well as the collection of informal requests filed by other researchers. In total, we have collected thousands of archival documents, which have been analyzed over the process of our research. A number of excellent researchers have advanced the case for using ATI/FOI as an archival research strategy over the past several years,[12] and we believe this project underlines the usefulness of ATI/FOI for work on contemporary issues that are prone to secrecy and obstructed access.

Our four case studies offer high-profile examples of Indigenous resistance and security state surveillance and suppression. Using resources that fall under the auspice of policing "extremism" in the "war on terror," we detail how Indigenous resistance movements are being increasingly framed as a threat to national security. We contend that, through these series of high-profile events and confrontations between Indigenous communities and the Canadian settler colony, the security state has solidified and made permanent an integrated policing model to mitigate and suppress instances of Indigenous dissent and assertions of sovereignty. Our case studies throughout this book integrate a number of themes, including settler colonial practices of divide and conquer as well as the manipulation of governance structures to ensure that Canada's version of treaty-making triumphs.

Treaties, or lack thereof, are a common feature running either prominently or subconsciously throughout the chapters. Where treaties exist, Indigenous and settler colonial interpretations differ greatly, as discussed briefly in Chapter 3, and when treaties do not exist, settler law and Indigenous law clash, often leading to violent conflict as we see in Chapter 4. A common thread throughout the text is the relationship of national security agencies and industry. In each chapter, we detail how policing and security agencies have established partnerships — particularly under the auspices of critical infrastructure — leading to situations where agencies like the RCMP embrace the role of industry advocate and enforcer.

A final and overarching theme is the abundance of resources within the "war on terror" that have been redirected at social movements, particularly those challenging extractive capitalism. A contemporary reality of the security state is that extremely localized conflicts, such as that of the Algonquins of Barriere Lake, become swept into the mechanisms of national security policing. We contend this is most visible with Indigenous activism that challenges Canadian sovereignty and settler economies. Not only do Indigenous movements present a distinct legal and political challenge to extractive capitalism, they also challenge the norms of settler sovereignty. The challenge to the very notion of Canada being a post-colonial society, and the extractive economics that underwrite these relations, is what elicits the vigilant and antagonistic policing responses that we detail in this book.

Notes

1. Our research cites heavily from government documents that have been produced through use of the *Access to Information Act* (ATIA). Our citation style uses the year of the request, the file number, then the page number. However, some files and departments do not provide page numbers for requests. In some cases, we have used a page number based on the original order of documents provided by the department. These page numbers correspond with our .pdf version of the files. Government documents used in this book are listed in the bibliography. All documents cited are publicly available using the same citation format on our website: <policingindigenousmovements.ca>. Throughout this book, we have reproduced quotations from documents received through the ATIA exactly as they appear, so as to depict the quoted material as accurately as possible. Other reproduced documents, such as those from various Indigenous activists and groups, are also left exactly as they appear. We are aware that this leaves multiple errors of grammar, spelling, and punctuation throughout the quotations in the book, but we have chosen not to indicate these instances with *[sic]*— except in a few instances where the meaning may be compromised — simply to reduce multiple interruptions of quoted text. At times, we have

made slight modifications to adjust verb tense.

2. There are many English transliterations of this word. We use Mi'kmaw to denote the singular form of the plural Mi'kmaq, as well as an adjective when it precedes a noun.

3. The term "settler colonial present" is largely acknowledged as an extension of Derek Gregory's (2004) book *The Colonial Present.* Lorenzo Veracini (2015) has used *The Settler Colonial Present* as the title of his recent book.

4. Our analysis draws from works such as Alfred (2005), Battell Lowman and Barker (2016), Boldt (1993), Coulthard (2014a), Deloria and Lytle (1984), Lawrence (2004, 2012), Manuel (2015), Monture-Angus (1999), Simpson (2014), Smith (2009), Turner (2006).

5. For an overview and a critique of these policing mythologies, see Francis (1993: 61–82), Graybill (2007), Mackey (2002), Monaghan (2013a), Walden (1982).

6. See Woolford (2015).

7. Our analysis is a synthesis of several recent works. For more detailed argumentation, see Battell Lowman and Barker (2016), Benvenuto, Woolford, and Hinton (2015), Hixson (2013), Veracini (2010, 2015), Wolfe (1999, 2006), as well as the journal *Settler Colonial Studies.*

8. We would like to stress that while "radicalization" is occasionally used against Indigenous or environmental movements, these occasional usages are often flippant and mostly about rationalizing funding or ongoing surveillance. However, the use of "radicalization" against Muslim populations is far more substantive. In its use by security actors against Muslims, "radicalization" is meant to describe a process — not just a label — that invites more surveillance and scrutiny toward a Muslim's citizenship and commitments to Canada. Though the citizenship loyalties are somewhat interrogated in relation to Indigenous protests, the procedural questions that attempt to trace "indicators" of a process of radicalization are not present. We therefore highlight, as others have, that "radicalization" is a highly flawed and racialized concept (see Kundnani 2014, also Monaghan and Molnar 2016).

9. Our understanding of these histories, as well as efforts to resist settler colonial control, have been advanced from writings such as Adams (1995), Borrows (2016), Carter (1990), Coulthard (2014a), Hall (2003), Lawrence (2004), Miller (1989), Monture-Angus (1999), Turner (2006).

10. We use the term survivity from Vizenor (2000), quoted in Tuck (2009).

11. We are indebted to many researchers and writers who have been documenting the surveillance and policing of Indigenous movements. In particular, we would like to acknowledge the work of Jorge Barrera, Russell Diabo, Tim Groves, Miles Howe, Martin Lukacs, and Shiri Pasternak.

12. In particular, see two edited volumes by Larsen and Walby (2012) and Brownlee and Walby (2015), as well as Dafnos (2014), Luscombe and Walby (2017), Monaghan (2017).

CHAPTER 1

"WELCOME TO ABL WORLD!!!!"

The Logic of Elimination and the Algonquins of Barriere Lake

Since Time Immemorial, we have used and occupied our lands for the pursuit of traditional activities, managing the lands and resources, as part of our way of life, on the basis of conservation and harmony with Mother Earth ... Impacts from flooding, logging, and wildlife depletion has devastated the lands and resources and disrupted our traditional way of life. (ABL 1992)

Plumes of tear gas billowed over Highway 117 in western Quebec on October 6, 2008, as a Sûreté du Québec (SQ) provincial police riot squad spanned the road. The paramilitary-like force faced off against an undeterred and defiant community of Algonquins, including Elders and youth, who blocked the highway to demand that the federal and provincial governments honour agreements they had signed regarding resource development on their territory and cease meddling in their internal affairs. "You want to keep us in this reserve, this tiny little reserve," community spokesperson Marylynn Poucachiche shouted with power and conviction at the wall of SQ, who had used force to push the community off the highway and onto the dead-end road leading to the reserve. "Well we're not going to stay here. You guys, you can stand here [for] maybe twelve hours. Us, we can be here another five hundred years," Poucachiche said (quoted in Stiegman 2008). True to her word, the community took over Highway 117 again in November, demanding the government send a negotiator. Instead of sending a negotiator, riot police were bussed in again from Montreal and Poucachiche and other community leaders were targeted for arrest.

This was not the first time that the Algonquins of Barriere Lake have experienced police repression for asserting sovereignty over their traditional lands and demanding that their rights and agreements be respected, and it would not be the last.

The Algonquins of Barriere Lake have been subjected to a series of overlapping and interconnected settler colonial techniques in a project of criminalization and elimination. Historically, these techniques have included settler encroachments, administrative and legal regimes to shrink the land base, and restrictions on Algonquin land-based activities such as hunting. In recent years, these techniques have been supplemented by political interference, concerted administrative and legal efforts to undermine the community's authority and traditional leadership, as well as police surveillance and repression. Because they refuse to capitulate to settler colonial power, the Algonquins of Barriere Lake have long been on the radar of the colonial bureaucracy centred in the Indian Affairs (INAC) offices of the federal government. As a result of their relentless blockades targeting settler economies and access to their lands, the community was labelled as a "hot spot" by the security state and subjected to various colonial interventions including a surveillance and control mechanism known as "third-party management." This technique is used by INAC to wrestle financial control and decision-making authority away from Indigenous communities who deviate from settler societal norms and prescriptions. When the Algonquins of Barriere Lake denied the third-party manager access to the community in October 2015, a senior INAC bureaucrat, André Bengle, expressed his frustrations to his colleagues in an email that said, "welcome to ABL World!!!! et ça commence aujourd'hui" (INAC 2015-1438: 29). The community's continued insistence on their treaty rights and control over lands has resulted in punitive measures and considerable repression. As the email from Bengle shows, the security state — and INAC as a member of the security state — expresses frustrations with the community, which are often animated by racist perceptions. The imagined "ABL World" that INAC bureaucrats reference with mocking disdain represents the space of resistance that is the thorn in the side of the bureaucracy's eliminatory project of settler colonialism: a small, impoverished Indigenous community that refuses to surrender its rights and land. "ABL World" exists and persists in and because of a settler colonial world, where only Indigenous non-compliance is highlighted while the normal violence of settler punishment remains ignored.

Barriere Lake encounters with the Canadian state reveal how the security state functions as the enforcement tool of settler colonialism. As is done with all communities that resist settler colonialism, policing and surveillance techniques target Indigenous land defence and challenges to settler sovereignty. In the case of the Algonquins of Barriere Lake, this includes police enforcement of government policies and *Indian Act* elections; facilitation of industry access to logging on Algonquin territory; and the monitoring, surveillance, and "threat" categorization of Barriere Lake activities associated with demands for recognition. The security state is also integral to administrative regimes of governance that are developed and employed to wrestle control away from the community, undermine their traditional leadership structures, and sever their relationship with the land — as well as criminalize those that stand in the way of these colonial efforts. The aims are straightforward: bring the Algonquins under the control of the *Indian Act* and modern treaty framework, which would extinguish their underlying title, for the larger purpose of securing and exploiting Algonquin lands and resources to enrich settler economies. As an eliminatory project, the practices of settler colonialism produce both an array of interventions by the security state and resistance from the Algonquins of Barriere Lake community.

LOGGING, RESISTANCE, AND THE TRILATERAL AGREEMENT

The Algonquins of Barriere Lake — *Mitchikanibikok Inik* (people of the stone weir) — refer to themselves as *Anishnabeg*, "which carries both the general meaning of 'human being', and the specific meaning of 'real (i.e., Indian) people,'" and are one of ten recognized First Nations comprising the Algonquin Nation (Morrison 2005: 2). Traditional Algonquin territory includes the land and water within and surrounding the Ottawa River *(Kiji Sibi)* watershed, straddling the Ontario/Quebec border and including Parliament Hill, yet the imposition of competing provincial jurisdictions and the use of the *Indian Act* to exclude two-thirds of the Algonquin from Indian status recognition have fractured their homelands (Lawrence 2012; Gehl 2014). Barriere Lake's territory comprises some 44,000 square kilometres in what is now known as western Quebec, the area in and around La Vérendrye Wildlife Reserve (Morrison: 7). They have been there for eight thousand to ten thousand years following the draining of the inland Champlain Sea, from which the Ottawa valley emerged (ibid.: 6–7). Their traditional settlement area lies in the heart of the watershed at a convergence of river systems where the Algonquins of Barriere Lake placed rocks across a ten-foot stretch of the river to catch fish. *Mitcikinabikong* (place of the stone fence or weir) was translated by the French as Lac Barrière (ibid.: 9).

Despite vast traditional territories, the "tiny reserve" that Poucaciche refers to is a fifty-nine-acre plot of sandy, eroding land, around 300 kilometres north of Ottawa-Gatineau. Created in 1961, the reserve was established without Band involvement or consent as part of a systematic attempt to eradicate the Algonquins' land-based subsistence lifestyle (ABL 1988). As a result of settler encroachment, erosion caused by fluctuations in water levels due to hydroelectric dams — which have flooded large portions of Barriere Lake territory — is symbolic of the Algonquins' shrinking land base. Despite settler policies and encroachment aimed to alienate and dispossess the Algonquins from their territory, community members still speak their Algonquin language and practise traditional activities on the land as they have done since time immemorial. Both of these mantras of Indigenous resurgence, described by Taiaiake Alfred and Jeff Corntassel (2005) as "land is life" and "language is power," are deeply embedded in the Algonquins of Barriere Lake's constitution and governance. The Algonquins of Barriere Lake have self-governed based on their constitution — *Mitchikanbikok Anishnabe Onakinakewin* — which is grounded in their language, culture, and relationship to the land. Their consensus-based customary governance model is comprised of community assemblies where the traditional Elders Council play a key leadership role in selecting and advising the Chief who requires the consent of the community to govern (Pasternak 2017). Until recently, the community was one of only a handful in Canada that maintained its customary government and constitution outside of the *Indian Act* Band Council system. Community members proudly speak their language, despite generations having been forcibly removed to Indian residential schools in a systemic effort to eliminate Indigenous languages and cultures. The community also maintains a strong, traditional, land-based economy despite government pressure for them to abandon it and embrace the welfare system centred on the reserve (Morrison 2005: 19–20).

The Algonquins have never ceded or surrendered any portion of their territory to Canada or its colonial predecessors. They entered into an alliance with the French in the early 1600s and then with the British in 1760 as part of the Covenant Chain treaty alliance. The alliance was formalized in 1764 at the Treaty of Niagara, which followed and affirmed the Royal Proclamation of 1763 that no Indian lands could be sold before first being ceded to the British Crown (Walters 2001).[1] According to Anthony Hall (2003: 155), the Niagara Treaty negotiations served to "entrench a regime of Crown recognition of existing Aboriginal and treaty rights" used as the basis for contemporary arguments against settler encroachments and the non-consensual theft of Indigenous resources. Unextinguished Algonquin rights are further recorded in the Three Figure Wampum Belt dating back to the 1760s, a treaty between the Algonquins, English, and French that stipulates Algonquin involvement in any questions related to land and that "the matter of jurisdiction was to be based on mutual respect and equality" (Shenkier and Meredith 1997: 71). Despite Canada's theft of land and efforts to disrupt their lives, the Algonquins still insist Canada and Quebec are bound to the terms of the original treaties.

Instead of honouring the original treaties, which established a nation-to-nation relationship framework, settler colonial authorities have layered laws, regulations, and informal enforcement, among other tactics, in a process of asserting control over the Algonquins' territories. Because these territories are located in proximity to major urban and industrial centres and possess an array of resources and wealth, the treaties have been systematically dishonoured in the expansion of settler colonialism. As Coulthard (2015) puts it, the structure of dispossession requires "the theft not only of the material of land itself, but also a destruction of the social relationships that existed prior to capitalism violently sedimenting itself on Indigenous territories." In defending their land and their way of life, the Algonquins of Barriere Lake have been forced to defend their territory for decades from resource development and settler encroachment (Aird 1990; Di Gangi 2003). Very few Bands have been able to hold on to their customary governance system into the twenty-first century, as Barriere Lake has, and this self-governance has allowed them to refuse to recognize settler control over their lands. Yet, despite their resistance, their territories are exploited by profitable forestry, hydroelectric, and tourist industries. The Algonquins of Barriere Lake receive none of the wealth extracted from their lands, are denied a say on how their land is managed, and are criminalized for asserting their rights to the land.

In the 1980s, logging companies invaded Algonquin territory. Clear-cutting and chemical spraying threatened to wipe out the animals and the land base (Matchewan 1989; Shenkier and Meredith 1997; Borrows 2005).

The Algonquins of Barriere Lake pleaded, in a series of letters to Quebec and Canadian political leaders, to work with them to develop a conservation strategy as the situation had become "almost unbearable" and their "survival [was] gravely imperiled" (ABL 1989b). Eventually, the Algonquins used blockades to force the Quebec government to stop chemical spraying, but the provincial and federal governments refused to come to the negotiating table in a meaningful way, and logging continued. Government refusal to meaningfully negotiate with the Barriere Lake community prompted more blockades and would set the stage for a protracted struggle between Barriere Lake and the policing agencies of settler colonialism.

Barriere Lake blockades signified a "disruptive counter-sovereignty" against the settler state's ambitions to clear-cut Algonquin forests for the exclusive benefit of settler society (Coulthard 2014a: 118). For Coulthard, the wave of Indigenous resistance against resource extractive industries in the 1980s "was an embarrassing demonstration that Canada no longer had its shit together with respect to managing the so-called 'Indian Problem'" (ibid.). It also signified the power of the blockade as an expression of Indigenous sovereignty "explicitly erected to impede the power of state and capital from entering and leaving Indigenous territories respectively" (ibid.). To regain control over the exploitation of Indigenous land, police violence was required to subdue blockades. How it played out on the ground reveals the intimate relations between the security state and resource extractive industries.

During a blockade in September 1989, an exchange between an SQ sergeant from the Maniwaki detachment and the Barriere Lake customary Chief revealed the stark contrast between settler and Indigenous approaches toward the land. The sergeant asked, "Do you have some document to prove you have the right to live here?" Chief Jean-Maurice Matchewan responded, "We've been around here for thousands of years. That gives us the right to live off this land" (Richardson 1993: 154). Unable to comprehend how small groups of Indians could challenge Quebec's jurisdiction and ownership over natural resources, the SQ grew frustrated and threatened to use whatever force was required to enable logging to proceed unabated. The same sergeant threatened, "We have four thousand officers in our force. If we need them, they will all be here" (ibid.). The following month, the SQ sergeant called for reinforcements, who violently broke up a logging blockade and arrested Matchewan. In a stark admission of collusion between the police and resource extractive industries, sq Captain Royal Gauthier admitted that the police operation was ordered by Quebec's Ministry of Energy and Resources in conjunction with the logging companies (ABL 1989a).

Aware of the imminent threats to their ways of life, the Algonquins of Barriere Lake had already proposed a trilateral process with Quebec and Canada to develop a conservation strategy for La Vérendrye Wildlife Reserve. Community spokesperson Norman Matchewan summarizes how it all unfolded:

> In the late 1980s, logging companies started spraying pesticides in our territory, making the animals and the people sick. The community was able to slow them down by taking a strong stand and blocking the logging roads, but they have cut over 50 percent of our territory. We pushed to sign the Trilateral Agreement to protect our way of life and to protect the animals and our land but the agreement has not been honoured. (Matchewan interview)

After further blockades, combined with political and diplomatic efforts by the community and their allies, the Trilateral Agreement was signed with the provincial and federal governments on August 22, 1991. The Trilateral Agreement is regarded as a "pioneering land management planning process" for 10,000 square kilometres of Algonquin territory (Manuel 2008). The unique approach to co-operative sustainable development was crafted and put forth by the Algonquins, who considered it a model of reconciliation (Notzke 1995: 89–90). The treaty requires that the community have a decisive voice concerning activities on their land and derive benefits from the use of their land or resources extracted from it (Notzke 1995; RCAP 1996: Vol. 2, Pt. 2, Appendix 4B).

However, the Trilateral Agreement was never implemented. Despite signing the agreement, settler authorities have shown no intention of honouring the groundbreaking deal. While the deal was reached to de-escalate the activism of the Algonquins, a land co-management agreement designed and demanded by an Indigenous Nation was far too radical a proposition to become meaningfully implemented. In large part, the Trilateral Agreement disrupted two main pillars of settler colonial power: it challenged the unconditional assertion of Canadian sovereignty and cut into logging profits made from exploiting Indigenous lands.

Colonial authorities have viewed the signing of the Trilateral Agreement in hindsight as a major blunder; it was a deviation from

Canada's unequivocal policy of denying and extinguishing Indigenous rights and title. Since its signing, both federal and provincial governments have demonstrated their contempt for the agreement by trying to ignore and undermine their commitments as well as the broader inherent principles characterizing the agreement. Stalling and backpedaling has since provoked the numerous conflicts and interventions that have ensued. At the centre of the protracted conflict is the federal government's push for the Algonquin Nation to sign a comprehensive land claim.[2] While the landmark Trilateral Agreement offered an alternative to the comprehensive land claims process, signing a new comprehensive agreement would formally — and finally — kill the more autonomous model established in the Trilateral Agreement. This agreement represents the antithesis of the land claims policy, which "rejects concepts such as co-management or sharing environmental management with First Nations" (Lawrence 2012: 69) and extinguishes Aboriginal title, offering a one-time payout and small portion of land in exchange for terminating title to the land. Mohawk policy analyst Russell Diabo describes the process as converting "pre-existing sovereign rights into post-treaty defined rights" (Diabo interview). Under the "modern treaty" approach, sovereign Indigenous nations are left with only "local or municipal-type powers left over to negotiate" (ibid.). Aboriginal title is subsumed under provincial jurisdiction and, therefore, industry interests. The Algonquins of Barriere Lake have vehemently opposed this model, insisting that Canada and Quebec honour the Trilateral Agreement.

ORCHESTRATING ELIMINATION USING ALL "INSTRUMENTS OF THE STATE"

Barriere Lake's insistence that governments honour the Trilateral Agreement (and other signed agreements)[3] and refusal to engage in Canada's land claims scheme is the underlying motivator behind persistent colonial interventions. Beginning in late 1995, Shiri Pasternak (2017: 165–81) documents how the federal government moved to destabilize the community rather than honour the Trilateral Agreement. Internal INAC documents demonstrate a series of tactics including codifying the community's constitution, collaborating with the SQ to exert control on the reserve, and taking over the community's finances and administration with third-party management.

Perfecting techniques of divide and conquer, INAC collaborated with the logging industry and advised a small faction, the "interim band council" opposed to the Trilateral Agreement, "how to seize power" and "become officially recognized" (ibid.: 172). Ultimately, the coup failed. Barriere Lake's customary government was restored and third-party management lifted, but only for the time being. Still under constant scrutiny from Indian Affairs, the community was coerced into codifying its constitution, which the Elders predicted would come back to haunt them. Codifying Barriere Lake's sacred oral law into writing could enable INAC to interpret the constitution to suit its interests and to exert control over the community and its governance (ibid.: 182, 299–300).

Having failed to subdue the community, Canada officially walked away from the Trilateral Agreement in 2001 citing a "lack of results" (Simard interview). INAC claimed the federal role was to provide funding, implying that $5 million had been squandered despite the extensive research and mapping work that had been carried out to create an Integrated Resource Management Plan, the equivalent of "binding an encyclopedia of oral knowledge of the territory" (Pasternak 2017: 153). The ultimate goal behind suffocating the Trilateral Agreement was to coerce Barriere Lake to negotiate away their title through the comprehensive land claims process. Michael Gratton, special representative to Barriere Lake at the time, described it this way: "They hate the idea of the Algonquins negotiating *not* a land claims agreement ... with the Trilateral, it was a different procedure and they hated it" (ibid.: 185). This was substantiated in a 2002 letter to the community from Canadian Prime Minister Jean Chrétien specifying that a long-term solution could only be realized through land claims negotiations outside of the Trilateral Agreement (ibid.: 173).

Despite years of protraction and disruption by Indian Affairs, Barriere Lake continued to demand that Quebec and Canada come back to the negotiating table to implement the Trilateral Agreement. A decade after destabilizing the community and perpetrating a major crisis, INAC once again began to meddle in the internal affairs at Barriere Lake in 2006. The renewed conflict began when INAC refused to continue recognizing the customary government, and then the conflict escalated when third-party management was imposed for the second time in ten years. This ultimately led to Indian Affairs recognizing an external Band Council in 2008, as they had done twelve years prior.

A number of provocations led to the 2008 government intervention, as detailed extensively in INAC documentation. Declassified documents accessed through the ATIA craft a counter-narrative of events that contradict the government's public relations messaging about how crises and interventions transpire and are acted upon. Internal reports from the summer of 2007 detail how INAC perceived mounting insecurities associated with protests by the Algonquins of Barriere Lake. These protests were sparked by INAC's 2006 decision to refuse to recognize the customary leadership, yet the demands from the community were grounded in long-standing assertions of autonomy and the respect of treaty commitments. Three core demands were put forward: the implementation of the Trilateral Agreement, recognition and respect for the customary Governance Code, and a rescission of third-party management. In a report prepared for the Minister on June 13, 2007, INAC acknowledges strong pressure exerted by the community, which included demonstrations, blockades of forestry roads, and appeals to the Minister of Indian Affairs (INAC 2010-2705: 69).

In 2007, INAC contracted former diplomat Marc Perron, as a special representative to the minister, to lead an alternative dispute-resolution process with the Algonquins of Barriere Lake.[4] Although Perron's mandate included evaluating the situation and providing a set of recommendations, his report and conclusions were predominantly informed from extensive consultations with INAC and other government officials, including the SQ, and minimal engagement with the community.[5] In a November 2007 letter to the Minister of Indian Affairs, the community outlined its opposition to the Perron appointment on the grounds of the latter's "disinclination to address the 'legalistic issues,' including the Trilateral Agreement" (Nottaway 2007).

Any skills of diplomacy obtained over his decades of public service did not apply to Perron's assessment of the Algonquins of Barriere Lake. Perron deployed innuendos and tropes steeped in racist stereotypes and settler myths to attack the community and discredit its customary leadership. Despite objections from Barriere Lake, Perron issued his final report to the minister in December 2007 (INAC 2010-2705: 89–109). The report has been described as laying out a "strategy for government subversion" (Lukacs 2009). Perron recommended the government permanently step away from the Trilateral Agreement and that this "*mythique 'traité*'" ("mythical 'treaty'")[6] should not be referenced in any future financial agreements. He wrote that INAC "*ne devrait contribuer à perpétuer cette utopie ... qui a servi essentiellement à nourrir des illusions dans la population et conforter ses promoteurs dans leur idéologie*" ("should not contribute to perpetuating that utopia ... which essentially feeds the population with illusions and strengthens those who promote it in their ideology"). Instead, Perron urged that Barriere Lake be coerced into entering Canada's modern treaty framework via comprehensive land claims negotiations.

During the reporting process, Perron doubled as a federally appointed negotiator in comprehensive land claims agreements and clearly vocalized his opposition to any alternative agreement that would retain Indigenous autonomy. Not surprisingly, INAC declared no conflict of interest,[7] and Perron's report expressed dismay over the customary government's insistence on the Trilateral Agreement and refusal to engage in the comprehensive treaty process. Notably, Perron cautioned that other First Nations may hesitate to engage in the land claims process if they saw communities like the Algonquins of Barriere Lake successfully negotiating agreements that do not extinguish Indigenous title. Perron argues that the Trilateral Agreement and land claims negotiations with other Algonquin communities have been unworkable because of *"un groupe restraint d'idéologues et de doctrinaires [qui] préfèrent la confrontation au dialogue, la théorie au développement"* ("a small group of ideologues and doctrinaires [who] prefer confrontation to dialogue, theory to development"). By challenging settler colonial authority and legitimacy, the Algonquins of Barriere Lake are characterized as the antithesis of progress and act as a hindrance to the realization of Canada's extinguishment process and thus its post-colonial status. Perron recommended that INAC revise the land claims policy to adopt a more flexible process so as to negotiate a land claim with those willing Algonquin Bands, citing an agreement with the Innu as an example. Doing so would allow the Bands to reach their *"plein épanouissement"* ("full potential") and would force the Algonquins of Barriere Lake to follow suit. Tony Wawatie from Barriere Lake interprets this type of logic:

> The government wants to wash their hands of the fiduciary responsibility they have to First Nations. They want to amend it and bring it down to the provincial governments to make us mainstream Canadian citizens. Get rid of the Indian problem and make us become citizens." (Wawatie interview)

INAC's land claims policy remains a potent aspect of the eliminatory project of settler colonialism with the aim of subverting Aboriginal title and asserting provincial and federal jurisdiction over Indigenous lands. Perron's report echos these long-standing efforts, while promoting policies that would further extinguish Algonquin land rights.

Perron's report also exonerated INAC of any blame regarding the community's destitute condition, insisting that the disastrous economic conditions were the responsibility of the community and due in part to *"l'attitude déplorable et peu constructive du Conseil"* ("the déplorable and unconstructive attitude of the leadership"). The community sees it differently:

> The federal government says that they want to improve our living conditions and yet they do not want to honour the agreement they signed, the Trilateral Agreement, which gives us a say in what goes on in our territory and a share in the revenue that they are extracting. The Quebec government makes over $100 million per year off our territory and nothing goes back into the community. (Matchewan interview)

This position is substantiated by the Royal Commission on Aboriginal Peoples (RCAP) Commissioner who stated in 1996 that "current levels of poverty and underdevelopment are directly linked to the dispossession of Indigenous Peoples from their lands and the delegitimization of their institutions of society and governance" (Pasternak 2014: 43). Ignoring this, Perron provided a long list of deficiencies in the community and, echoing long-established tropes of settler colonialism, wrote that poverty was due to *"une culture de dépendance, de négligence, d'irresponsabilité flagrantes"* ("a culture of dependency, negligence and flagrant irresponsibility"). Parroting a long tradition of settler stereotypes of Indigenous communities in Canada, Perron describes the Algonquins of Barriere Lake as embodying a *"culture du misérabilisme"* ("culture of cultivating one's own miserable condition"). Perron admits that INAC "committed errors" over the years but he insists that those errors were made in good faith.

Underscoring the settler colonial representation of Indigenous deficiencies, Perron underlines that INAC has a duty to intervene because of the incompetent and confrontational attitudes of the community's leadership and the inability of traditional Indigenous customs to provide prosperity. Perron wrote that there was no short-term solution to improve the situation, which he describes as on a path of "auto-destruction" fuelled by an intransigent leadership and exacerbated by conflict surrounding the Governance Code. Perron contended that *"la direction de la communauté est au coeur même des problèmes. J'en conclus qu'il n'y a pas, ou si peu, de chance d'améliorer la situation, à moins d'un renouvellement complet du leadership"* ("the community leadership is at the heart of the problems. I conclude that there is little or no possibility of remedying the situation unless there is a complete change in leadership"). His report implored the federal government not to bow to pressure and advised that any negotiations be contingent on the cessation of blockades. Perron urged INAC to use all tools at its disposal to impose a new collective discipline on the Algonquins of Barriere Lake.

Armed with the Perron Report, INAC had the pretext required to forcefully intervene and destabilize the community as it had done in 1996. The Trilateral Agreement could finally be quashed, and steps could be taken to extinguish Algonquin title through manipulation and coercion. However, INAC was well aware of the potential fallout. A secret departmental briefing note from February 18, 2008 recalls INAC's destabilization efforts surrounding the 1996 intervention "to 'recognize' the opposing Council instead of the one in place," which resulted in a "major crisis in the community" where "barricades were erected and all activities in Barriere Lake were stopped during several months" (INAC 2010-2705: 88). The "major crisis" — limited access to food, electricity, and medical services in winter conditions — was caused by INAC, not the "barricades" as claimed. Despite acknowledging that another potential "major crisis" could materialize as a result of once again meddling in the community's internal affairs, the briefing recommends that the INAC Minister recognize a new Band Council whose members were seen as more agreeable. The briefing note stated that "the improvement of the situation in Barriere Lake depends on ... a Council willing to work with the Department and its other partners in capacity building" (ibid.: 87). An annex to the briefing note claims there will be "positive impacts" of working with "a new council less dogmatized," including "improved collaboration ... with INAC, the third-party administrator and other partners," although INAC acknowledges that it may not be able to exercise "an effective control on the reserve"[8] (ibid.: 90).

In a coordinated effort to bring the reserve under control after the decision to recognize a new Band Council, police harassment escalated in the community beginning in March 2008 (Pasternak 2017: 236). INAC secret documents from March 3, 2008, reveal the justification. INAC anticipated "strong reactions" and the emergence of new tensions, including violence, legal action, media pressure, and blockades. In a section appearing under the headline "Road block/violence/protests," INAC anticipated vandalism, highway blockades, and protests at INAC offices in Maniwaki, Buckingham, and Gatineau, as well as at Parliament Hill. The document suggests "close collaboration for a number of months" between INAC and provincial police, who replaced the community police force on the reserve in 2006 (INAC 2010-2705: 203). Matchewan recounts: "After the provincial police moved in ... people were getting harassed. People were getting pulled over and having their licences checked. Any Natives driving on the highway were harassed" (Matchewan interview). The SQ further maintained a regular presence at the end of the reserve road at the Highway 117 junction. By doing do they could observe everybody who entered and left the reserve and pull over and harass and intimidate whomever they pleased (Pasternak 2017: 235). According to INAC, the SQ agreed to "act firmly against perpetrators of violence in the community," "not tolerate any traffic disturbance on Highway 117" and "proceed with arrest if required" (INAC 2010-2705: 203). With Perron's report having concluded that INAC should study all possible forms of intervention, *"en utilisant tous les instruments de l'État"* ("using all the instruments of the state"), the colonial bureaucracy helped orchestrate a coup d'état and placed the security state on alert.

SECURITY STATE REPRESSION AT BARRIERE LAKE

In the context of mounting antagonisms provoked by settler colonial interference in the Algonquins of Barriere Lake's customary system of governance and ongoing resistance to resource extraction, the small community became increasingly scrutinized by the security state. As a fusion of security governance agencies, the security state has an array of resources that can be directed toward perceived threats. Although efforts at social control have been directed in various forms at Indigenous resistance for centuries, the contemporary incarnation of the security state is characterized by trends in the "war on terror" that aim to integrate policing, intelligence, and governmental resources with the objective of pre-empting and disrupting activities that are defined as threats.

With the focus of the "war on terror" experiencing a spatial shift from international to domestic threats, the discourse of extremism emerged in the mid to late 2000s (Monaghan 2014; Monaghan and Walby 2017, 2012). As "extremism" is a flexible label that can be disconnected from its original association with Islamic fundamentalist militancy, the security state quickly expanded the term's applicability to categorize and frame domestic protest groups as threats to national security, blurring the boundaries between protests and terrorism, as well as violence and non-violence (Monaghan and Walby 2012). As a rhetorical device that immediately extends the retributive politics of the "war on terror," this effort to blur protests and national security threats were quickly taken advantage of by the security state in constructing the notion of "Aboriginal extremism." The security state has redirected policing and intelligence resources toward new threat categorizations such as "domestic extremism" or "Aboriginal extremism," words that are now used for actions — like those of the Barriere Lake community — that challenge resource extractive industries and the authority of settler governments.

Barriere Lake was listed as a potential domestic security threat through the "hot spot reporting system" in 2006. Diabo and Pasternak described the hot spot system as a "blueprint for security integration on First Nations issues" (FNSB 2011, Vol. 9). Barriere Lake was identified as a "hot spot" and an "Aboriginal community of concern" as community resistance efforts to settler authority were increasingly monitored by national security and counter-terrorism agencies. There are at least five presentations released through the *Access to Information Act* (ATIA) that detail how security state infrastructures were developed around the "hot spot" surveillance and information sharing system.[9] These presentations highlight the need to integrate government and policing resources to monitor, mitigate, manage, and catalogue Indigenous dissent.[10] For instance, INAC's "Aboriginal Hot Spots and Public Safety" presentation dated March 30, 2007, outlines the function of the hot spot reporting system as comprising continuous monitoring of existing and emerging risks and information dissemination using police intelligence in "synergy" with security agencies including CSIS, ITAC, the GOC, and the RCMP (INAC A0240846: 951). Supplementing the INAC presentation is an RCMP slide deck addressing the "Response to Aboriginal Occupations and Protests" (RCMP 2015-9455). To mitigate against protests and their potential economic impacts the RCMP formed a National Steering Committee with policing partners and INAC to manage Indigenous dissent (ibid.: 28). An RCMP presentation on "Aboriginal Occupations and Protest" to CSIS on April 3, 2007, detailed how the fusion of intelligence and policing resources directed at Indigenous populations was prompted by "a growing concern among high-level government officials and the policing community about the potential for unrest in Aboriginal communities, and an increasing sense of militancy among certain segments of the Aboriginal population" (INAC A0240846: 963). This growing concern is contextualized in the RCMP admission that "The assertion of rights is a fundamental and defining characteristic of Aboriginal protests," amidst a "difficult history of relations between police and Aboriginal people" (ibid.: 964). Describing future risks, the RCMP reference "Aboriginal and non-Aboriginal extremists" as escalating or agitating conflicts. Likewise, CSIS assessments of "the threat from terrorists and extremists" justify ongoing surveillance that perceives Aboriginal extremists as increasingly willing to resort to direct action tactics on issues related to sovereignty, land claims, natural resources, and environmental concerns (CSIS 2012-222: 62, 67–8, 91). A separate draft of the RCMP presentation to CSIS highlights the security state's primary concern under "present and future considerations" as potential "negative economic impacts for Canada" (RCMP 2015-9455).

While acknowledging "difficult relations," the RCMP leave the particulars of these difficulties ambiguous. Yet, they underline Canadian sovereignty when stating that protests often take place "off-reserve on 'traditional lands' held by the Crown or non-Aboriginals" (INAC A0240846: 964). The presentation suggests that the "sense of militancy" and "assertion of rights" are policing matters that require urgent attention from the security state. Under the heading "Criminal Intelligence," one slide offers a staggering police re-imagination of history when it emphasizes that incidents at "Oka, Ipperwash, Burnt Church and Caledonia have validated the threat and/ or use of violence among Aboriginal militants" (RCMP 2015-9455: 20). As Indigenous communities like the Algonquins of Barriere Lake continue to assert their rights and self-determination, "hot spot" systems of monitoring and information sharing emerge as new tactics to organize and coordinate interventions against Indigenous communities.

Communities that appear in "hot spot" reports are sites of struggle, typically over land and resources that challenge Canada's post-colonial image and claims of settler sovereignty. Similar documents show how Barriere Lake resistance efforts, along with those of other Indigenous communities, were a catalyst for security state integration efforts. In an April 3, 2007 presentation titled, "Aboriginal Hot Spots and Public Safety," INAC (2015-1603) cited a number of "unpredictable protests" led by "splinter groups," which we discuss further in the following chapter, as prompting the fusion of security intelligence on Indigenous resistance. These "unpredictable protests" included Barriere Lake's blockade of Highway 117, the Six Nations occupation of the Douglas Creek Estates in Caledonia, the Mohawk blockade of a Montreal/Toronto rail line in Belleville, and the highway blockade at Grassy Narrows First Nation (ibid.: 23).

Given INAC's contention that the "vast majority of hot spots are related to land and resources" and "most are incited by development activities on traditional territories" (ibid.: 21), the Algonquins of Barriere Lake and dozens of other communities contesting Canadian sovereignty over Indigenous land have been swept up in the vast surveillance and profiling regime of the security state. After being first mentioned in weekly "hot spot" reports in July–September 2008 for what INAC called "governance disputes," the Algonquins of Barriere Lake became a regular fixture in a series of "burst" reports from October 2008 to January 2009. These reports detailed how the community erected barricades on Highway 117, and carried out further protests in Ottawa/Gatineau, Cantley, and Montreal. Barriere Lake was further labelled as a major source of "civil unrest"[11] (INAC 2016-448: 3) and community members faced criminalization for their insistence on asserting their treaty and territorial rights.

Coinciding with the emergence of an integrated approach to policing Indigenous resistance, Indigenous communities who resisted settler colonialism were classified as potentially violent, militant, and extremists. Categorizing those who defend their territories against resource extraction as such enables police repression and criminalization, as Barriere Lake has been subjected to time and again since commencing logging blockades in the 1980s. Practices of criminalization were prominent during the 2008 blockades where, from April 2008 to January 2009, all but one of the community's leaders and spokespeople were targeted for arrest. In addition to arrests and police harassment, Crown lawyers demanded that the leadership of the community be handed harsh sentences and strict release conditions.

Among those arrested was traditional Chief Benjamin Nottaway, who was specifically targeted for arrest by riot police during a Highway 117 blockade and sentenced to sixty days in jail. A press release issued by the Algonquins of Barriere Lake (2008) claimed that the Crown asked for a one-year sentence to send a "clear message" to the community. The imprisonment of Nottaway prompted further protests at INAC headquarters in Gatineau. Yet, the costs of defending their land and rights was high: over forty members of the community had been arrested and charged for actions stemming from various blockades since 2008 (ibid.). For Tony Wawatie, the government's objective is straightforward: "They want to criminalize First Nations because we are taking a stand on our Aboriginal rights and title toward the land. We are trying to protect our identity and our homeland" (Wawatie interview). Despite facing criminalization and police violence on the remote highways and courtrooms near Maniwaki, Quebec, the Algonquins of Barriere Lake took to Ottawa and other cities after their demands for respect and recognition continued to be refused.

MAKING THE ALGONQUINS INTO NATIONAL SECURITY THREATS

As protests mounted, Barriere Lake efforts were monitored and tracked by Canada's anti-terrorism agencies, promoted from a regional threat to lumber barons to a national security threat. Their activities were closely monitored by CSIS' Integrated Terrorism Assessment Centre (ITAC),[12] a central agency within the security state for tracking and information sharing about threats that are deemed as terrorism. ITAC's central function is to aggregate security intelligence then distribute its assessment of national security threats to other — if not all — partners within the security state. Focusing on the Algonquin's plan to take their protests to Ottawa, ITAC monitored and reported on a protest at Conservative Member of Parliament (MP) Lawrence Cannon's Maniwaki office (CSIS 2016-47: 159). At that protest, Cannon's assistant invoked long-held racist settler stereotypes by telling Matchewan to "come back when he was sober" (Pasternak 2013: 170). Afterward, Cannon (2008) publicly slandered the community as "dissidents." Matchewan (2008) publicly called out Cannon's attempt to discredit the community and its traditional leadership: "First his aide insinuates we're alcoholics; now he vilifies our community's majority as 'dissidents.' How much more racist contempt can we expect from his office?" ITAC continued to track protests, including those at INAC's Ottawa office. Documents describing the protests refer to demands to honour the Trilateral Agreement and customary Governance Code as emanating from "dissident" community members; because the surveillance reports were disseminated through security state agencies, using this language can be see as an effort to delegitimize, marginalize, and discredit the community (CSIS 2016-47: 386–87).

Keeping a watch over a number of Indigenous-related protests that were being framed as issues of national security, ITAC surveillance was particularly scrutinous of the May 29, 2008 National Day of Action (NDA) in which Barriere Lake members and allies were involved. In their reports circulated to other security agencies, ITAC admits that it was monitoring peaceful protests, yet simultaneously labels those participating as "extremists." One report from May 7 notes that Aboriginal leaders expressed that the NDA would be peaceful, however "non-Aboriginal residents of

contested areas [were] becoming increasingly frustrated with the protest actions and demonstrations by Aboriginal extremists" (ibid.: 123).
Framing protests under the banner of "extremism," ITAC reports discredit
Indigenous grievances and instead legitimize criticisms from non-Native
communities. These discursive practices of bolstering the complaints of
non-Indigenous people offer insights into the normative environments
of policing operations, where — perhaps unconsciously — the way that
events are reported on constructs a narrative that normalizes settler views
of Indigenous nuisance and delegitimizes Indigenous efforts to challenge
the settler colonial status quo. Nowhere in the documents do the analysts
at CSIS show concerns for the grievances of Indigenous Peoples. Instead,
security agencies treat non-Indigenous grievances as legitimate and non-
threatening, while Indigenous grievances are framed by agencies of the
security state (especially ITAC) as disruptions to settler colonial authority
and as national security threats under the framework of "extremism." In
these framing practices, national security agencies consider community
protests, in which children and Elders often participate, under the rubric
of anti-terrorism.

Classified as threats to national security, Indigenous self-determination
struggles and demands for rights recognition are subjected to ongoing surveillance. Leading up to the 2008 National Day of Action, ITAC catalogues
a list of ongoing Indigenous protests as "NDA related activities impacting
on national security" (ibid.: 154). In a section detailing policing measures
to prepare for the three thousand to five thousand protesters expected
to march in Ottawa, ITAC reveals the extent of security state surveillance
and issues a fuzzy warning that "Barriere Lake First Nation members have
indicated they may set up a Parliament Hill NDA encampment" (ibid.:
175–76). Although a Parliament Hill camp on unceded Algonquin territory
is framed as a potential national security threat, it reveals the fragility of
settler claims to Indigenous lands and the methods invoked to mitigate
displays of defiance.[13]

Another ITAC report, *Aboriginal Militancy — The National Security Factor,*
makes this more explicit (ibid.: 80). This report quotes Liberal Senator
Roméo Dallaire saying that "growing Aboriginal unrest may constitute an
internal security risk" and warning that Indigenous mobilizations could
bring the country to a "standstill" (ibid.). Representing an "internal security
risk" to the Canadian state, the Algonquins of Barriere Lake constitute
a threat to settler colonialism. Settler fears surrounding countrywide

disruptions would materialize through the Idle No More movement (detailed in Chapter 3), which was used as a further pretext to entrench and expand the security state. National Day of Action mobilizations demanding treaty rights and justice on Indigenous land were used by the security state to categorize Indigenous communities that challenged Canadian sovereignty and settler economies as a source of threat, which justified pervasive and perpetual surveillance.

PERPETUAL SURVEILLANCE AND THE EXTRACTIVE ECONOMY

Once classified as extremist and a national security threat, the Algonquins of Barriere Lake became a focus of constant scrutiny as a potentially deviant Indigenous community who refused to conform to the eliminatory prescriptions of settler society. The Algonquins of Barriere Lake appeared in an RCMP report called *Aboriginal Communities, Issues, Events and Concerns 2009/10*, produced by the Criminal Intelligence Division of the Aboriginal Joint Intelligence Group (AJIG).[14] In the report the AJIG "summarizes eighteen Aboriginal communities with existing issues and conflicts which could escalate to various forms of direct action" (RCMP 2013-5595: 8). The AJIG justifies profiling the Algonquins and other communities defending their land and rights with the following criteria: "history of violence, history of tension or conflict towards police involvement; militants operating within the community; threats against critical infrastructure, and; external influences (i.e. activist groups, government policies, major events)" (ibid.: 13). The report's executive summary highlights a number of upcoming, high-profile events where the RCMP feared "violence and criminal acts" could be committed, as Indigenous Peoples could attempt to raise "national and international attention" surrounding "ongoing unresolved issues" in their communities (ibid.: 8). Noting a series of events in 2009–10, including the NDA, the report warned of "increased uncertainty and concern" surrounding Indigenous protest activity (ibid.). These unresolved issues were categorized as grievances predominantly related to "federal government strategies and decisions" such as environmental disputes, treaty rights disputes, sovereignty disputes, economic disputes, internal conflict, lands claims, and social issues (ibid.: 19–20). Not surprisingly, the majority of the communities under scrutiny have grievances related to land rights and resistance to settler colonial resource extraction in the form of road and rail blockades.

As another information-sharing agency within the security state, the

AJIG extensively documented and reported on Indigenous activities that challenged settler colonialism. Similar to ITAC, AJIG reports express a logic of divide and conquer to marginalize and delegitimize resistance movements, referring to "small factions within a community, representing their own interests" and to "further their own agendas" (ibid.: 14–16). The AJIG paints Barriere Lake with this brush while acknowledging the role of Indian Affairs in fomenting division by having "appointed" an opposing Band Council at Barriere Lake in 2008, and indicating "that they [Indian Affairs] would no longer work with previous leadership" (ibid.: 22). In a context of INAC destabilization efforts, AJIG justifies ongoing surveillance and criminalization through a strategy of divide and conquer. AJIG and other actors of the security state reinterpret demands for autonomy and the upholding of treaty rights into the actions of "dissidents," "factions," or "splinter groups" who are delegitimized as rogues within the post-colonial imaginary.

After itemizing a host of communities that threaten the post-colonial order, the AJIG report then lists the Algonquins of Barriere Lake as an example of a community engaged in criminal actions by blocking Highway 117. Demonstrating how security agencies have utilized new concepts of national security to redirect resources against Indigenous and environmental movements (a topic we explore in depth in the next chapter), the AJIG put forward the facile claim that Highway 117 represents "major critical infrastructure" (also a topic we explore in depth in the next chapter) (ibid.: 14). For the Algonquins of Barriere Lake, the construction of the Mont-Laurier–Senneterre Highway (now Highway 117) in 1938 deeply impacted their lands and way of life by opening up their territory to further settler encroachment in the form of tourism and sport hunting.[15] This piece of "major critical infrastructure" was used to displace and dispossess the Algonquins from their land, as they were excluded from a ten-mile corridor on either side of the highway (Pasternak 2017: 66–67).

In addition to representing a threat to Canada's "major critical infrastructure," the community's resistance to settler colonialism is illuminated in an RCMP rubric that catalogues "issues that contribute to unrest in Aboriginal communities" (RCMP 2013-5595: 18–20). The RCMP describe the "root causes of unrest" as "either real or perceived," and the subsection describing "sovereignty disputes" succinctly illustrates how settler colonialism rationalizes the RCMP's antagonistic conceptualization of Indigeneity as hostile to the settler order (ibid.). Describing the need for increased policing over troublesome Indigenous communities, the RCMP claim sovereignty disputes transpire when "members of an Aboriginal community do not recognize the primacy of provincial and federal laws, and contravene these laws" (ibid.: 20). Reflecting how settler colonialism delegitimizes actions that challenge the "primacy" of Canadian sovereignty and the notion of Canada as a post-colonial society, these Indigenous communities are categorized as illegal and criminal. This suggests that these communities are themselves opposed to the rule of law, and they are therefore marked as priorities for intervention from the security state. Notwithstanding that, settler colonialism is itself opposed to the rule of treaty law when the logic expressed by settler colonial justice holds that Indigenous Peoples can only have "claims" to land, which can then be recognized by settler authorities.

Surveying the multiple security reports produced from monitoring and tracking Barriere Lake activity, the most common threat associated with the Algonquins of Barriere Lake stems from their disruption of extractive economies by denying access to their traditional lands. For example, a July 9, 2009 presentation from Indian Affairs provides an update on the department's approach to the Algonquins of Barriere Lake and references how INAC has put in place *"en mesure de contenir les 'débordements'"* ("measures to contain outbursts") including *"tolérance zéro pour barrage routier"* ("zero tolerance for blockades") as part of *"renforcement de la securité — une condition gagnante"* ("a winning condition for strengthening security") (INAC 2010-2705: 114–23).

Working with police and other actors of the security state, INAC describes how these "winning conditions" were in fact the goal of opening Barriere Lake territory for resource extraction. The July 9 presentation provides further insight into the role that industry plays in governmental calculations and interventions. One slide lists *"securité"* ("security") and *"accès aux ressources naturelles"* ("access to natural resources") as two key areas of coordination with the Quebec government (ibid.: 121). A subsequent slide highlights the necessity of protecting logging operations, noting *"opérations forestières et 'récoltes' à surveiller"* ("surveillance of logging operations") (ibid.: 122). A follow-up briefing dated July 30, 2009 notes that the "situation remains calm in the community," and that "forestry work [is] proceeding without hindrance" (INAC 2015-1265: 1068). For the security state, notions of "calm" are associated with unimpeded resource extraction, while blockades and disruptions are associated with crime, violence, and insecurity. In October, INAC again illustrates their role as a mechanism for the logging industry to take wealth from the community when they claim that the "current situation" includes "minimal disruption of forestry operations" (INAC 2010-2705: 29).

INAC's preoccupation with logging activities is made clearer in a briefing note to the Minister on January 29, 2010. The briefing highlights that "Quebec's main preoccupation in regard to Barriere Lake relates to forestry operations by Bowater around the community" (INAC 2015-1265: 1296). The briefing note indicates that logging company Bowater pleaded for INAC's Minister to act, citing 130 potential job losses if a permit was not issued (ibid.). Highlighting the perceived and ongoing menace of the Algonquins of Barriere Lake to settler economic interests, an August 6, 2010 briefing note emphasizes INAC's concerns about "mill closure threats in Maniwaki" (INAC 2010-1809: 460). With a friendlier Band Council in place, the briefing indicates that logging permits were indeed issued to Bowater and Domtar, demonstrating the necessity of having a Council installed that is willing to facilitate industry operations, outside of the Trilateral Agreement.

As we saw during INAC's 1996 intervention, the threat to settler economic interests in the form of job losses and potential mill closures prompted collaboration between the federal government, police agencies, and resource extractive industries. INAC's claims of *"progrès accomplis"* ("progress made") reflect some advancements in guaranteeing settler industries access to the forest (INAC 2010-2705: 117). These efforts were made possible as a result of the criminalization of many within the Algonquins of Barriere Lake community and an intervention into the traditional leadership selection process that appointed a new (more business friendly) Band Council. Matchewan explained, "Quebec is now using the leadership confusion created by the federal government's interference in our internal affairs as an excuse not to implement the [Trilateral] Agreement and to let forestry companies have their way on our land" (Matchewan interview). However, the new Council claimed authority based on the customary Governance Code. Given that the Algonquins of Barriere Lake continued to resist INAC intrusions, INAC decided to move forward with plans to eliminate the Code altogether.

THE ULTIMATE POLICING TOOL:
SECTION 74 *INDIAN ACT* ELECTIONS

Barriere Lake protests continued throughout 2008–09, challenging resource extractive industries and the INAC-recognized Band Council, which maintained its legitimacy based on the customary Governance Code. Alongside surveillance, criminalization, and police repression, INAC cemented plans to overhaul Barriere Lake's traditional governance structure. Eliminating customary governments has been a long-standing practice and legislative policy effort of the settler state. Shortly after the *Constitution Act* of 1867 created the federal dominion of Canada, colonial leaders moved to dismantle the traditional leadership structures of Indigenous Nations in favour of an elective system. The "gradual enfranchisement of the Indians" legislation was designed to give Indians "the benefits of municipal government" (Milloy 1983: 62). This and other settler colonial legislative measures served to eliminate Indigenous nationhood and bring Indigenous governance under the full control and jurisdiction of Indian Affairs. Barriere Lake's customary government system is based in the *Mitchikanibikok Anishnabe Onakinakewin*—an oral system of law based on the nation's connection to the land. INAC's assault on it was meant to disrupt the community's social and legal orders, from which the leadership derived its authority to govern and assert Algonquin jurisdiction over lands coveted by settler governments (Pasternak 2017: 163–65). After INAC's insistence that Barriere Lake's sacred constitution be codified in writing, steps were taken to manipulate and eliminate the legalities of the Code, claiming it was "weak and deficient" (INAC 2015-1265: 1552–53).

To eliminate the Code altogether, INAC resorted to drastic measures and invoked section 74 of the *Indian Act.* Section 74 gives the Minister of Indian Affairs the power to unilaterally depose traditional Chiefs and Councils and force new elections under INAC rules.[16] Though INAC has wide powers for controlling Indigenous governance, the imposition of section 74 is perhaps the most authoritarian — and perhaps the least frequently exploited — technique. Exemplifying the "shape shifting" (Alfred and Corntassel 2005) character of settler colonialism, INAC proceeded with the imposition of section 74 while at the same time acknowledging the measure as a "last resort" and the "antithesis of self-government" (INAC 2015-1265: 1055). Indian Affairs claims to only use the section 74 provision when "a community is in chaos," and the situation is "so volatile that no other option is viable," recognizing that "such an action ... would be viewed very negatively as an intrusion into the affairs" of a community (ibid.). However, it is INAC's penchant for intervention that instigated the so-called "chaotic and volatile" situation in Barriere Lake. INAC reasoned that "taking no actions would perpetuate the governance imbroglio" without acknowledging that security state interventions and refusal to honour signed agreements created the "chaos" and "crises" in the community (INAC 2010-2705: 32). In reality, the use of section 74 was viewed by colonial administrators as a necessary action to break the will of the Algonquins of Barriere Lake to continue demanding control over their lands. INAC's true motive is to work with those in communities who are willing to establish "practical working relationships" with the department and work together to "keep the reserve 'trouble makers' quiet" (Horn 1983: 39).

Following recommendations made in Perron's report, INAC decided it was worthwhile to use section 74 and eliminate the customary system of governance for the Algonquins of Barriere Lake. Unlike customary elections that are based on selection processes outlined in the Code, section 74 elections are governed through the *Indian Act*. Internal INAC documents reveal how the imposition of section 74 was utilized. A secret briefing note to the Minister on March 3, 2008 outlines INAC's rationale for instigating the leadership crisis, which is then used to justify imposing section 74 elections. INAC first acknowledges the decision to recognize a new Band Council headed by Casey Ratt, anticipating "strong reactions" from the current traditional Council headed by Benjamin Nottaway. INAC further anticipates the Nottaway Council laying claim to its legitimacy and blocking the arrival of the new Ratt Council. INAC then maps out how the traditional Elders Council would most likely initiate a leadership review process to challenge the government's move, which INAC could take as an opportunity to delegitimize the Code and "confirm the whole problematic with the current selection code which contributes greatly to the governance imbroglio" (INAC 2010-2705: 202). The Minister could then request both groups review the selection process "or be faced with the imposition of the election regime under the *Indian Act*, in accordance with section 74 of the Act" (ibid.). Using underhanded legal tactics and the power of colonial law, INAC believed it had outmaneuvered the Algonquins and, by implementing section 74, would not only revive the possibilities of bringing the community into the land claims termination tables, but also do away with the Trilateral Agreement once and for all.

As INAC predicted, the community challenged the Ratt Council's legitimacy. As a result, on August 11, 2009 INAC's Quebec regional office prepared a memo to the Minister where they recommended he impose section 74 elections on the Algonquins of Barriere Lake. Within, INAC reveals that carrying out such a drastic measure will require the collaboration and coordination of actions "with other federal departments, law enforcement agencies, and the Government of Quebec" (ibid.: 195). In preparation to execute the order, INAC bureaucrat Nathalie Nepton was tasked with preparing a backgrounder on the process. In a September 17, 2009 email, she reached out to her colleagues to share the information noting that if section 74 was used it "will require our collective efforts (misery loves company!)" (INAC 2015-1265: 1288). Although paid handsomely to carry out settler colonial policy from their cubicles in urban centres, colonial bureaucrats evidently resent their self-inflicted existence in "ABL World." Though bureaucrats at Indian Affairs make light of their "misery" in having to intervene in Indigenous communities by undoing traditional governance regimes, empathy is rarely displayed toward the Algonquins of Barriere Lake community.

Following the advice of INAC bureaucrats, INAC Minister Chuck Strahl notified the community on October 30, 2009 of his intention to impose a section 74 election in five months. The notice also states that "the Minister does not know anymore who the duly selected council is in Barriere Lake," knowingly creating and perpetuating a scenario that created its own justifications for increasingly dramatic interventions. Addressing this claim in a letter to INAC's Regional Associate Director General Pierre Nepton (relation to Nathalie Nepton unknown), the Algonquins of Barriere Lake state, "we do not believe that it is a matter of the Minister not knowing who to deal with; we believe it is more a function of 'who he wants to deal with.' It is clear that INAC is adverse [sic] to dealing with a council which refuses to comply with INAC's agenda" (ibid.: 2086). Strahl's letter, along with INAC documents, underline that INAC viewed the community's existing customary Governance Code as inadequate and required modification on INAC's legislative terms.

Draft speaking notes prepared for Pierre Nepton for a community meeting on December 19, 2009 further illustrate the contempt of settler colonialism toward Indigenous expressions of self-determination. Nepton's notes claim that the Code had "weaknesses" and "deficiencies" and was not compliant with the principles of "modern democracy" (with an emphasis on the secret individual ballot) (ibid.: 1552–53). INAC's conceptualization of "modern democracy" was juxtaposed with the "ambiguity" of the Code, which they said must be replaced with something "transparent, democratic, and accessible" (ibid.). Moreover, INAC's democratic prescriptions required that the community open voting to anyone claiming community membership, regardless of whether they live on the traditional territory and know the language and Algonquin customs, as required by the Code. The community responded to Nepton's visit with a letter dated January 13, 2010 (ibid.: 2084–89). The letter refutes INAC assertions, claiming that INAC has never presented any evidence or explanation for how Code "ambiguities" or "deficiencies" lead to governance disputes. Instead, Barriere Lake asserts that their "customs are not the problem; the problem is INAC's interference" (ibid.: 2086). Moreover, the community claims that it is disingenuous for the department to make such claims when it had insisted on the codification of the *Mitchikanbikok Anishnabe Onakinakewin* in 1996 and was involved in the process, accepting subsequently that the 1997 leadership selection process was "transparent and legitimate" (ibid.: 2087).

Regardless, INAC had no intention of allowing room for modification; elimination was the only prescription. Anticipating strong resistance, Indian Affairs prepared a host of techniques to fortify the legal manoeuvres required to impose section 74. The community had been undertaking a reconciliation process and developed a "broad consensus ... in favour of retaining our customs and against a section 74 order" (ibid.: 2086). They pleaded with INAC for an extension of the section 74 order so that the Code could be modified rather than eliminated. INAC regarded the community's gestures as "rhetoric," claiming "we have not seen any signs of reconciliation" (Simard interview). Declaring that "no extension will be granted" (INAC 2015-1265: 1061), INAC had no interest in negotiations. In preparing for potential legal actions, INAC claims any "injunction/stay will be appealed by Canada," with a motion made to "suspend the injunction until the appeal is disposed of" (ibid.: 1063). INAC preparatory documents further detail that even if those elected through the section 74 process do not live in the community, the Council will still be declared duly elected with no option for appeal. The internal process reveals INAC's determination for eliminating Barriere Lake's traditional leadership.

Through letters and INAC directives, the colonial bureaucratic strategy displays a consistent intent to undermine the Trilateral Agreement by negotiating exclusively with what Tony Wawatie from Barriere Lake referred to as a "puppet Council" (Wawatie interview). Criminalizing and

suppressing those that would not accept extinguishment, INAC systematically plotted to eliminate the traditional governance practices of the
community. Wawatie explained that, according to the Code, the leadership has to be connected to the land and speak the language; he saw INAC
efforts as an "excuse to undermine and sever our connection to the land ...
They want to deal with a weak Council and to undermine the agreements
that they have signed," with the purpose of controlling the community
and exploiting their resources. Preparing for community resistance to the
elections, INAC documents show that if there were attempts to "prevent the
holding of the election," arrangements had been made for the "electoral
officer [to call] upon the law enforcement agencies to deal with the situation" (INAC 2015-1265: 1066). With the security state placed on alert, INAC
imposed elections under section 74 of the *Indian Act* under ministerial
order on April 1, 2010. As a culmination of years of antagonisms toward
the community, the ministerial signature authorizing section 74 signified
the most explicit attempt to eliminate Barriere Lake's traditional government, and levied a form of collective punishment against the community.

Following the imposition of the section 74 election process, the
Algonquins of Barriere Lake wrote a series of letters to the Minister
rejecting the legitimacy of the ministerial order (ibid.: 1461–66, 2013–
18). Within them, they expressed a willingness to co-operate with INAC
demands to clarify the Code. For the Algonquins of Barriere Lake, section
74 represented not just an attack on their customary government, but an
attempt to sever their connection with the land and their language. Elder
Michel Thusky explained that their ancestors taught them to preserve their
language through the continuous use of traditional territory:

> We want to be able to preserve and protect our land, sustain our
> language, and conduct our assemblies in our own language. That's
> what we want to protect, the language, because a nation without
> its language is not a nation, and a nation without its territory is
> not a nation." (Thusky interview)

With their efforts ignored, the community protested and boycotted the
election process.

During that time, the Algonquins of Barriere Lake consistently reap-
peared on INAC "hot spot" notifications regarding protests in Ottawa and
blockades on the reserve obstructing the section 74 election process. The SQ
was called upon throughout the process to enforce INAC policy, evident in

Electoral Officer Bob Norton's emails. On August 1, he met with sq Acting Commander Robert Chaifaux in Maniwaki to make a formal request for extra police presence at the nomination meeting and assurance that "band members can access the meeting site with no interference" (INAC 2010-1809: 118). INAC files detail the monitoring of protests, including a blockade on July 22 as well as a demonstration planned for August 12, to which Norton indicated in an email that, "I have had discussions with the sq and requested that only four to six police officers be present. I explained that we will not be requesting road clearance and/or large number of arrests" (ibid.: 205). Norton's email suggests that INAC has the authority to direct policing operations, including the dismantling of blockades and ordering of mass arrests. As seen consistently over the historical course of settler encroachment on Algonquin land, governments and industry either direct policing operations or are accompanied by police to carry out resource extraction and enforce settler policy. Various emails from Norton reveal that, to circumvent protests on reserve, election meetings were held outside the community (ibid.: 103–04, 117, 410).

In the effort to further circumvent the section 74 protests and community support for their customary governance, INAC accepted nominations for the new leadership only via mail. Norton received five valid written nominations — one for Chief and four for Councillors — and acclaimed the individuals concerned, which was a sufficient enough process of "modern democracy" demanded by INAC to establish an *Indian Act* Band Council. However, the acclaimed Chief Casey Ratt refused the nomination on the grounds that it violated the traditional customary Governance Code (Ratt interview). In a letter to INAC, Ratt noted that less than ten people participated in an election that brought "serious harm to the social fabric" of the community because of the annulment of the customary Governance Code (INAC 2015-1265: 2019–2020). Ratt attributed the push for section 74 elections because

> they wanted to go ahead with their forest activities as soon as possible. Because if not a lot of mills would have closed in the surrounding area, Maniwaki, Buckingham and all those places would have closed down if there wasn't any volume of wood being provided to these mills ... Quebec played a big part in pushing the federal government to impose section 74. (Ratt interview)

Regardless, INAC declared that a quorum of four Councillors with no Chief was in compliance with *Indian Act* electoral regulations. Following careful planning, INAC's use of section 74 elections had succeeded in eliminating the Algonquin's sacred constitution. Norman Matchewan explained,

> Section 74 is erasing our identity. Our identity and our language have always been connected to our customs and our land. Section 74 ignores our relationship with the land and the animals. We're protecting it for future generations. To take that away is like taking someone's beliefs and religion. (Matchewan interview)

INAC's use of section 74 elections had succeeded in subverting the traditional practices of the Algonquins of Barriere Lake, which had been in place since time immemorial. Immediately following INAC's recognition of an absent government, the community reported that the new Band Council had held consultations with Quebec and logging companies. As agreements were signed, opening up Barriere Lake lands to the foresty industry, the community was compelled to continue resisting extractive industries as well as INAC's ongoing interference.

THIRD-PARTY MANAGEMENT:
"A COLONIAL STATE OF ARRESTED DEVELOPMENT"

The Algonquins of Barriere Lake remain under a section 74 *Indian Act* Band Council system; the erasure of the customary Governance Code has forced the community to engage in the colonial election process to regain control over decisions that impact their reserve and their territory.[17] Although INAC succeeded in eliminating the customary Governance Code, it did not succeed in ridding itself of the traditional leadership. As a result, conflict between the Algonquins of Barriere Lake and colonial authorities continues, predominantly surrounding the imposition of third-party management. Third-party management is controlled by a private-sector firm who is selected by the colonial bureaucracy to administer a First Nation's resources, and whose salary is paid for by the community.[18] As an additional level of surveillance over the community — intended to ensure their compliance with resource development and other financial requirements from INAC — the third-party management system has functioned as an extension of the security state.

In a May 2016 newsletter, the community outlines the decade-long government assault, describing the imposition of third-party management and section 74 as well as the criminalization of community members as being placed into "a colonial state of arrested development" (ABL 2016: 14). Third-party management was met with vehement opposition including numerous protests and legal actions, which were "not well received by INAC" and closely monitored by the security state (INAC 2015-1265: 994). Community opposition to the eliminatory prescriptions of settler sovereignty was viewed by the RCMP as a source of insecurity and unrest. In reference to a judicial review hearing regarding the legality of third-party management on March 16, 2009, the RCMP express concern that "the federal court's decision concerning INAC third-party management will influence future action by community members" (RCMP 2013-5595: 23). The RCMP conclude that "future protest action, both peaceful and non-peaceful is likely" (ibid.).

The Algonquins of Barriere Lake's ongoing struggles demonstrate the punitive nature of settler colonialism. The failure of the Algonquins of Barriere Lake to conform to settler norms and prescriptions — by demanding that settler governments honour signed agreements and revoke external administrative control — informed the policing response in the form of a series of overlapping punitive sanctions. Under the auspice of increasing "transparency" to appease mythical settler constructions of corruption on reserves (Palmater 2015), the Canadian government imposed the *First Nations Financial Transparency Act* (FNFTA) in 2014. The legislation targeted uncooperative Indigenous communities including the Algonquins of Barriere Lake and others under third-party management. INAC documents contain a report on outstanding financial submissions and list the Algonquins of Barriere Lake as "high risk" while outlining steps involving court action to enforce compliance (INAC 2015-1156: 1327–29). INAC emails show that the community last submitted consolidated financial statements in 2005–06, before third-party management was imposed. In typical fashion the community was blamed and sanctioning was required, even though an external firm managed the community's finances.

An INAC letter to the Barriere Lake leadership in November 2014 outlined a series of punitive sanctions for failing to comply with the FNFTA. Under the supervision of Regional Director General Luc Dumont and Senior Funding Services Officer André Bengle — author of the "ABL World" email — these punitive measures included withholding $18,708 for "non-essential programs, services, and activities" and that "further funding halts will continue to be applied" for continued non-compliance (INAC 2014-1546: 357). Dumont and Bengle also directed the third-party manager to "withhold any payment related to the Band Council members' retribution and travel expenses" (ibid.: 357–58). As delegated under the FNFTA, INAC officials planned to name Band members and display financial reports for non-compliant First Nations on their website — a typically settler colonial gesture of shaming intended to perpetuate racist settler stereotypes of backwards, corrupt Indians. A memo to INAC's deputy minister in September 2015 outlines "further action for willfully non-compliant First Nations" and the pros and cons surrounding options for halting all "non-essential funding" (INAC 2015-1156: 1542).

The community's ongoing opposition to third-party management prompted the colonial bureaucracy to threaten to cut health services, in addition to cutting "non-essential funding." A memo to Health Canada's deputy minister in November 2015, which outlines the implementation of a unilateral policy intervention regarding the reduction of "non-essential" health services for the community, notes that Barriere Lake's *"dettes demeurent"* ("debts remain") (ibid.: 2038). In a feat of morally bankrupt colonial calculus, INAC and Health Canada claimed they were owed over $750,000 from the Algonquins of Barriere Lake. The colonial bureaucracy continued to blame ongoing conflicts on divisions within the community and an unwillingness to take responsibility (ibid.: 2038). Demonstrating Janus-faced colonial power, the memo claims that the new Council restricts access to the third-party managers *"lorsqu'il est contrarié"* ("when it is annoyed") and uses this as a justification for pulling access to health care services (ibid.: 2039). The memo indicates that the community was warned that continued refusal to allow third-party manager access to the community would result in the suspension of non-essential services. Under the heading "Considérations," Quebec's First Nations and Inuit Health Branch threatened an unprecedented move: *"Si la situation se détériore davantage ... ce serait la première fois au Canada que Santé Canada suspendrait certains services essentiels dans une communauté des Première nations"* ("If the situation deteriorates further ... it will be the first time in Canada that Health Canada will suspend certain essential services in a First Nations community") (ibid.: 2042). Taking the unprecedented move of suspending a First Nation's essential health services coincided with preparations for security state responses to anticipated protests. An INAC email in January 2016 notifies bureaucrats that a "heads up" will be given to Public Safety's

Government Operations Centre and the Privy Council Office's Crisis Management Cell of upcoming protests in Ottawa (INAC 2015-1438: 163).

Third-party management, in tandem with a host of overlapping intervention techniques and punitive sanctions, has explicitly targeted the Algonquins of Barriere Lake's struggles for self-determination and maintenance of their traditional Indigenous lifeworlds. As an extension of settler colonialism's policing and surveillance techniques, third-party management is a mechanism to subvert Indigenous traditional governance structures. It is often used as a punitive tactic to destabilize communities and is enforced in part through police power. As an aspect of the security state, third-party management works in tandem with other intervention techniques, activating a surveillance apparatus to monitor Indigenous resistance to settler colonialism. As elements of the security state, these mechanisms are intended to ensure compliance with resource development and other settler colonial ambitions.

ON THE FRONT LINES OF "CANADA'S LOW-INTENSITY WARFARE ON FIRST NATIONS"

As a result of the decades-long struggle against settler colonial authorities, the Algonquins of Barriere Lake have been subjected to a series of security measures and punitive intervention techniques. The security state's primary objectives are facilitating access to their land while eliminating their traditional systems of governance; the targeting and criminalization of the Algonquins of Barriere Lake has been mobilized through the conflation of land defence with violence, militancy, and extremism. As fundamentally colonial practices, the interventions against the Barriere Lake community are part of an ongoing project that Russell Diabo has coined "Canada's low-intensity warfare on First Nations" (Pasternak, Collis, and Dafnos 2013: 80). These interventionary practices, increasingly framed around perceived Indigenous threats to national security, are used in tandem with a host of techniques to delegitimize and destabilize communities that resist settler colonialism.

For decades, the Algonquins of Barriere Lake's approach has remained consistent, reasonable and level headed. In 1989, after peaceful Barriere Lake blockades were met with police violence coordinated by the Quebec government and logging companies, national Chief George Erasmus explained in a press release that, for years, the Algonquins had tried to negotiate a conservation strategy with Canada and Quebec in "a very reasonable and level-headed way," despite accelerated logging and "strongarm tactics" (National Indian Brotherhood 1989b). Simply, the community does not want their land base to be destroyed; they want a definitive say in how the land is used; and they want to maintain their culture, language, and traditional governance. The community has never wavered from these demands despite seventy years of collaboration between settler governments, the logging industry and police agencies to suppress their rights. While the community has remained reasonable and steadfast, it has been the security state that has accelerated underhanded tactics with contempt and without remorse. The community is under constant surveillance, justified in part by the vicious cycle of security state reporting that marginalizes and criminalizes them as an internal security risk. The reasonable efforts of the Algonquins can be juxtaposed with the underhanded efforts of the security state — the collusion of a multitude of actors who work together to undermine and discredit a small community.

Barriere Lake resistance prompted the intense development of security state infrastructure surrounding the hot spot reporting system and fusion of policing and intelligence resources to respond to Indigenous dissent. Despite the enormous efforts and resources of the security state, the Algonquins of Barriere Lake have consistently defied and resisted settler colonial interventions. They continue to demand that settler authorities recognize and respect their self-determination outside of Canada's eliminatory logics and policies of extinguishment, and they serve as an example that shatters Canada's image as a post-colonial society.

The Algonquins are far from the only example of Indigenous communities that refuse persistent settler colonial interventions. Resistance to pipeline expansion emanating from Alberta's tar sands has provoked the security state to direct more resources into monitoring and stifling dissent in Canada's pursuit to claim ownership over Indigenous lands and resources. As we examine further in the next chapter, many of the tools of control utilized (and honed) against the Algonquins of Barriere Lake have been deployed against other Indigenous movements challenging settler authority and extractive capitalism. We focus on the rapid expansion of "critical infrastructure" as a technique for the security state to expand policing and surveillance practices, particularly against Indigenous movements.

Notes

1. However, scholars like Howard Adams (1995: 144) argue that constitutional documents like the 1763 Royal Proclamation "declared British ownership of Indian territory" and were deployed by colonial officials to "further encroach upon Native governments, to weaken them, seize Aboriginal land and resources, and to proclaim absolute control" over Indigenous Peoples. While the Royal Proclamation gave Indians the right to hunt on their territory, Adams argues that it stripped them of their rights to possession and control of their land.

2. The original comprehensive land claims policy of 1973 contained "blanket extinguishment" provisions, which required Indigenous Peoples to "cede, release and surrender" Aboriginal rights and title. While modified over the decades, the underlying "assumption of Crown sovereignty" in treaty making remains (Lawrence 2012: 71–72).

3. In addition to the Trilateral Agreement, the Algonquins of Barriere Lake signed an agreement with Quebec in 1998 outlining "co-management, revenue sharing and land-use" on their traditional territory (ABL 2016).

4. INAC records indicate Perron was paid handsomely. As a "higher rate appointment," one Perron invoice dated September 20–October 31, 2007, totals $20,224.97 (INAC 2016-847: 150, 207).

5. A copy of Perron's schedule from November 14–22 shows that while only three and a half hours were dedicated as an "official meeting" (original: *Réunion officielle*) with community members, Perron spent more time meeting with INAC officials as well as the third-party manager. Interestingly, Perron met with SQ Sergeant Nault on the evening before and the morning after his day on reserve, with the latter framed as a "debrief" (original: *débreffage*) (INAC 2016-847: 254).

6. This and all of the following French translations are the authors'.

7. From the outset, the community claimed Perron had a conflict of interest because of his role as a federal negotiator in a comprehensive land claim with the Atikamekw Nation in northern Quebec, whose territorial claim overlaps with that of the Algonquins of Barriere Lake (Nottaway 2007). INAC emails show that the department identified this possible conflict of interest in the lead up to Perron's nomination yet in the end shrugged it off as insignificant (INAC 2016-847: 208).

8. The new Band Council was led by Casey Ratt. In an interview, Ratt explained that at the time his Council had been offered large sums of money in exchange for "peace in the forest" and assurances that blockades and disturbances would cease (Ratt interview).

9. These include two INAC presentations on "Aboriginal Hot Spots and Public Safety" on March 30 (A0240846) and April 3, 2007 (2015-1603), and well as drafts of three RCMP presentations: "RCMP Response to Aboriginal Occupations and Protest" (February 2007 and April 21, 2008) (2015-9455) and "RCMP Operational Response to Aboriginal Occupations and Protest" (April 3, 2007) (INAC A0240846).

10. Under the slide heading "Criminal Intelligence," the RCMP proposes the "building of an intelligence network (i.e., INAC, CSIS, OPP, SQ, CBSA, DND, NRC, Transport, Health & DFO)" (INAC A0240846: 976).

11. In 2009–10 INAC identified "civil unrest" as a major concern and source of risk, which included demonstrations, occupations, blockades, marches or rallies, traffic slowdowns, hunger strikes, and even instances when the media are contacted to "speak of the community's grievances" (INAC 2016-448: 2). In addition to identifying the Algonquins of Barriere Lake as one of the top three most involved communities, INAC admitted that disputes with the government were a major motivator for civil unrest (ibid.: 3, 6).

12. Referred to at the time as Integrated Threat Assessment Centre.

13. In September 1988, the Algonquins of Barriere Lake set up camp on Parliament Hill. The RCMP swept through the camp, making numerous arrests for trespassing, and permanently confiscated tents and sleeping bags (Pasternak 2017: 129–30).

14. According to the report, the AJIG was created in 2007 "to collect and analyse information, and produce and disseminate intelligence concerning conflict and issues associated with Aboriginal communities" (RCMP 2013-5595: 12).

15. Highway 117 enabled the creation of La Vérendrye Wildlife Reserve, which comprises much of the Algonquins of Barriere Lake's traditional territory. Both sadly and ironically, there are no mechanisms in place to protect wildlife at all; instead, the land has become a haven for loggers and hunters.

16. Section 74 of the *Indian Act* states, "Whenever he deems it advisable for the good government of a band, the Minister may declare by order ... elections to be held in accordance with this Act."

17. When the section 74 Band Council's term expired, the community selected Council members approved by the Elders, which included Casey Ratt and Norman Matchewan (Pasternak 2017: 217, 269).

18. According to INAC, there were eleven First Nation Recipients under third-party management as of February 1, 2012 (INAC 2011-1703: 74).

CHAPTER 2

NORTHERN GATEWAY PIPELINES

Policing for Extractive Capitalism

Our people have had enough. We're not gonna just stand here and take the bullying and take it without a fight. We've had enough of these spoiled brats stealing off our lands and not accepting no for an answer. We're going to be the stern parent and say, "No, you're not coming in." (Unist'ot'en spokesperson Freda Huson, quoted in Lopez 2014)

A wooden bridge on a forestry road over the Morice River is the only transit route into Unist'ot'en territory. The Unist'ot'en Clan's — (C'ihlts'ehkhyu/ Big Frog Clan) of the Wet'suwet'en First Nation — territory is located in what is commonly referred to as northern British Columbia, at a critical juncture of multiple proposed oil and gas pipeline projects. Their territory has experienced multiple incursions over the years by energy companies and the RCMP, who have been working closely with other security state agencies toward the realization of the Enbridge Northern Gateway Pipelines project. As the frequency of these incursions increases, the Unist'ot'en and other Indigenous communities have been peacefully evicting industry workers and police from their territories, over a time period spanning almost a decade. In relation to the proposed Gateway pipelines, members of the community persistently travelled to meetings with local settler governments, company representatives, or shareholders to reiterate time and again that the energy company Enbridge does not have consent to build the pipeline on their territories and that it will never be built, period.

During one of these meetings, on August 24, 2010, two Hereditary

Chiefs of the Likhts'amisyu Clan — Hagwilakw and Toghestiy — delivered a clear warning to two Enbridge representatives at a meeting with the town council in Smithers, B.C., to cease further trespassing on their unceded territories:

> We cannot be clearer about our position, there will [be] NO PIPELINES like Enbridge ... going through our territories. Enbridge ignored our last statement at the Hudson's Bay Lodge (on December 9, 2009) where they were warned not to trespass onto Wet'suwet'en territories ever again. Because of your return, we are issuing each of you an eagle feather for trespass. This is the last warning that you will receive. If you are caught trespassing with plans to come onto our territories again, you will be dealt with according to Likhts'amisyu Law. Municipalities, Provincial Governments, and Federal Governments have no jurisdiction or authority over our unceded lands. The jurisdiction and authority belong to the title holders of the Wet'suwet'en House Groups and Clan Groups and nobody else. (Hereditary Chiefs of the Likhts'amisyu Clan 2014)

Despite numerous public iterations like these, Enbridge, settler governments, and agencies of the security state would not accept no for an answer. This is described by Wet'suwet'en Hereditary Chief John Ridsdale (Na'Moks), a member of the Tsayu Clan, House of Tsa K'ex Yex, who works in Smithers at the Office of the Wet'suwet'en's Natural Resources Department:

> I'll never forget what was said to us, [Enbridge] said, "Oh, we want to change your 'no' into a 'maybe' into a 'yes.'" And I just had to remind them — I think my grandson was five years old when they said that to me — and I said, "You know my grandson is five years old and he understand what 'no' means. He knows that 'no' does not mean 'maybe' and it certainly does not mean 'yes.' And you who are older than five years old and multimillionaires don't understand 'no.'" They were offended. And I really don't care if they are offended, no still means no. (quoted in Bowles and Veltmeyer 2014: 59)

Unist'ot'en leadership had previously sent letters to all parties informing them that no pipelines would be crossing their territory, and that they had constructed a permanent camp that blocks the proposed path of the pipelines.

These displays of defiance against the assertion of settler authority and extractive capitalism sparked an intense surveillance campaign directed at the Unist'ot'en and their supporters, which comprised one aspect of a broader security state campaign against all Gateway opponents. RCMP officers with the Critical Infrastructure Intelligence Team (CIIT) and Aboriginal Intelligence Group (AIG) closely monitored the Unist'ot'en's every move (RCMP 2013-5745: 453–56). As with the Algonquin resistance at Barriere Lake, the Unist'ot'en were constructed as a national security threat to justify the campaign of harassment and intimidation. A secret risk assessment compiled by Public Safety's Government Operations Centre (GOC) of pipeline blockades in B.C. even branded the camp as the "ideological and physical focal point of Aboriginal resistance to resource extraction projects" (PSC 2015-104: 2325). Unable to take no for an answer, the security state mobilized behind the forces of industry in a multi-year process that would ultimately be defeated.

EXTRACTIVE CAPITALISM AND THE
NORTHERN GATEWAY PIPELINES

As settler colonialism in Canada revolves around accessing Indigenous land, security state practices are deeply embedded in extractive capitalism. Vast accumulations of wealth by non-Indigenous people have derived directly from the "hyper-extraction of natural resources on Indigenous lands" over a centuries-long process of "colonial pillage" (L. Simpson 2013b). Recent iterations of settler colonial wealth extraction from Indigenous lands is particularly visible in the rapid expansion of the tar sands megaproject in northern Alberta as part of the "northwestern energy frontier," which includes the massive development of natural gas infrastructure in northeastern British Columbia (Barker, Rollo, and Battell Lowman 2016: 159). Indigenous communities on these territories have been systematically oppressed to ensure the plunder necessary for the accumulation of settler wealth, which is what former prime minister Stephen Harper romanticized when describing Canada as an emerging "energy superpower." In addition to an array of negative health impacts on Indigenous communities in and around the tar sands, wildlife populations and ecosystems have been devastated.

The rapid expansion of the tar sands and fracking infrastructure can be understood as a new model of extractive capitalism, or "extractivism" (Bowles and Veltmeyer 2014: 139–43). Extractivism involves creating frameworks to open lands for natural resource extraction (like mining, which Canadian companies dominate on a global scale), as well as rapidly developing extractive capitalist infrastructure that can export commodities to markets (ibid.). This demands that Indigenous communities abandon their way of life and connections to the land — their laws, governance, and title — as well as producing an onslaught of health problems from environmental pollution (Willow 2016; Preston 2017). To continue the expansion of the tar sands, government and industry wish to export the "slow genocide" of extractive capitalism by way of pipelines to foreign markets (Barker, Rollo, and Lowman 2016: 161). Indigenous communities most impacted by extractivism are on the front line, refusing pipeline projects that facilitate expansion of destructive megaprojects like the tar sands and refusing to accept notions of monetary value being able to offset the associated risks of oil spills on their waterways and the division of their territories. Mel Bazil of the Wet'suwet'en and Gitxsan Nations explains:

> The main reason we oppose these projects is because this is the dirtiest project on the planet, the tar sands. We are standing in solidarity with people affected and impacted currently by tar sands developments. We understand that the volumes proposed to be transported through our territories either by pipelines or rail would facilitate the expansion of the tar sands. (quoted in Lopez 2011)

Although the environmental consequences of the tar sands are well known by Canadian governments who claim leadership on climate change issues, political parties across the spectrum have supported corporate efforts to expand production and market to overseas consumers. Pipelines have become the signature mode of expanding production and with this comes the resistance efforts against new (or retrofitted) pipelines.

Enbridge's proposal for Northern Gateway emerged as one of the first and most elaborate pipeline proposals that aimed to expand tar sands production. As early as 2002, the Calgary-based multinational gas and pipeline corporation proposed a pipeline to transport stolen oil resources from Treaty Seven territory (Alberta) to the West Coast, which would then be transported by equally excessive tankers to the markets of the Pacific. A massive project in scope, the proposed pipeline is worth billions of dollars to the petroleum industry looking to open markets for the tar sands. Enbridge formally presented their proposal for construction to the National Energy Board (NEB) for consultation in May 2010. Enbridge's proposal included a marine terminal with two ship berths, eleven oil storage tanks, three condensate storage tanks, and a utility berth for tugs and other vessels. The facility would receive approximately 220 ship calls per year, including some supertankers. Per day, the twinned pipelines would carry 525,000 barrels of diluted tar sands bitumen and synthetic crude west and 193,000 barrels of toxic bitumen-thinning diluent east. The Northern Gateway Pipelines proposal is one of many — alongside Trans Mountain (west), Keystone XL (south), Energy East (east), and others including the recently approved Line 3 — all of which aim to secure foreign markets for the tar sands. Hyped by media and the petroleum industry as a $5.5 billion project, the proposal called for 1,177 kilometres of pipelines from northern Alberta to a port in Kitimat, British Columbia. Travelling over and through some of the most pristine and remote wilderness in the B.C. interior and Pacific Coast bioregions — and almost exclusively over unceded and unsurrendered Indigenous territories. Popular resistance to the Gateway proposal was immediate and widespread.

Indigenous communities opposing Northern Gateway put forth a number of concerns about the proposal. These included inadequate consultation and lack of consent for use of their land; a murky history of pipeline spills and industry/government spill response; tanker traffic on the coast; and all the interrelated effects on wildlife, culture, and water and food sources sustaining Indigenous communities. The pipeline route would cross 785 rivers and traverse three watersheds key to salmon habitat — Fraser, Mackenzie, and Skeena — as well as the Great Bear Rainforest, meaning that a spill could devastate local ecosystems (Swift et al. 2011). According to Enbridge data, the company spilled over 25 million litres of fossil fuels in 804 separate spills between 1999 and 2010 (Girard and Davis 2012). This data excludes the four million litres of tar sands crude spilled in Michigan's Kalamazoo River in 2011 from the ruptured Line 6B pipeline. Enbridge was widely criticized for its response to the spill, which has cost over $1 billion in cleaning efforts, and their negligence in correcting a "corrosion fatigue" issue that had been detected three times prior to the rupture (Brooks 2014). Researchers have also shown that Enbridge's Northern Gateway proposal was unequipped to deal with a pipeline spill (Gunton and Broadbent 2013).

In March 2010, a group of nine Coastal First Nations declared a ban on oil supertankers on the Pacific North Coast according to their traditional laws. Harold Yeltatzie, president of the Coastal First Nations, stated, "The consequences of a catastrophic oil spill on our people and our culture cannot be calculated or compensated" (Yinka Dene Alliance 2011). Later that year, sixty-one First Nations centred in the Fraser River watershed signed the *Save the Fraser Declaration*, which in upholding their ancestral laws, title, rights, and responsibilities, declared, "We will not allow the proposed Enbridge Northern Gateway Pipelines, or similar Tar Sands projects, to cross our lands, territories and watersheds, or the ocean migration routes of Fraser River salmon" (*Save the Fraser Declaration* 2010). Indigenous communities have united against tar sands pipelines and infrastructure given that they all depend on the water that connects their communities (Bowles and Veltmeyer 2014). Ridsdale stated,

> We won't let government and industry play First Nations off one another with their usual divide and conquer strategies. We are drawing the line in B.C. and First Nations are more united than ever before to stop the threat of oil spills. (Yinka Dene Alliance 2011)

Despite the substantive issues raised surrounding Indigenous jurisdiction and environmental impacts, a state–corporate collaboration emerged to mitigate opposition and try to push the pipeline through, demonstrating the pivotal role of extractive capitalism to settler colonialism in Canada.

Both historic Indigenous declarations on the comprehensive ban against tar sands–related pipelines and infrastructure were not well received by Enbridge or the security state. Rather than taking a step back to review the legal and international implications of defying Indigenous law by proceeding with the proposal and review process, Enbridge and the security state moved to undermine Indigenous land and treaty rights. Enbridge's Vice-President Commercial of Northern Gateway Pipelines Inc. Paul Fisher framed it this way:

> Aboriginal treaty rights are not absolute … Rights may be infringed upon. If infringement does occur, consultation is required. A project proponent has the obligation to mitigate infringement or provide accommodation, but that must be proportional to the scope and scale of the infringement. Accommodation can be reduced by a court. (Uechi 2012)

Representing Indigenous rights and claims as subordinate to their corporate or extractive development agenda, Enbridge moved quickly to consolidate support from government actors in an effort to delegitimatize Indigenous opposition. Facing well-organized and near-unanimous Indigenous opposition along the pipeline route, Enbridge and the federal government undertook the classic settler colonial strategy of divide and conquer.

A primary tactic has been offering economic enticements to Indigenous groups for participating in extractive capitalism on the contested lands. By offering marginal investment opportunities to First Nations leaders, the company and the government have prioritized these investment options as a development strategy meant to alleviate economic and social problems produced by settler colonialism. Following a typical development model, these options are supported (and often organized) by government agencies — in this case INAC — in collaboration with corporations. Corporations are enticed by the prospect of obtaining government support and approvals, as well as the promise of using this divide-and-conquer strategy to produce Indigenous "buy in." Briefing notes prepared for senior INAC officials for a series of meetings with Enbridge representatives convey how government and corporations collude in these efforts for promoting extractive capitalism. In the typical government language of settler colonial development, the note reads as follows:

> There are about 100 Aboriginal communities potentially affected by the project. At the same time, there is potential for the project to generate significant economic benefits for Aboriginal groups, including job creation and equity partnerships offered by the proponent. Such economic benefits can create support for the project among Aboriginal groups. (INAC 2012-88: 3)

In entirely downplaying the unanimous Indigenous opposition, the discussions between Indian Affairs and the corporation focus only on strategies to foster extraction. Nowhere has Indian Affairs defended claims to land, or Indigenous rights.

The focus of INAC meetings is exclusively to support Enbridge in their efforts to build pipelines. In doing so, INAC positions themselves as allies of Enbridge — and in opposition to Indigenous groups who resist the practices of extractive capitalism. Moreover, bureaucrats lend particular expertise within the INAC–Enbridge alliance in transmitting tactics for undermining Indigenous communities. For the Gateway pipelines, a key component of the INAC–Enbridge strategy was the development of a unique investment opportunity known as an equity stake. Developed through consultations with INAC, Enbridge offered First Nations who supported the pipeline a 10 percent equity in the project. This would allow First Nations to literally "buy in" as part owners of the pipeline with the possibility of sharing in lucrative petroleum profits from the state-supported tar sands economy. This was certainly a lucrative offer — a large amount of money combined with additional financial rewards — but the equity stake was twinned with a required gag order for those groups that signed on. An Enbridge presentation to the industry-friendly Canadian Council of Aboriginal Business in November 2010 detailed the range of economic incentives — equity shares, employment, contracting opportunities — offered to First Nations who surrendered land to the project. In return, the presentation detailed, "Participating Groups may raise legitimate, specific concerns via JRP [Joint Review Panel] process, but cannot proactively oppose project" (ibid.: 15).

The efforts of Enbridge — supported by INAC — to purchase the participation of some First Nations leaders shows they recognized that the major impediment to the project was the threat of Indigenous opposition. As a project of extractive capitalism within a long continuity of settler colonialism, the prospect of Indigenous resistance risked highlighting the dubious ethical and political character of the pipeline megaproject. In recognizing that Indigenous movements could present a moment of rupture by contesting the use of unceded land and the unfinished character of settler colonialism in British Columbia, Enbridge and the security state began to focus on suppressing the mobilization of Indigenous communities against the pipeline.

A "VESTED INTEREST": CORPORATE–SECURITY COLLABORATION AGAINST "ABORIGINAL SOVEREIGNTY CONCERNS"

Settler colonial desires to develop Gateway as an aspect of promoting Canada as an energy superpower had a profound and potentially unprecedented effect on security state dynamics. Enbridge, itself an energy superpower boasting a net worth of $166 billion, would play a central role in the policing efforts against pipeline opponents, chiefly Indigenous Nations invoking traditional laws to ban the company from their territories. Following Enbridge's NEB application and Indigenous legal declarations, the security state began to take steps toward a program providing policing assistance to the corporation as it progressed through the application and consultation process. Understanding the breadth of the opposition posed by multiple Indigenous communities asserting their sovereignty and rejecting the pipeline, the security state began to prepare to confront pipeline opponents.

A first step to coordinate policing efforts to support Enbridge was the convening of a national security stakeholders meeting at the Ottawa headquarters of the RCMP in August 2010. Under the title of "Enbridge Northern Gateway Pipeline Project — Intelligence Production Meeting," the RCMP's national security unit convened a broad array of actors to "provide a forum to discuss security concerns" related to the pipeline "with the objective of developing an integrated intelligence production plan" (RCMP 2013-5745: 229). Ches Parsons, the director of National Security Criminal Operations, sent a letter of solicitation to other policing agencies and partners, which shows the priorities of the meetings. The letter reads,

> Currently we assess the potential criminal threats to the Project as those associated to Aboriginal sovereignty concerns, environmental extremists and lone wolves; each having the potential and capability of conducting acts of unlawful civil disobedience, sabotage, vandalism, thefts and other criminal actions. (ibid.: 234)

The invitation sent to stakeholders contained no further information about specific threats or other participants. Simply listing "Aboriginal sovereignty concerns" as possessing an inherent element of criminality was explanation enough. In some instances, participants responded by email to ask specific questions. These informal communications shed more light on who the participants were; one email says "this is our initial meeting and will include RCMP representatives from 'E' [B.C.], 'K' [Alberta], 'HQ' [Ottawa], CSIS and Enbridge" (RCMP ibid.: 235). The direct involvement of Enbridge in the intelligence meeting is not mentioned in any other documents, including the summary document that was circulated post-meeting.

Though there are only a few declassified records regarding the substantive contents of this intelligence meeting, the summary document does provide further information about the integrated security apparatus that was under construction around the Northern Gateway proposal. Moreover, the tone of the RCMP summary illustrates the close relationship between the national security agencies and Enbridge. These close relationships between the policing agencies and a major corporation are key aspects of the security state, showing how industry and police integrate and share surveillance and intelligence in a coordinated effort to further settler colonialism. As a project to access Indigenous lands for the benefit of capitalist extraction, these close collaborations demonstrate how resources of the "war on terror" become reframed to police Indigenous dissent. While security state agencies such as the RCMP never hesitate to publicly declare their neutrality or impartiality, internal files show the extent to which the RCMP consider their role as a cheerleader of industry and an active enforcement arm supporting Enbridge's efforts. This is particularly evident in the Aboriginal Policing Services monthly reports, discussed further in the next section, which, over a number of years, tracked industrial projects in British Columbia and Indigenous opposition to them. Consistently outlining economic benefits while framing opposition as unreasonable, the collaboration between government and corporations is more than a friendly interaction. It reveals the ability of corporate power to command policing resources in the objective of advancing extractive capitalism.

During the national security stakeholders meeting in Ottawa, Timothy O'Neil, the coordinator of the meeting and a senior member of the National Security Criminal Intelligence division, acknowledges that "we all have a vested interest in the Enbridge Northern Gateway Pipeline Project" (ibid.: 245). Outlining how the "vested interest" is represented by the wealth produced by the pipeline project, O'Neil's summary of the meeting begins by saying how "the financial benefits of the pipeline ... [are] well documented" but acknowledges that there remain "many who oppose" its construction (ibid.: 178). O'Neil notes that "associated criminal activity" with pipeline opponents "will be experienced" during the NEB process (ibid.). Under the "Discussion" section of the meeting summary, O'Neil again outlines the benefits from the pipeline — in a way that could easily be mistaken as a clip from Enbridge promotional materials — including how the NEB process will be approved "in accordance with strictly enforced federal government regulations which will include consideration for the health and safety of Canadians, Aboriginal concerns, and the safety of the natural environment" (ibid.: 179). Dispensing with legitimate concerns about Enbridge's less-than-stellar environmental record (Girard and Davis 2012; Gunton and Broadbent 2013), O'Neil mentions recent oil spills from Enbridge piplines only in the context of how such disasters might bolster "physical/violent opposition" to pipelines (RCMP 2013-5745: 179). Though it should have absolutely no bearing on questions of public policing, the summary goes on to list advantages and disadvantages of the pipeline. Under the heading of "wide support" for the pipeline, the document lists trade union member employment, pipe manufacturing employment, support and service industries, as well as "many spin-off jobs" and "legacy jobs" (ibid.). Under the heading "those opposed to the pipeline project," the RCMP list three general categories "associated" with Aboriginal sovereignty concerns, a variety of environmental awareness groups, and others who may be impacted during the construction and the subsequent life of the pipeline (ibid.).

None of the items are explained any further than their categorization as "opposed to the pipeline." Leading the list was "Aboriginal sovereignty" — a term that is often used by security agencies as a code for radical Indigenous movements. Unlike the discussion of the noted "wide support" for economic growth and jobs offered by Enbridge, there are no additional points about the legitimate land claims grievances, lack of consultations even by settler colonial standards, or the history of land theft. Though the majority of First Nations were emphatically (and publicly) opposed to the pipeline — despite the efforts to buy off Nations with lucrative enticements — the notion of "sovereignty" is invoked to suggest these are the irrational and uncompromising Indigenous Peoples who have not been adequately assimilated into settler society. In addition to the backward Indigenous sovereignty opponents, the other two opponents are presented as pests or nuisances. No explanation is offered regarding the claims from "environmental awareness groups," and the final group of those impacted by construction are construed as NIMBY-esque complainers.

As an aggregate, the opponents of pipelines are represented by meeting participants as unruly and unreasonable outsiders. Given that Enbridge is the "stakeholder" with whom the security state explicitly voices support, the outsiders are cast as the villains who present a threat to the prosperity and development of the megaproject. The conclusions of the meeting notes represent how these meetings foster close corporate–state relations. Under "recommendations," the summary states that "E, K, and HQ, [redacted], will collaborate in the production of associated classified and unclassified intelligence products for the benefit of the RCMP and other law-enforcement agencies; other federal and provincial departments; related stakeholders and, not exclusively: [redacted]" (ibid.). As a stakeholders meeting, the inclusion of the redacted entities — elsewhere listed as Enbridge — illustrates the integration of corporate influence into the policing of Northern Gateway protests. Rarely, if ever, are Indigenous or environmental groups considered stakeholders. Yet, corporate interests get to sit at the table and strategize with the security state about how to promote pipelines as an integral aspect of the Canadian economy. Further recommendations from "E" Division note that each detachment in the North District "will identify one member to be the equivalent of a Counter Terrorism Information Officer (CTIO) ... responsible to provide detachment members with intelligence and information from a national security and critical infrastructure protection perspective" (ibid.: 180). By the conclusion of the meeting, coordination of this security hub was tasked to Timothy O'Neil under the office of critical infrastructure protection, as a long-term project that would integrate multiple departments and agencies.

CRITICAL INFRASTRUCTURE AND THE THREAT OF "ENVIRONMENTAL CRIMINAL EXTREMISTS"

Surveillance of Northern Gateway opponents involved intelligence sharing across a range of agencies in the security state. Coordinated by the RCMP, this network also included CSIS, the NEB's security personnel, local and regional police, petroleum firms, and private security firms. Not coincidentally, the Northern Gateway policing effort was organized under the growing rubric of critical infrastructure that had been emerging as a central node in reorganizing national security bureaucracies toward domestic surveillance (see Monaghan and Walby 2017). "Critical infrastructure" is an organizational mechanism of the security state that redirects the vast resources of the "war on terror" toward a broad spectrum of domestic actors. It was used to characterize the Gateway pipelines proposal. Despite the pipeline not being an actual piece of infrastructure, the policing agencies operating under the protection of critical infrastructure share close relationships and an ideological partnership with the corporate world of extractive capitalism, as discussed at the shareholders meetings. Given these affinities, the banner of critical infrastructure has been a prominent category by which Indigenous communities that assert their rights and self-determination can be labelled as national security threats, which then allows the security state to intensify the surveillance and policing of these movements.

A useful articulation of how critical infrastructure shapes collaborations between the security state and extractive corporations is provided by director of CSIS, Dick Fadden, at the Canadian Association of Petroleum Producers (CAPP) annual meetings in April 2012. As a major annual event for the energy industry, the guest list featured many major corporations. The headline speech from Fadden begins with lamenting encryption technologies; then, he delves into general statements about the potential criminality of Indigenous and environmental movements, or groups who "oppose issues such as the perceived oppressive effects of capitalism" (CSIS 2012-27: 5). Importantly, the specifics of criminality were not mentioned — because the specifics are likely trivial — and the thrust of the speech was grounded on the understanding, like the RCMP's "intelligence production" meeting, that the threat from social movements is a threat against the profitability of the tar sands. Moreover, the speech suggests that the purpose of Fadden's attendance was to develop systematic surveillance collaborations between the security state and extractive corporations as "corporate partners" (ibid.: 8). In detailing a new CSIS Liaison Awareness Program, he says,

> These developing relationships, we hope, will not be a one-way dialogue. We feel we also can benefit from the insight and experience of our partners. The entrepreneurial or private sector community has its own considerable expertise in risk assessment, and has much to contribute to the dialogue about threat management and mitigation. (ibid.)

Underlining the benefits from private-sector partners, Fadden emphasizes how agencies like CSIS and the RCMP have sought to bring corporations into an intelligence sharing "dialogue" through more formal mechanisms.

Transforming national security practices around the theme of critical infrastructure protection has cemented the position of corporations within the security state. Although critical infrastructure protection only began to be formalized after the National Strategy for Critical Infrastructure was published in 2009 (Canada 2009a, 2009b; Monaghan and Walby 2017), the organizational approach has evolved quickly due to the resources given to national security policing, as well as the benefits for private corporations. In large part, the high priority for "partnerships" with the private sector has been rationalized because over 90 percent of what is considered critical infrastructure is claimed to be owned and operated by private corporations (Canada 2009a, 2009b). Given these institutional arrangements, the corporations have become more than merely stakeholders — they are now active policing partners. The implications of the partnership are profound given the impacts on targeted social movements, or democratic practices more broadly. After all, it is in Enbridge's best interest to ignore Indigenous law declarations since they are a corporation whose primary concern is bolstering profits. Yet, provincial and federal governments are bound by the Canadian constitution and numerous court rulings to consider the implications of contestations over lands unceded by treaty. However, within the broadening domain of the "war on terror," security state officials can easily evade or ignore any responsibility toward Indigenous communities. Moreover, given the close relations between the security state and tar sands corporations, Indigenous communities have become increasingly surveilled and criminalized by the security state through the framing of pipeline opponents as "environmental criminal extremists." In 2012, the federal government established an RCMP counter-terrorism unit (INSET) in Alberta to "protect" the energy industry.

The security state focused particularly on environmental movements opposed to tar sands development that aligned themselves with Indigenous movements. For the security state, a well-organized and globally connected environmental movement working in solidarity with the decolonial praxis of Indigenous communities represented a significant threat to critical infrastructure and the development of extractive capitalism. On January 9, 2012, one day before the NEB hearings commenced, Natural Resources Minister Joe Oliver issued an open letter targeting Northern Gateway opponents. Oliver labelled Indigenous communities and environmental groups as "radical" enemies of progress acting against the "national interest" (Oliver 2012). Outlining the Harper Government's unconditional support for energy corporations and extractive capitalism, Oliver claimed that "these groups threaten to hijack our regulatory system to achieve their radical ideological agenda" (ibid.). Glossing over the billions in tar sands foreign investment and government subsidies, Oliver proclaimed, "They use funding from foreign special interest groups to undermine Canada's national economic interest" (ibid.). Oliver declared that long delays for major projects were no longer acceptable, thereby justifying the government's upcoming gutting of environmental legislation (that would, in turn, help spark the Idle No More movement). This was the result of a collaborative effort emanating from energy industry interests directly linked to tar sands pipelines proposals.

Though environmental movements have a poor track record of

recognizing their own settler colonial characteristics, the movements against the Northern Gateway Pipelines provided elements of the environmental movement the opportunity to place a critique of settler colonialism at the forefront of their political struggle. Although there is still much to be resolved between Indigenous and environmental movements, the solidarity between them that was evident in the early stages of the campaign against the pipeline captured the attention of security agencies who recognized the power of the coordinated opposition to the pipeline. A slide deck from Enbridge that was provided to INAC's Deputy Minister Michael Wernick during an unofficial lobbying meeting on September 21, 2011, expresses these concerns from the vantage point of Enbridge and the government.[1] Under the headline "New challenges," one presentation details the growing threat of international funding to "green lobbyists" (INAC 2012-88: 29). Without a trace of irony from a department thoroughly embedded into the network of energy lobbyists, the presentation highlights the threat of U.S. funding and provides an itemized list of environmental and Indigenous entities who have received funds from U.S. foundations (ibid.). Moreover, a separate briefing note to the Minister of Indian Affairs outlines that "One of the main obstacles for the project is the unsettled land claims in BC" (INAC 2011-1387: 2). It concludes by warning, "Opposition to oil sands projects including the Northern Gateway has become a big fundraiser for environmental non-governmental organizations" (ibid.).

With an acceleration of collaborations between the security state, Indian Affairs, and tar sands corporations, the framing of opponents as foreign agitators hedged against the national interest contributed to an overall narrative of pipeline opponents as serious threats to national security. In an email to colleagues from multiple agencies in the security state, O'Neil from the Critical Infrastructure Intelligence Team notes that "Canadian law enforcement and security intelligence community have noted a growing radicalized environmentalist faction within Canadian society who is opposed to Canada's energy sector (RCMP 2013-5745: 156). Using language developed in the context of the "war on terror" to describe domestic threats to national security, O'Neil claims that "environmental extremists associated to well funded NGOs have the expressed intent and demonstrated capability to engage in criminal activity to prevent and disrupt the development of the Alberta Oil Sands" (ibid.). In his assessment, O'Neil identifies "environmental extremists including Greenpeace as credible criminal threats to Canada's energy sector" (ibid.). In a clear attempt to transplant the language of terrorism into a social context of protest and democratic dissent, O'Neil concludes, "Environmental criminal extremists have ... the objective of influencing government policy, interfer[ing] within the energy regulatory process and forc[ing] the energy industry to cease operations that they assess as being harmful to the global environment" (ibid.: 157).

An irony of O'Neil's statement is that his policing efforts have explicitly facilitated industry lobbyists becoming more intimately embedded in the bureaucratic and regulatory framework of the settler state, which has had profound influence on regulation, legislation, and policing. Demonstrating how the security state has branded protests as forms of crime (and terrorism) for attempting to influence government, while considering corporate collaborations as an integral aspect of national security policing, O'Neil writes the following to his peers:

> While the private sector is required to be prepared for all hazards, most often in accordance with federal and provincial regulations, it does not have ready access to criminal intelligence that will identify potential and/or credible criminal threats. Therefore it is incumbent upon the appropriate federal and provincial authorities to share responsibility for the protection of Canada's energy sector with the private energy sector stakeholders. (ibid.)

With a deepening of the alignment between the security state and extractive corporations, threats to pipeline development allowed for an extensively broad program of surveillance.

Given that the Gateway pipelines were only proposed, the security state was not merely protecting a material piece of infrastructure but promoting the proposal to create the infrastructure. In doing so, the security state began collecting information on any activities that represented opposition to the tar sands, often combining environmental movements and Indigenous groups into aggregated databases. Despite many overlaps and shared affinities between these movements, they are nonetheless distinct movements with differing constituencies and allegiances, differing places in the social hierarchy, differing decision-making structures, and distinct approaches to strategies and tactics. The environmental movement commands strong mobilization capabilities and many of the reports highlight a potential threat where movement resources support Indigenous rights. Cognizant of the influence of the environmental movement, the security state was particularly attentive to situations where environmentalists would advance the claims of Indigenous communities. For example, an entry in the March 2011 *Aboriginal Issues Bulletin* notes the following:

> Enbridge experiences some form of opposition at many of their community presentations throughout North District. Media coverage on the perils of pipeline development has resulted in a grassroots alliance of First Nations and environmental groups working together in opposition to the proposal. Enbridge will likely continue to face protest and possible direct action as they attempt to garner support in First Nations communities for the pipeline proposal. (ibid.: 543)

With a focus on "garnering support" from Indigenous communities, Enbridge — and the security state — recognize that the pipeline requires the theft of land or the use of unceded land in typical settler colonial fashion. Although settler colonial authorities have a long history of using legal techniques of land theft to promote development, the moral authority to carry out these practices must be managed to confer a legitimacy to this project. As articulated by the security state, a "grassroots alliance" between environmentalists and Indigenous communities might disrupt the efforts of Enbridge to "garner support." Again demonstrating how security state agencies like the RCMP become supporters and facilitators for large tar sands corporations, specifics about the political opposition are ignored and the protests are represented as merely criminal.

This tacit rationalization of pipeline development works simultaneously to disqualify legitimate land claims made by Indigenous groups (and supported by environmental groups). Unlike the summary of Enbridge claims regarding economic development and pipelines that are articulated by the security state, Indigenous claims to land, or expressions that contest the logic of settlement and development, are never mentioned. Instead, they are presented as a panoply of irrational grievances. Little has changed in the representation of Indigenous grievances from the land expropriations of the nineteenth century (see Carter 1990) and Canadian civilizing missions that required the assimilation of Indians of "good moral character" (Lawrence 2004: 30); contemporary police continue to rationalize ongoing surveillance efforts against pipeline opponents on the basis that opponents are unreasonable and are enemies of development, progress, and Canadian values.

To support extractive capitalism, the security state circulates disparaging claims of Indigenous groups by presenting them as irrational and potentially violent, as with the Unist'ot'en Camp. Adding the potential threat of an alliance with environmental groups further reinforces the potential for political opposition against the corporate members of the security state. Under the expanded rubric of national security, these opponents of extraction are deemed to be potentially criminal and worthy of intensified surveillance and policing. In a typical illustration of the normality of monitoring potential tar sands protests, Aboriginal JIG analyst Catherine Greenley circulates warnings such as the following:

> While most of the protest activity has been peaceful and within the law, [redacted] this issue has the potential to cross the line from peaceful protest, to civil disobedience or acts of violence. The situation continues to be monitored for development. (RCMP 2013-5745: 600)

With such an extensive mandate, the security state has placed the entire political spectrum opposing the tar sands under scrutiny. Though protest may be entirely peaceful, opponents cannot escape the label of violence and criminality — and the resulting policing efforts of the security state.

The scope of the surveillance regime attached to the Northern Gateway proposal was widespread, casting intense scrutiny toward any groups or persons contesting the norms of energy extraction and tar sands development. A central theme, or fear, articulated by the RCMP was the "growing" movement, as well as the twinning of environmentalists with Indigenous groups. The following "analysis" was provided by the RCMP at the beginning of the NEB hearings:

> Analysis: Two weeks of protest against KEYSTONE XL PIPELINE in Washington, D.C., followed by the large Ottawa protest on Sept 26, 2011, indicates a growing group of protesters are willing to not only protest, but risk arrest in order to oppose pipeline development in North America. ENBRIDGE will experience increasingly intense protest activity due to the environmental sensitivity of the NORTHERN GATEWAY path, combined with the fact that the territory has never been ceded to the Crown by First Nations in B.C. (ibid.: 641, emphasis in original)

Acknowledging the settler colonial reality of land theft and the mobilization capacities of the environmental movement, the document provides a lens into the concern — even care — that the security state extends to Enbridge. At the other end of the police–Enbridge friendship is hostility toward those who "oppose pipeline development." Under the mantle of protecting critical infrastructure, the security state has rationalized a widespread surveillance program targeting opponents of tar sands development and, to legitimize these practices, has also engaged in the construction of a quasi-criminal identity under the "war on terror" rhetoric of extremism. As we detail, the elastic construction of protest activity as national security threats illustrate the animosities of the security state toward opponents of tar sands development, as well as the terms of reference that justify widespread and pervasive surveillance practices under the banner of national security.

"SECURITY PEERS" PREPARE FOR ENBRIDGE HEARINGS

To undertake a joint environmental and regulatory review of the proposed Gateway pipelines, a three-member review panel was established by the NEB. The NEB scheduled hearings for 2012 and 2013 on Enbridge's Gateway proposal in seventeen communities across British Columbia. However, to fulfill Canada's "energy superpower" ambitions, the NEB had lost any legitimacy it may once have enjoyed. Adam Barker, Toby Rollo, and Emma Battell Lowman (2016: 159) describe the NEB as "a facilitator for Enbridge and other energy corporations, in many cases rubber stamping approval for pipeline construction." Many Indigenous communities boycotted the "consultations," citing a lack of free, prior, and informed consent. Jasmine Thomas, a Dene woman and Frog Clan member from the Saik'uz First Nation, describes how the Yinka Dene Alliance — a group formed in 2010 that includes Indigenous Nations whose territories comprise 25 percent of the proposed pipeline project — asked for a separate First Nations review process that would not only recognize the cumulative impacts of climate change and the expansion of the tar sands as related to the pipeline project, but also respect Aboriginal rights and title (Bowles and Veltmeyer 2014: 28). Thomas stated,

> They are not respecting our ways of how we govern ourselves here and because of the lack of treaties in the area, we are still the sovereign stewards of this land. There is no bill of sale to say that they are allowed to proceed. (ibid.)

Given the strong opposition to the NEB process, the security state made preparations to control any outbursts or displays of resistance associated with upcoming NEB "consultations" and the various related decisions that would unfold. Further, Indigenous communities asserting legal jurisdiction over territories coveted by Enbridge came under increased surveillance and were framed as criminal, economic, and national security threats.

In preparing for the pipeline hearing process, the security state and their peers from Enbridge and the NEB engaged in extensive collaborations. These collaborations provide an illustration of how the security state — particularly under the banner of critical infrastructure protection — functions as an enforcement arm of extractive capitalism. A prominent venue for these state–corporation relations — uncovered by investigative journalist Tim Groves (2012) — was known as the semi-annual classified briefings for Energy Sector Stakeholders. Emerging in parallel with the Gateway hearings, the Energy Sector Stakeholders meetings fused national security bureaucracies with critical infrastructure corporations into an institutional hub for security intelligence sharing. The meetings were organized by Natural Resources Canada (NRCan) but coordinated and chaired by the RCMP's Timothy O'Neil. Importantly, these meetings served as an official platform to merge the energy companies into the security state.

Held at the CSIS headquarters in Ottawa, the meetings had approximately one hundred participants, half of whom were from energy corporations. Representatives from the energy sector were authorized with at least Level II (secret) security clearance, allowing them to view classified intelligence. According to the RCMP, the briefings were intended to "provide intelligence to select energy representatives so they are able to implement the required security precautions to protect their assets" (RCMP A008499: 2). Granting high-level security clearance to former police officers who went on to work for energy companies allowed for more effective, two-way exchanges of security intelligence, where corporations like Enbridge could in turn share the information it gathered on pipeline opponents with law enforcement agencies. These exchanges furthered the working relationships between the security state and the corporations and, as O'Neil expresses in his invite to energy sector participants, ensured that the national security police were equals with their energy counterparts. Describing the "purpose of the panel," O'Neil describes how the meetings "provide a briefing to the Government of Canada so that it is aware of your initiatives, and secondly and of more value to your security peers, discuss your security procedures, lessons learned, etc." (RCMP 2012-7489: 5). The meetings served to consolidate security peerships between law enforcement and the energy industry, further embedding the latter into the security state.

Critical infrastructure protection has served as the institutional rationalization to fuse the national security apparatus with the energy corporations as "security peers." Energy Sector Stakeholders meetings are highly illustrative of this fusion because so many of the meetings focus on social movements as threats to critical infrastructure. Meetings have highlighted the Northern Gateway Pipelines, protests against nuclear energy, the G20 and G8 protests in Toronto, "eco extremism," and "aboriginal land issues." Given growing opposition to extractive projects, one of the meetings featured a workshop with the theme "North American Resource Development at Risk," which featured a number of sessions on potential threats to energy development. One set of meetings concluded with a panel on the "legal challenges of infrastructure protection: collecting evidence for prosecutions in Canada" (NRCan 7040-12-214: 13–17). Providing more than two-way security intelligence transfers, the meetings also function to entrench the relationships between the security state and energy corporations.

As preparations for the NEB hearings got underway, the Energy Sector Stakeholders meetings focused on how to direct more resources toward policing Gateway opponents, as well as how to improve the monitoring capacities of environmental and Indigenous groups. Leading up to the May 2012 meetings, O'Neil wrote to Denis Rivais (Alberta) and Dan Bond (B.C.) to ask that "E/INSET [Integrated National Security Enforcement Team] provide a briefing in collaboration with 'K' NSES [National Security Enforcement Section] regarding the RCMP's plans for the Northern Gateway Project, and other projects associated to the Oil Sands" (RCMP 2012-7489: 3). The email added that O'Neil will "also be soliciting the assistance of Enbridge and the National Energy Board to impart from their perspective how the Project has evolved including lessons learned thus far" (ibid.: 4). Underlining the importance of including the oil sands corporations, O'Neil adds that "there will be many petroleum representatives from Alberta and B.C. in attendance — most of who are retired members" (ibid.). Referring to how many of the energy corporations have representatives who are former RCMP members illustrates the close relations between the security state and the petroleum economy.

The institutional formation of the Energy Sector Stakeholders meetings further affirms these relations. In another example of close relations between the security state and extractive corporations, agendas for subsequent meetings in May 2013 (NRCan 7040-13-094: 1) included advertisements that note receptions for the meetings are to be co-hosted by the companies Bruce Power and Brookfield, while breakfast, lunch, and coffee was sponsored by the Gateway pipelines applicant, Enbridge. As an illustration of the rapid expansion of powers and collaborations under critical infrastructure, the Energy Sector Stakeholders meetings demonstrate how the security state has integrated extractive corporations. Liaising as "security peers," the flow of surveillance information becomes far more fluid as do the capacities to deploy national security resources toward protest groups or pipeline opponents. As a mechanism that clearly creates an us-versus-them view of environmental protests, the repercussions of the state–corporate fusion are significant. Opposition to the hearings became an acute focus of the security state that, as we detail below, set in motion plans to monitor and mitigate any opposition to the pipeline.

PIPELINE OPPONENTS UNDER SURVEILLANCE

As soon as the NEB announced the public consultation process, referred to as the Joint Review Panel, the security peerships formed over the course of multiple meetings over multiple years were put into practice. A major result of these relationships was the ability to engage in widespread surveillance of the Northern Gateway consultation process, the extent of which involved the collection of information — through public and covert mechanisms — of almost any protests against the pipeline. Much of the information collected on individuals involved highly mundane activities, but was nonetheless pervasive. Policing bodies were most attentive toward Indigenous protests, as well as environmental movements that allied with or supported Indigenous struggles. The RCMP's "E" Division Aboriginal Policing Services devoted their monthly intelligence reports (also known as strategic outlook reports, but specifically titled *Aboriginal Issues Bulletin* in 2010 and early 2011) to tracking pipeline opposition, warning that "Opposition to the project is growing" (RCMP 2013-5745: 428). The report warned that a Wet'suwet'en protest in Smithers, B.C., and a mock oil spill and occupation of Enbridge's office by Greenpeace in Vancouver "indicate there is a diverse grassroots opposition to the proposed pipeline" (ibid.). The assessment concluded that "increased protest activity and media attention is likely with the commencement of the Joint Panel Review public sessions" (ibid.).

In addition to Aboriginal Policing Services, the RCMP's CIIT and AIG took the lead in monitoring and tracking the daily activities associated with the Northern Gateway resistance. As the main contact and information liaison of the AIG, Catherine Greenley maintained a calendar of all Indigenous protest activity related to energy extraction and circulated these monthly calendars to members of the AIG. Under a preface that says, "This report is for law enforcement use only, and is not to be disseminated externally," (ibid.: 495) the scope of activities and groups featured in these reports expands far beyond national security issues, or even issues of supposed criminality. The reports consist entirely of organizations and actors that were at odds with the extraction and energy agenda supported by the RCMP and their "security peers" within major corporations. Often threat reports would mention items like an "all-native basketball" tournament, youth protests, or the No Tanks Flotilla.

Some of the declassified calendars contain a colour-coding system that uses a red highlight to denote potentially contentious events. These red events are almost exclusively Indigenous events. Highlighted in red in one monthly calendar are the "pipedreams project" (kayakers paddling to raise awareness about the Enbridge proposal), the NEB hearings in Prince George, and an event under the name "Stop the Site C Dam — Paddle to the Premier." Other non-red events also under scrutiny included a "Rally with Betty," the Enbridge presentation to the Chetwynd Chamber of Commerce, a B.C. Salmon Farmers AGM, the Sea to Sands Conservation Alliance anniversary meeting, and the Wild Salmon Circle.

Many of the calendars consisted of repeated information, or new events with no criminal or national security impacts. Some of these included the Bringing our Sisters Home vigil, a Global Day for Climate Justice, the Mission Film Festival (where Greenpeace representatives, as well as Chief Marilyn Baptiste and Chief Joe Alphonse "will be in attendance"), a Day of Action for Ashley Machisknic (young Native woman who was killed in Vancouver's Downtown Eastside), a Paddle for Wild Salmon, the Think Pipeline Tour, and a panel discussion hosted by Forest Ethics, among other similar events. As an aggregate, the calendars contain no events that present significant security threats. Instead, the calendars illustrate a comprehensive surveillance project monitoring all activities that oppose resource extraction. Most are innocuous and rather mundane gatherings but nonetheless critical of Enbridge and the politics of the tar sands.

In addition to the blanket and indiscriminate surveillance of any activities that seem to indicate opposition to the tar sands or pipelines, the security state also engaged in highly discriminate surveillance against specific organizations and individuals who took prominent public roles against the Northern Gateway proposal. As detailed in a court challenge against pipeline-related surveillance filed by the British Columbia Civil Liberties Association (BCCLA 2014a, 2014b), this surveillance campaign relied on widespread open-source surveillance and also the use of covert, undercover methods. Comprising multi-level aspects of the security state, the resources dedicated to tracking anti-pipeline activism took place at the highest levels of the national security apparatus. This is demonstrated, for example, by a series of intelligence reports that described how "a known member of the Indigenous Environmental Network will be heading to Northern B.C. tomorrow for a planned Wet'suwet'en Direct Action Camp" (RCMP 2013-6936: 17). The files are contained in a secretive national security databank known as Secure Police Reporting and Occurrence System (SPROS).

Records indicate that the file was opened specifically in relation to the movement of a "known" Idle No More activist, corresponding with planned demonstrations against the Northern Gateway Pipelines (see Barrera 2014). The SPROS entry was described as an information file opened "at the request of the District Ops Officer" to "gather and monitor information on possible protests about the Northern Gateway Pipeline from Edmonton to Kitimat by Enbridge" (RCMP 2013-6936: 2). Accessed through the ATIA, the file contains a disclaimer that says, "Forwarded for your info only folks. Please do not disseminate further" (ibid.: 6). It is unknown how the RCMP national security teams located the movement of the Idle No More activist — other than the likelihood of continuous surveillance — but the file notes that information has been transferred "direct from Enbridge."

Underlining the widespread and continuous surveillance of Indigenous groups that challenge settler colonial land theft, the national security investigation notes that "Although there is no specific criminal threat," the police have opened an investigation file because it "pertain[s] to extremist groups organizing training for potential disruption of Enbridge pipelines" (ibid.: 4). Filed in the national security database as a "suspicious incident" threatening critical infrastructure, the investigation file also included almost a dozen "involved persons." The list includes the Direct Action in Canada for Climate Justice ("protest group"), Ruckus Society, Global Justice Economy Project, Defenders of the Land, Sea to Sands Conservation Alliance, Ontario Public Interest Group (OPIRG), Indigenous Action Movement, Wet'suwet'en Direct Action Camp, and the Canadian Youth Climate Coalition. Beside the entry listing the OPIRG as "involved persons" the database states, "(Position: Co-Chair of the International Conference were several co-sponsors of the event)" (ibid.: 1). In a separate example, criminal intelligence and critical infrastructure analysts tracked a Decolonization Teach-In organized by the Vancouver Island Public Interest Research Group (VPIRG), which included organizers of the Unis'to'ten Camp (RCMP 2015-9616: 2954). RCMP monitoring events such as these on university campuses demonstrate the broad scope of surveillance by national security agencies.

Another noteworthy aspect of the report is its demonstration of the resources involved in these surveillance efforts: at least fourteen RCMP officers are listed as "involved officers" in the tracking of one targeted Indigenous activist. Their listed positions included intelligence analyst, assisting units, and investigators from the B.C. "E" Division (including the counter-terrorism unit INSET), as well as three branches of the headquarters of the National Security units in Ottawa. At the conclusion of the investigation of the activist, the "E" Division wrote that "A SIR [Suspicious Incident Report] report was not completed, as the incident refers to possible planned protests and does not fall within the suspicious incident categories as designated by the critical infrastructure criminal intelligence section" (RCMP 2013-6936: 4). Yet, after a review of the files, national security analysts at RCMP headquarters in Ottawa overruled the original decision and placed the report as describing a potential terrorism incident regarding critical infrastructure. A final entry in the report requests a SIR on the incident "to capture information of analytical value that pertains to pre-incident training that targets a critical infrastructure sector" (ibid.). A central component of these national security surveillance practices has been to aggregate intelligence data on prominent activists. This surveillance data is uploaded into national security policing databanks (like SPROS) which are not subject to evidentiary rules of criminal law. No warrants are needed to engage in this surveillance; individuals are not notified when they are under surveillance; oversight bodies monitoring these surveillance practices are very limited; and targeted individuals have no realistic venues or meaningful mechanisms through which to stop this surveillance, challenge it, or cross examine the police engaged in this surveillance.

In a widespread effort to track activists, which includes receiving covert surveillance as well as intelligence "direct from Enbridge," the security state has actively branded opponents as security threats while solidifying their support for the creation of a pipeline as future critical infrastructure. Moreover, the breadth of actors integrated into the security state is notable not only because it includes traditional policing actors as well as extractive corporations, but also because it has integrated the supposedly "independent" and "neutral" regulator: the NEB. Emails from the NEB reveal that they too collaborated with the security state to conduct surveillance on Indigenous rights and non-profit groups. An email from the NEB's Group Leader of Security Rick Garber notes, "the Security Team has consulted today with CSIS at national and regional levels; RCMP at national, regional and local (Prince Rupert Detachment) level and conducted a thorough review of open source intelligence, including social media feeds" (Millar 2013). Revealing how the NEB worked closely with Enbridge and the security state as a security peer to assist in the coordination of intelligence and mitigation of opposition to Enbridge's pipeline project proposal, Garber notes, "The Security Team, together with our police and intelligence partners, will continue to monitor all sources of information and intelligence" (ibid.). Of particular concern was security around the contested and controversial Joint Review Panel hearings, where the NEB hired a private security contractor and actively coordinated "security plans" with CSIS and the RCMP, including requesting a visible uniformed presence from the Prince Rupert Detachment to deter "illegal activities" (ibid.). The circulation of intelligence on Indigenous and environmental groups is particularly troubling in this case given the alliances between Enbridge and the security state. While the NEB is intended to be an independent entity, it has been incorporated into a security partnership that systematically favours Enbridge as the applicant. In doing so, the NEB security wing reports on the activities of tar sands opponents directly to the security state, which includes Enbridge. Simultaneously, the NEB hearings become enshrouded in the language of national security and supposed "illegal activities," including the many suggestions that the Board members were at risk.

Despite the resources of surveillance devoted to catching potential crimes — or terrorism — reports from the NEB and the CIIT repeat analysts that state "no intelligence indicating a criminal threat to the NEB or its members. I could not detect a direct or specific criminal threat" (ibid.). Yet, an absence of crimes never correlates with a diminished level of surveillance. In fact, an absence of crime is only interpreted by security state actors as a need for more scrutiny. Particularly high levels of scrutiny were applied along the pipeline route. One RCMP report warned of Wet'suwet'en protests and the response to Enbridge officials trespassing on their traditional territory. Given the "extreme nature of the warning," the RCMP note that "Wet'suwet'en involvement against Enbridge should be monitored very closely due to the potential for violent confrontation" (RCMP 2013-5745: 465). As Indigenous communities like the Unist'ot'en and others began enforcing their own Indigenous laws and restricting industry access to their territories, they were interpreted and framed by the security state as a national security threat to the settler state's energy ambitions.

"LAWS OF THE LAND": CRIMINALIZING THE UNIST'OT'EN AMID INTENSIFIED SURVEILLANCE

Opposition to the Gateway proposal has included protests staged at government buildings, Joint Review Panel hearings, and at Enbridge meetings, as well as direct actions on unceded territories along the pipeline route. As mentioned in the introduction to this chapter, the Unist'ot'en Clan of the Wet'suwet'en Nation have established their own self-described "critical infrastructure" in the form of an official settlement camp to prevent industry representatives from entering their territories and carrying out the survey work required to push various pipelines forward. Unist'ot'en spokesperson Freda Huson explains the rationale for the strategic placement of the original cabin:

> this was the initial route for the Pacific Trails Pipeline and Enbridge. So, we put the cabin right here in the GPS route of the pipelines ... Everywhere they lay that pipe we will no longer have access to our territory. We use this territory for berries, for medicines, for hunting. (quoted in Lopez 2015)

According to the Unist'ot'en Declaration,

> The Unist'ot'en settlement and camp is a peaceful expression of our connection to Unist'ot'en territory. It is also an expression of the continuing and unbroken chain of use and occupation of our territory by our clan. Flowing from this continuous use and

occupation, our traditional structures of governance retain complete jurisdiction in our territory and further, dictate the proper
use and access to our lands and waters. (Unist'ot'en Declaration
2015)

In asserting sovereignty over their lands and threatening to block the
building of the Gateway pipelines, the Unist'ot'en have been interpreted
as a national security threat, and the security state has monitored every
movement associated with the Wet'suwet'en and the Unist'ot'en Camp.

Aboriginal Policing Services of RCMP's "E" Division in B.C. tracked
Unist'ot'en Camp activities on a monthly basis from at least 2010 to the
end of 2015. The monthly strategic outlook reports regularly comment on
mundane activities like upgrades in camp infrastructure, noting that "a
traditional pithouse, a root cellar and garden were constructed to support
more camp participants" (RCMP 2016-1140: 160) or describing the construction of a gate, healing centre, hall, and kitchen (ibid.: 393). Reports warn
that "The camp is occupied year-round by the Unist'ot'en, however, the area
hosts a yearly *Action Camp* which includes hundreds of participants" (ibid.:
579, emphasis in original). As a result of bridging movements and providing the tools and resources to challenge the energy industry, Unist'ot'en
activities were under intense scrutiny by the security state.

Over a period of many years, numerous work crews and the RCMP have
attempted to enter unceded Wet'suwet'en territories for pipeline-related
activities, but have been turned away time and again because they do not
have the consent to enter the territories. Asserting that the lands are under
Wet'suwet'en sovereign title, Mel Bazil of the Wet'suwet'en and Gitxsan
nations puts it bluntly: "This is Wet'suwet'en land. This is not Canada, this
is not B.C." (quoted in Lopez 2011). Wet'suwet'en Hereditary Chief Toghestiy
does the same: "We have never ceded or surrendered our lands to anybody
here. There's no treaty. There's no relationship built with any government in
the past. None of our people signed anything to let them make decisions on
our territory" (quoted in Lopez 2014). Such iterations of self-determination
serve to challenge settler sovereignty and assert Indigenous jurisdiction over
lands coveted by Enbridge, accelerating attention from the security state.
RCMP documents refer to the Unist'ot'en Camp as a "physical impediment"
to pipeline development and the Wet'suwet'en were listed as a top threat.
Given the community's strong opposition and claims to self-determination,
the security state proceeded to delegitimize the group, fearing they could
influence further opposition to extractive development.

Knowing the Unist'ot'en Camp could stoke settler colonial anxieties surrounding Indigenous resistance to the Northern Gateway Pipelines, Public Safety declared, "The Unist'ot'en Blockade Camp is the ideological and physical focal point of Aboriginal resistance to resource extraction projects" (PSC 2015-104: 2325). As a hub for the integrated approach to intelligence sharing, the Public Safety's GOC — which we detail further in the next chapter — circulated this representation of the Unist'ot'en Camp throughout the security state. Identifying the Unist'ot'en Camp as not only the physical focal point blocking the proposed pipelines but also the *ideological* centre demonstrates settler colonial authorities' fear of having provincial and federal jurisdiction challenged by the assertions of Indigenous Nations. While these warnings illustrate how the direct action of the Unist'ot'en can challenge resource extraction practices as well as disrupt the post-colonial imaginary, they also show how the security state honed their efforts to suppress the Unist'ot'en by labelling the Clan as a "splinter group" (RCMP 2016-1140: 160).

In using the label of "splinter group," RCMP reports attempt to delegitimize the Unist'ot'en by claiming that they "have a long history of opposing pipelines, mines and non–First Nations resource extraction in general on their territory" (ibid.). As detailed by Diabo and Pasternak (2011), the use of the "splinter group" category is a divide-and-conquer tactic deployed by settler colonial authorities to undermine Indigenous demands for self-determination and the recognition of land and treaty rights. Instead, the colonial bureaucracy prefers to work with "duly elected leaders" under the *Indian Act* system so as to "negotiate" settler and industry access to Indigenous land. Constructing Indigenous opponents to "non–First Nations resource extraction" as enemies of progress, the security state actively sought to characterize the Camp as irrational and potentially criminal — thereby rationalizing intensified surveillance regimes.

The Unist'ot'en Camp drew considerable scrutiny from the security state due to their assertion of sovereignty over unceded land and the refusal to allow industry representatives and the RCMP onto their territory. Following the province's issue of temporary use permits to Enbridge, RCMP reports noted increased confrontations on and evictions from Unist'ot'en territory. One report warned, "B.C. First Nations' opposition shows no sign of abating; further 'evictions' and protests are expected" (ibid.: 582). A video of an eviction of a TransCanada Coastal GasLink crew arriving by helicopter captures why the Unist'ot'en refuse to allow crews onto their land, as a worker tries to justify their presence by suggesting they're doing "non-invasive work." Huson countered,

> Non-invasive work leads to permits. Permits lead to projects that we do not approve of. It's going to destroy our lands. And the company has already been told you don't have permission to be here so I'm going to ask you guys to leave. (quoted in Lopez 2015).

Puzzled, the worker asks, "So is our crew safe to be here?" Huson replies, "Do I look like I am trying to harm you? I am peacefully asking you to leave because you're trespassing. So please get back in your chopper and leave" (ibid.). Peaceful evictions were construed by the security state as threats that challenged Canadian sovereignty and, as such, opponents were framed as criminals within the discourse of the "war on terror." A Government of Canada risk assessment on the blockade of the proposed TransCanada pipeline referred to the Unist'ot'en as a small faction "led by an aboriginal extremist who rejects the authority of the Crown over his perception of what constitutes traditional territories" (PSC 2015-104: 2323). RCMP reports warn that Enbridge employee evictions have been occurring, including at the Gitga'at First Nation, as well as noting a warning from the Yinka Dene Alliance that trespassing Enbridge employees would be prosecuted under Indigenous law (RCMP 2016-1140: 594).

Reports produced and circulated by security state actors note that, at the Unist'ot'en Camp, a chain was erected across the Morice River Bridge. The RCMP reproduced a quote from Huson, which was printed in a local newspaper, where she refused Enbridge entry to their territory by saying, "they will be considered trespassers. And we'll enforce Wet'suwet'en law against any trespassers. You bring any equipment on here, it's going to belong to us. You're going to be walking out" (ibid.: 253). When Enbridge was presented with an eagle feather and informed that they were no longer allowed to continue trespassing on unceded territories, the security state further fixated on the Wet'suwet'en threat. The RCMP's AJIG analyst Catherine Greenley circulated an email that said, "Quite the threat these individuals provided to the Enbridge reps. According to the Wet'suwet'en website 'Laws of the Land' a further infraction is punishable by death. I've posted this below" (RCMP 2013-5745: 448). Though the protests had been entirely without violence and the Wet'suwet'en have significant legal authority over the territories — though never acknowledged by the security state — analysts like Greenley abstract notions from Wet'suwet'en law to represent their claims as hedged on violence against settler development.

As a result of continuous evictions of pipeline crews, the RCMP increased their presence around the territory, set up checkpoints, and attempted to enter the territory on multiple occasions. An exchange between Sgt. Steven Rose of the RCMP and Freda Huson in the summer of 2015 captures an element of the conflict. Two RCMP officers were stopped by camp volunteers after they tried to enter the territory without consent. Sgt. Rose attempted to lecture Huson: "The interaction with one of your people was not appropriate. It's not appropriate for him to stand in front of police and suggest that we can't cross the bridge or can't cross the public road way." At that point Huson interjected, "It's not a public road way, this is Unist'ot'en territory." Rose conceded, but at the same time revealed that the RCMP-attempted incursion was on behalf of industry interests:

> I mean, legally it's your right as the First Nations people if this is your territory to represent that, to voice that, to express that to anybody that wishes to come in to the territory. Or, if they want to do work in the territory to settle that matter through the courts. (quoted in Lopez 2015)

Huson then shut him down:

> We don't need that to prove that this is our land; it always has been. The province and everybody else needs to prove why they think they can access our land. We don't trust police because we're suspicious that your forces will come in to scope out our layout so that if there is an injunction, you guys will be better prepared on how you're going to deal with us. (ibid.)

The exchange was one of many in what the Clan characterized as "a campaign of harassment and intimidation on and around Unist'ot'en territory" (Toledano 2015). Huson and others had to repeatedly intercept energy company workers, who attempted multiple fly-ins to bypass the bridge and work on the territory, and peacefully evict them from unceded and unsurrendered Unist'ot'en territory.

The security state's extensive surveillance campaign against the Unist'ot'en demonstrates the material and immaterial threats to the settler colonial project by the Clan and other Indigenous communities refusing industry access to their land. This was not based on a threat of physical violence, as the security state fixates on, but a material threat in the form of challenging Canada's energy superpower ambitions and set-tler sovereignty claims over unceded Indigenous territories, as well as an immaterial threat to Canada's post-colonial status.

"A TOUCHSTONE FOR OPPOSITION"

From the outset of Enbridge's efforts to push through the Gateway pipelines, the security state recognized the need for an integrated and coordinated policing strategy. Under the institutional umbrella of critical infrastructure and with an expansion of national security resources under the "war on terror," extractive corporations became formal participants of the security state. As these collaborations developed over a multi-year period, the security state established itself as an advocate of tar sands development and a political antagonist to opposition to the Gateway proposal, with CSIS describing the pipeline as becoming "a touchstone for opposition to oil sands development" (CSIS 2015-54: 16). Despite widespread opposition amid accusations of a flawed consultation process, the NEB's JRP reached a decision on December 17, 2013 recommending that the federal government approve the Northern Gateway Pipelines project.

Following the December 2013 NEB decision, the Canadian government immediately indicated its intention to approve the pipeline, regardless of widespread opposition. A January 6, 2014 memo to Prime Minister Harper referencing the NEB recommendation declared the pipeline as being in the "public interest" despite "potential effects on land, water and resource use" which "can be mitigated, and where immitigable, are justified in the circumstances" (PCO 2013-898: 1). Notably, the report makes no mention of Indigenous land. An RCMP strategic outlook report notes that the Prime Minister addressed the Vancouver Board of Trade the following day, on January 7, where he declared, "if handled correctly, this is an unprecedented opportunity for aboriginal people and their communities to join in the mainstream of the Canadian economy" (RCMP 2016-1140: 162). Insisting that consent could be purchased, the RCMP note that $1 billion in benefits will be available to First Nations and Métis communities. In a highly disingenuous statement that nonetheless illustrates how the RCMP regard themselves as promoters of the Gateway pipelines, the report claims that "they [Enbridge] have full First Nations and Métis participation" (ibid.: 161–62).

After a brief period of promotion by politicians and industry, the federal government approved the project a few months later in June 2014, with an anticipated start date for 2017. Yet, despite the wishful thinking of "full First Nations and Métis participation," the Gateway approval was immediately met by numerous legal challenges led by First Nations. By RCMP estimation, this included at least nine First Nations court challenges out of a total of thirteen lawsuits aimed at the Joint Review Panel (ibid.: 275). Given the close relationships between the security state and Enbridge, developed through monitoring and disrupting the opposition to the Gateway proposal, the RCMP kept close track of the lawsuits and regularly disparaged the efforts of Indigenous Nations to stymie the project. One document claims hubristically that Gateway is "one of the most consulted on projects in Canadian history" (ibid.: 254). Another RCMP note claims "lawsuits are unlikely to kill the project however may buy the litigants more time" (ibid.: 255). As a demonstration of how the Gateway process produced shared identities and interests between agencies of the security state and extractive corporations, these expressions of support are also twinned with a sense of cheering on the economic growth of Enbridge as a market player. An RCMP strategic outlook report from May 2014 celebrates that, "Despite facing an uphill battle," Enbridge reported a 56 percent jump in first-quarter earnings (ibid.: 234). In these declarations of support, we can see how the Gateway proposal — and the organizational structure of critical infrastructure — resulted in an institutional partnership where the profitability of Enbridge is translated into a matter of national interest. On the other side of the coin are the Indigenous movements that the security state has branded national security threats for potentially disrupting the profitability of Canada's resource extractive industries.

Notwithstanding the efforts and confidence of the security state who felt their assistance in suppressing Indigenous movements would translate into the fulfilment of the pipeline, the fate of Gateway took an abrupt turn in June 2016. Despite the hubris and cheerleading of the RCMP, industry, and the federal government, the Federal Court of Appeal ruled that the company and the Crown had not obtained the free, prior, and informed consent of First Nations impacted by the project (*Gitxaala Nation v. Canada* 2016). As a combination arising from the court ruling and the staunch opposition from Indigenous communities and allied environmental groups, the federal government formally abandoned the Gateway project in December 2016. The pipeline was stopped. Yet, this tremendous victory for Indigenous movements was quickly overshadowed by new machinations to promote extractive capitalism. When announcing the final rejection of Gateway in December 2016, the federal government used the opportunity to approve two other tar sands pipeline projects. This included the Trans Mountain pipeline from Alberta to the southern coast of B.C. These announcements have, not surprisingly, spurred a new round of Indigenous mobilizations, legal challenges, and security state preparations.

As we further demonstrate in the subsequent chapter, the fusion of corporate interests with the security state has been accelerated by the discourses of extremism as well as the organizational framing of critical infrastructure. Further characterizing Indigenous movements as antithetical to Canadian interests and values, the developments that arose from the security–corporate collaborations during Gateway provided an integrated and intensive policing response to Idle No More, when the movement erupted in late 2012. As noted in an RCMP daily situation report, "Ongoing protests against this project [Gateway] have merged with the Idle No More movement, with the changes to federal environmental laws arising as a common focal point for the two groups" (RCMP 2015-9616: 322–23). Gateway opposition served as a catalyst for the surveillance practices deployed during the Idle No More movement, particularly given that the "changes to environmental laws" were heavily influenced — if not ordered — by a conglomeration of energy industrialists. The groups, which included CAPP, the Canadian Energy Pipeline Association, the Canadian Petroleum Products Institute (now the Canadian Fuels Association), and the Canadian Gas Association — under the banner Energy Framework Initiative (EFI) — sent a letter to the Ministers of Environment Canada and Natural Resources Canada in December 2011 that urged dramatic reductions to environmental protections and regulations (Paris 2013). The Harper Government's 2012 omnibus bill incorporated the EFI's recommendations and would spark the Idle No More movement. In what was initially viewed as a potent movement of Indigenous resistance to settler sovereignty, these nationwide Indigenous mobilizations struck fear in the heart of the settler colonial bureaucracy. In contrast to the somewhat slow-moving surveillance and policing that developed against Gateway opposition, the policing of Idle No More was pervasive — quite possibly exceeding any other examples of surveillance against a social movement in Canada.

Note

1. No communications between Enbridge and INAC are reported in the federal Lobbyist Registry for September 21, 2011. A recorded communication has been noted for September 9, 2011, between Enbridge and Deputy Minister Wernick. However, the September 21 meeting appears to be considered a government business meeting — as opposed to an instance of formal lobbying. Such spurious categorization and recording of meetings between corporate interests and senior officials is illustrative of corporate lobbying as a system of legalized corruption and its near-absence of substantive oversight mechanisms.

CHAPTER 3

IDLE NO MORE AND THE "FUSION CENTRE FOR NATIVE PROBLEMS"

The impetus for the recent Idle No More events lies in a centuries old resistance as Indigenous nations and their lands suffered the impacts of exploration, invasion and colonization. Idle No More seeks to assert Indigenous inherent rights to sovereignty and reinstitute traditional laws and Nation to Nation Treaties by protecting the lands and waters from corporate destruction. Each day that Indigenous rights are not honored or fulfilled, inequality between Indigenous peoples and the settler society grows. (Idle No More n.d.a.)

Treaties are largely fulfilled ... [Canada has achieved] unfettered access for settlement and development; Full ownership of all resources and benefits; Only need to consult in cases relating to defined treaty rights. (INAC 2017-311: 21)

From the entrance to Victoria Island on the river between Ottawa and Gatineau, the steady beating of drums could be heard in the distance. It was March 23, 2013, and a mass procession of youth was marching toward the Portage Bridge through the patchwork of drab federal government office buildings. The Cree youth had arrived, completing a 1,700 kilometre walk south from their home community of Whapmagoostui to Canada's colonial administrative centre. The "Quest of Wisjinichu-Nishiyuu" (Quest for Unity) was joined by hundreds of Anishnabe and other Indigenous youth along the way as part of the burgeoning Idle No More movement.

The air was electric, as it had often been during the winter of 2012–13 that saw tens of thousands march in Ottawa on multiple occasions in a unifying struggle against settler colonialism. Inspired by Attawapiskat

Chief Theresa Spence's six-week hunger strike on Victoria Island a few weeks earlier, the youth and their supporters stopped there before continuing down Wellington Street to Parliament Hill. Eighteen-year-old walker David Kawapit explained that they were trying to "achieve unity with other nations and to secure a future for our children and their children's children" (quoted in Masty 2017). The small group had departed from their home on January 16, a significant date. On that day, a national shutdown disrupted the everyday economic exploitations of settler colonialism, as Indigenous Peoples blocked roads, rails, borders, ports, and airports — causing panic in the colonial bureaucracy and the security state. Instead of meeting the movement's demands of instituting a nation-to-nation relationship, the security state scrambled to establish techniques of surveillance and police intervention. The Journey of the Nishiyuu and hundreds of other Idle No More–related actions inspired the world and charted a new path of resurgence toward realizing Indigenous nationhood. For the security state, Idle No More inspired the further integration of policing and security resources in a centralized surveillance hub with the purpose of responding to and mitigating potential outbursts that challenged settler authority and the settler colonial practices of wealth extraction from Indigenous lands.

Idle No More was a national uprising of Indigenous resistance that commenced in December 2012 and peaked in January 2013, remaining a preoccupation with security agencies ever since. Arising in response to legal efforts to erase Indigenous connections to traditional territories, Idle No More was quickly marked by policing agencies and the Indian Affairs (INAC) bureaucracy as a source of threat. Serving as an example of how the colonial bureaucracy mobilizes against Indigenous movements asserting sovereignty and self-determination, the response toward Idle No More demonstrates the extensive systems of surveillance and intervention that characterize settler colonialism. Given the prominence of Idle No More and the radical politics of decolonial resistance that the movement articulates, settler colonial authorities interpreted the movement as both a criminal and a national security threat (see also Crosby and Monaghan 2016). In detailing the extensive surveillance of the movement, we describe the policing of Idle No More as a continuation of colonial governance practices that target — with the objective of eliminating — Indigenous movements that challenge extractive capitalism and the legitimacy of settler colonialism.

Drawing upon a broad collection of internal documents, this chapter shows how the movement unfolded and evolved through the interpretive gaze of the security state. Like resistance to the Northern Gateway Pipelines project, settler colonial agencies increasingly characterized Idle No More through the lens of critical infrastructure protection, used by security agencies to mobilize resources against Indigenous disruptions to the Canadian economy. Attempting to mitigate economic disruptions as well as ruptures to Canada's fragile post-colonial imaginary, a multitude of actors and intelligence networks consolidated colonial practices of security governance and integrated into what CSIS coined a "central fusion centre for Native problems" (CSIS 2016-93: 1). Given the scope of Indigenous mobilizations — more than a thousand actions across the country — the response involved potentially unprecedented resources dedicated toward a campaign of mass surveillance. This campaign was centred in entities like the Government Operations Centre (GOC) that embraced the "fusion centre" approach, acting as a hub for intelligence sharing across all levels of the security state. Given the importance of Idle No More as a force of Indigenous self-determination over land and resources, the efforts to develop integrated policing activities to undermine the movement demonstrate the central role of the security state as an enforcement tool of settler colonialism.

IDLE NO MORE ORIGINS AND THE SOCIAL MEDIA SCARE

Idle No More represents a powerful example of resistance to practices of settler colonialism. However, Indigenous Peoples have never been idle in resisting settler colonialism (see McMillan, Young, and Peters 2013), even in the presence of Indian agents on reserves who conducted surveillance and attempted to restrict movement under the authority of the "pass system," as well as legislation outlawing political activities and association (Manuel 2015; as well as Barron 1988; Jennings 1986; Monaghan 2013a). For Sylvia McAdam, one of the Idle No More co-founders, "Idle No More resistance began long before in different names, different locations through the generations since the arrival of Europeans" (McAdam 2015: 86–87). Describing the continuation of resistance, Leanne Simpson describes Idle No More as "an ongoing historical and contemporary push to protect our lands, our cultures, our nationhoods, and our languages" (Simpson 2013b). The movement emerged in late 2012 as a form of grassroots opposition to various pieces of federal legislation that eroded environmental protections and Indigenous land and treaty rights. With the objective of supporting resource extraction industries, the federal government pushed through the pieces of legislation without consultation. McAdam (2015: 90) has said that the legislation was designed to "undermine the sovereignty and inherent rights of Indigenous peoples by focusing on individual rights, legislatively extinguishing treaty and Indigenous sovereignty." In particular, the 2012 omnibus budget Bill C-45 contained a number of provisions that would significantly impact Indigenous communities and the protection of the environment from development and industry, as well as ownership of reserve lands.

While one piece of legislation (Bill C-45) served to ignite the movement, Idle No More put forward a much broader politics against settler colonial governance practices. At the centre of the movement is the notion of honouring existing treaties and the right to Indigenous self-determination based on an equal nation-to-nation relationship encapsulated in Idle No More's vision "to honour Indigenous sovereignty, and to protect the land and water" (Idle No More n.d.b.). The decolonial politics put forward by Idle No More presented a direct challenge to Canadian sovereignty and settler society's post-colonial imaginary by demanding

> a commitment to a mutually beneficial nation-to-nation rela-
> tionship between Canada, First Nations (status and non-status),
> Inuit, and Métis communities based on the spirit and intent
> of treaties and a recognition of inherent and shared rights and
> responsibilities as equal and unique partners. (Kino-nda-niimi
> Collective 2014: 22)

Though Idle No More began as a small, grassroots series of teach-ins held in Saskatchewan, within a few weeks the movement spread throughout North America and was characterized by hundreds of disruptive protest actions and solidarity demonstrations, from flash mob round dances and marches to Parliament Hill in Ottawa, to economic blockades of railroads, highways, and international border crossings, as well as international soli-darity actions abroad (ibid.). McAdam argues, "What began as a series of teach-ins to educate about and mobilize around the erosion of Indigenous sovereignty and environmental protection has changed the social and political landscape of Canada" (McAdam 2015: 92). While McAdam describes the movement as providing "hope and energy to millions of people" (ibid.), corporations, policing and security agencies, and settler colonial bureaucracies felt differently. Given the power of the movement to unsettle settler authority and challenge Canadian sovereignty, combined with the threat posed to the national economy by such disruptive actions, the movement immediately caught the attention of the security state.

In mid-December 2012, an intelligence report prepared by the RCMP's Protective Investigation Unit tracks the movement's emergence. On December 4, around three hundred First Nations Chiefs adjourned the AFN Special Chiefs Assembly meeting in Gatineau to attempt to "instigate action" on Parliament Hill (Nepinak 2014: 85). Some Chiefs who tried to enter the House of Commons were forcefully turned away by RCMP. Chief Derek Nepinak of the Assembly of Manitoba Chiefs said the move was in solidarity with Idle No More and an opportunity to bridge the disconnect between the *Indian Act*–based leadership and the grassroots. For the security state, the confrontation was a worrying escalation of tactics. With hundreds of Chiefs throwing their support behind the grassroots opposition, the movement continued to rapidly develop momentum. This moment triggered a larger mobilization that culminated in the December 10 National Day of Action, which brought people out in the thousands. The Protective Investigation Unit warned that frustration levels among Indigenous populations had reached an all-time high surrounding Bill C-45, due to the absence of consultation and potential negative impacts on Indigenous communities (RCMP 2012-7309: 10–20). In addition, the RCMP and the Indian Affairs bureaucracy began to take note of Idle No More's successful social media mobilizations and the "real-time issues management challenges" posed as the movement gained momentum (INAC 2013-719: 11).

The escalation of #IdleNoMore on social media in December 2012 prompted INAC to pay close attention.[1] Internal emails give a sense of the department's rising concern: "maybe we should be commissioning someone to monitor the social media around this more systematically than we can do"[2] (INAC 2012-1391: 11). By late December, INAC officials had compiled an extensive report analyzing Idle No More social media, tracking tens of thousands of tweets of the #IdleNoMore hashtag between December 16–23 and noting that "the hashtag has been 'trending' within Canada for the last few weeks" (INAC 2012-1322: 22). The report also mentions the 8,525 tweets calling on Prime Minister Stephen Harper to meet with Attawapiskat Chief Theresa Spence who had been on hunger strike on Victoria Island in Ottawa since December 11. Since Idle No More had caught INAC off guard, their internal reports emphasize the size of the movement. One INAC document notes,

> Organized and promoted through social media, Idle No more has
> been able to do something that other movements in the past have
> not been able to do or manage to sustain. It has people leaving
> their homes to participate. More than 100 events have taken place
> in Canada, including rallies, flash mob round dances, teach-ins
> and blockades. Actions have been held in every province and
> territory. (ibid.: 23)

Recognizing the potency of Idle No More, the INAC report underlines a
need to gain control over the movement, yet the wording also relies on a
characteristically colonial assumption that "people" (i.e., Indigenous people) do not "leave their homes to participate" in demonstrations. Written
explicitly about why Indigenous people protested Bill C-45 (and settler
colonialism more broadly), this disparaging remark stands in stark contrast to how movement participants eloquently described Idle No More as
a continuation of Indigenous struggles. As the Kino-nda-niimi Collective
(2014: 21) put it, "Indigenous peoples have never been idle in their efforts
to protect what is meaningful to our communities — nor will we ever be."

INAC monitoring and reporting do, however, shed light on the power
of social media as an anti-colonial organizing tool. The Kino-nda-niimi
Collective (ibid.: 25) articulates this point further:

> This was the first time we had the capacity and technological tools
> to represent ourselves and our perspectives on the movement and
> broadcast those voices throughout Canada and the world — we
> wrote about the movement while it was taking place. Through
> social media ... these words spread quickly and dynamically, trend-
> ing through venues like Twitter and Facebook. During the winter
> we danced, the vast amount of critical and creative expressions
> that took place is like the footprints we left in the snow, sand, and
> earth: incalculable.

The impact of Idle No More footprints — both digital and physical — were
under intense surveillance and coded as threat by the security state. The
report quoted above also includes both a North American map of Idle No
More–related events and rallies and a global map of tweet origins, which
were summarized as follows:

> The map demonstrates that the tweets are not just coming from
> Canada, but worldwide. There are a number of international "hot

spots" on the map such as London, Cairo and Geneva where there have been rallies in support of the movement. It has also generated international press in papers such as The Guardian and Al Jazeera. (INAC 2012-1322: 27)

As discussed in the chapter on the policing of the Algonquins of Barriere Lake, the language of "hot spots" to describe international solidarity practices is highly illustrative. Indian agents use this term as a discursive device to categorize groups or regions as threats, often blurring political protests with violence and criminality. Similar to how the colonial bureaucracy and security establishment have historically used euphemisms like "squaws" (Sangster 2002), "trouble-makers" (Tobias 1983), or "Indian troubles" (Monaghan 2013a), the use of "hot spots" confers a label onto communities that challenge the normalcy of settler colonialism.

Documents released by the department of Public Safety Canada's (PSC) GOC further highlight the success of Idle No More's social media campaign. A heavily redacted secret document entitled "GC Contingency Planning Scenario — FN Protests & Potential Escalation," notes that "social media has been key to the founding, growth and success of Idle No More, and the current Aboriginal protest movement generally. Idle No More (INM) boasts some 45,000 'Friends' on it *[sic]* Facebook page and numerous Twitter followers" (PSC 2013-160: 422). Underlining the concern with international attention, an INAC report further documents the movement's reach by stating, "Events have also been held in United States with solidarity rallies also held in Stockholm, Sweden, London, U.K., Berlin Germany, Auckland, New Zealand, and Cairo, Egypt, and messages of support have come from Croatia, Ukraine and Palestine" (INAC 2012-1322: 23). Following the peak months of Idle No More demonstrations, INAC compiled a social media analysis report, *Evolution of the #idlenomore hashtag on Twitter,* which tracked the movement from Dec 1, 2012 to March 13, 2013 (INAC 2013-361: 1–8). The report noted that the volume of #IdleNoMore tweets reached one million within ninety days and warned that the "impact of the movement will extend far beyond its tweets" (ibid.). Given how Idle No More used social media to mobilize people on the ground, actors within the security state recognized the powerful dynamics at play with the movement. Demonstrations that people participated in — the rallies, flash mob round dances, teach-ins, and blockades — in turn mobilized the capacities of the security state's surveillance regime to monitor the growing movement as a security threat.

MAPPING THE EXTENSIVE SURVEILLANCE OF IDLE NO MORE

Due to Indigenous Peoples' historical and ongoing experience with settler authorities, surveillance was anticipated. McAdam (2015: 94–95). acknowledged, "In the midst of Idle No More, we knew we were watched and monitored by the government; we expected it. Law has always been used as a weapon against those who stand against colonial mechanisms and genocidal practices." Despite this history of surveillance, the policing efforts to monitor Idle No More were extensive — and potentially unprecedented because of the use of social media monitoring[3] and databank technologies. The surveillance practices targeting Idle No More incorporated a fusion centre approach that involved dozens of policing agencies, from local to national security agencies, with the purpose of integrating intelligence capabilities with numerous other settler colonial entities that monitor Indigenous Peoples. Departments including INAC, PSC, the Canadian Border Services Agency (CBSA), Department of National Defence (DND), the Canadian Security Intelligence Service (CSIS), and the RCMP each produced their own matrixes cataloguing events associated with Idle No More, with the RCMP acknowledging that they monitored around a thousand events.

From the East Coast to the West Coast to the Far North, Indigenous communities were taking to the streets, shopping malls, legislatures, roads, and rails in unprecedented numbers. The movement was decentralized, non-hierarchical, and leaderless, yet hundreds of actions were coordinated in a way that mobilized the scrutiny of the security state. In maintaining a systemic surveillance effort on Idle No More, Indian Affairs bureaucrats prepared weekly situational awareness reports to monitor and share information with government departments and law enforcement agencies. As with the Algonquins of Barriere Lake and other communities who challenge Canadian sovereignty through land-based direct actions, hundreds of communities were monitored and labelled as "hot spots." Between December 14 and 28, a number of Emergency and Issues Management Directorate reports featured titles such as *Hot Spot Summary* and *Protests in Opposition to Bill C-45 Situation Report* that functioned as catalogues of Idle No More protests. These situational awareness reports detail an array of activities and present a graph of Idle No More protests by date and location (see INAC 2012-1322; INAC 2016-765). Reports catalogue information on numerous blockades including the Sandy Bay First Nation on the Trans-Canada Highway, the Stoney Nakoda First Nation on Highway 1 and the Samson First Nation on Highway 2A in Alberta, the Listuguj Mi'gmaq on Highway 132 in Quebec, the Kahnawá:ke First Nation on the Mercier Bridge ramp in Montreal, and the Athabasca Chipewyan First Nation on Highway 63 in Fort McMurray. Also detailed were partial blockades of the Winnipeg and Iqaluit airports, the St. Mary's First Nation partial blockade of the New Brunswick legislature, a partial blockade of Highway 401 near London, partial blockades of Highway 102 and the Canso Causeway in Nova Scotia, as well as various highway and rail blockades in Saskatchewan and Quebec (INAC 2012-1322: 831).

In addition to extensive surveillance conducted through INAC, the Canadian military also closely monitored Idle No More–related events which were construed in DND reporting as a "domestic security threat." Documents obtained from DND illustrate that the military routinely monitored Idle No More protests and shared their intelligence with the GOC. In preparing for the January 16 National Day of Action, DND reports voiced concerns of an "economic slowdown" (DND 2013-679: 215) and anticipated "interruptions to passenger and freight trains, disruptions to traffic and potential delays at border crossings/ports of entry" (ibid.: 6). Sensing potential public displeasure with the military involvment in monitoring social movement activities, the high-level Canadian Forces National Counter-Intelligence Unit's (CFNCIU) spokesperson was coached to use as a "Key Message" that "The Canadian Armed Forces (CAF) are not in the business of spying on Canadians" (ibid.: 1). However, hundreds of pages of DND files reveal that various units engaged in routine surveillance of Idle No More demonstrations, producing weekly intelligence reports by the CFNCIU, Joint Task Force North, Land Forces Central Area, and the special forces unit Joint Task Force 2. Frequent mentions of Idle No More are contained within the CFNCIU's *Threat Information Collection in Support of Domestic Security Threats* reports. An extensive email chain regarding the disruption of DND activities by Idle No More demonstrations clarifies what DND believe to be permissible monitoring activities, but also illustrates the elaborate scope of surveillance targeting Idle No More activities in that virtually any demonstration that threatens roads, waterways, or economic assets falls under the matrix of potential threat.

Complementing the military intelligence resources directed toward Idle No More, Canada's national police force played a pivotal role in the surveillance network targeting the movement. Almost immediately, the RCMP created daily situation reports on "Aboriginal-based issues" and protests related to Idle No More. Prepared by RCMP HQ Criminal Intelligence, these reports are contained in hundreds of pages and date from January 2 to June 26, 2013. The reports contain broad overviews of Idle No More activities, as well as extensive and intimate summaries of activities ranging from pickets and pow wows to round dances and blockades, often followed by an event summary that details protest actions by province as well as noting international events (see RCMP 2013-1554; RCMP 2015-9616). RCMP surveillance efforts show that no matter how mundane or seemingly unthreatening an event, Indigenous actions challenging settler authority require scrutiny, cataloguing, criminalization, and ongoing surveillance, particularly when Indigenous actions threaten settler economic interests.

Like the policing of Northern Gateway protests, the RCMP voiced a central concern with protecting economic interests from the emerging Idle No More demonstrations. Glen Coulthard (2014b: 36) explains the thought process behind blockades and the security state's reaction:

> If history has shown us anything, it is this: if you want those in power to respond swiftly to Indigenous peoples' political efforts, start by placing Native bodies (with a few logs and tires thrown in for good measure) between settlers and their money, which in colonial contexts is generated by the ongoing theft and exploitation of our land and resource base.

Documents note the blockades that have garnered the most attention, including the Aamjiwnaang rail blockade (discussed further below); the rail blockades in Belleville, Ontario, which affected two thousand passengers; the January 5 coordinated border crossing protests; and the January 11 rail blockade in Millbrook, Nova Scotia. As a strategic consideration, an RCMP briefing note indicates that "Major Highways, Bridges, Railway Routes, Marine Ports/Ferry Terminals, Airports and Government Buildings (DFO, Offices of MP's, CBSA, etc.), are most vulnerable to disruption/protest" (RCMP 2015-9616: 108). Though the RCMP have deeply embedded peerships with the extraction companies and big businesses that may be impacted by the blockades — many of which were established during their policing of the Northern Gateway protests — the documents are illustrative of the powerful socializing forces of settler colonialism that have long imagined the police as claiming to remain "neutral" and "objective" about protests. Yet, the movement itself is viewed exclusively as a criminal and disruptive group of Indigenous people who threaten settler colonial stability.

Indigenous groups who advance their claims of self-determination are unambiguously characterized as threatening and deserving of more pervasive policing. Although seemingly impossible given the magnitude of surveillance targeting Idle No More, the RCMP claim they "are prepared to increase national monitoring should Idle No More actions escalate" (ibid.: 106).

Similar to other agencies, the RCMP created a nationwide matrix consisting of dozens of pages tracking Idle No More-related protests from December 2012 to June 2013 (ibid.: 177–243). Through this catalogue of activities, the RCMP map out the location of Idle No More protests as well as providing estimates for the number of participants and on-site notes from policing and intelligence partners. As another illustration of the extensive surveillance targeting Idle No More, RCMP "D" Division (Manitoba) created a matrix of protests that tracked "event organizers or people affiliated," as well as a catalogue of the latest intelligence to share with partners in the security state (ibid.: 1407–1416, 1920–1926). In the monitoring of Idle No More, the security state has accumulated vast amounts of personal information on organizers and supporters — much of which is catalogued in national information databanks. While the contents of these policing efforts are shielded by the opaqueness of Canadian policing agencies, their methods for gathering intelligence often retains a typical colonial character of divide and conquer.

The use of divide-and-conquer tactics as a technique of settler colonialism characterizes a long and continuous history of settler–Indigenous relations (Hall 2003). For example, an email from the National Operations Centre notes: "RCMP will continue to liaise with FN communities in an attempt to gather intelligence on upcoming protests" (RCMP 2015-9616: 3752). In another example of how RCMP try to exploit divisions and gather covert intelligence from within Indigenous communities, a briefing note from "E" Division (B.C.) claims that "comprehensive information gathering still remains with working level relations between First Nations and detachment/district-level resources" (ibid.: 1366). Using local points to exploit intelligence on the movement, the circuits of information sharing allowed the most mundane examples of protests and disruptions to be shared across the network of agencies within the security state. While Idle No More certainly did put forward a politics that challenged the settler colonial establishment, the policing of Idle No More reflected none of the political demands of the movement. The security state hollowed out any substance and replaced it with a litany of petty disturbances, innuendoes and rumours, and a caricature of Indigenous threat.

As a circulation of surveillance that had extensive reach within Indigenous communities and across the country, the fusion structure of the security state aggregated all of the information at the colonial centre: Ottawa. At the core of the demands of Idle No More was the establishment of sovereign-to-sovereign relations and the undoing of the settler colonial infrastructures of Canada. In other words, direct challenges to the political legitimacy of Parliament and the Prime Minister. Of course, the Ottawa establishment was paying close attention to the surveillance of the movement. The Privy Council Office (PCO) — the bureaucratic arm of the Prime Minister's Office — produced documents relating to Idle No More, including multiple memos to the Prime Minister (PCO 2012-678; PCO 2013-226). This included the involvement of the PCO's Crisis Management Cell in monitoring and reporting to the Prime Minister. The Prime Minister received debriefs on rail and road blockades, threats of an "economic slowdown," and updates regarding the history and trajectory of the movement, including a fixation on the international attention garnered by Attawapiskat Chief Theresa Spence.

"FIRST NATIONS 101" AND SETTLER COLONIAL DIVIDE-AND-CONQUER PRACTICES

The security state's preoccupations with Idle No More accelerated with the dramatic hunger strike by Chief Spence on Victoria Island in Ottawa. Chief Spence's six-week-long hunger strike inspired numerous Idle No More solidarity protests and "galvanized the movement" (Kino-nda-niimi Collective 2014: 25). The movement rallied around Spence's demand to meet with representatives of the Crown (specifically the governor general and prime minister) to demand substantial changes in the relationship between the Canadian state and Indigenous Nations (L. Simpson 2014: 155). Pam Palmater highlights the stark symbolism surrounding Spence's hunger strike and the situation faced by Indigenous communities under settler colonialism. "For every day that Spence does not eat, she is slowly dying, and that is exactly what is happening to First Nations, who have lifespans up to 20 years shorter than average Canadians" (Palmater 2014: 40).

RCMP emails and intelligence reports obsessed over potential divisions between the grassroots movement and the *Indian Act* Chiefs, highlighting every instance where there may be disagreement on tactics or meetings with the state and Crown. Likewise, the authors of these intelligence reports would fixate on Chief Spence's support base, who she may or may not support, and criticisms of her hunger strike.[4] Historic tensions have existed surrounding the Band Council leadership system, and for good reason. Colonial legislative measures aimed to eliminate traditional governance structures so that Indigenous leadership could be controlled by Indian Affairs. Pam Palmater (2015: 3) explains that successive Indian Affairs ministers under the authority of the *Indian Act* "imposed multiple election-based systems in many communities within our larger Nations — not only dividing us geographically but politically as well." Palmater describes this form of erasure targeting traditional governance structures as "One of the most devastating impacts to our nation" (ibid.). Ongoing tensions surrounding *Indian Act* leadership came to the forefront during Idle No More and were the subject of intense debate and struggle.[5]

Idle No More protests associated with Chief Spence's hunger strike on Victoria Island were the subject of intense scrutiny and reporting. Major demonstrations were held in Ottawa at various times in December and January, drawing thousands of people to the streets. RCMP emails reveal close monitoring of events on the ground as well as efforts to track buses and walkers travelling to Ottawa. However, the accuracy of the RCMP's monitoring is somewhat dubious. For example, one day before a large protest on December 21, 2012, the RCMP's Aboriginal Liaison, Cpl. Wayne Russett predicted a turnout of a thousand to fifteen hundred people. The following day, Russett had to admit that his intelligence reports were far off when over four thousand people attended (RCMP 2015-9616: 684).[6] In a not-so-subtle display of settler colonial racial stereotyping, Russett's animosities toward Indigenous Peoples and his willingness to mischaracterize the movement are expressed when he dedicates much of an email to supposed alcohol consumption at the protest (ibid.: 682). The reports provided by Russett demonstrate that the surveillance measures from the RCMP are far from simply a matter of "objective" public order policing, instead betraying deeply embedded hostilities and racial stereotyping that get played out against the movement.

In an email to Mike LeSage, the acting director general of National Aboriginal Policing, Russett underlines why Idle No More is a threat to settler society and must be contained and suppressed. Russett described Idle No More as follows:

> This Idle No More Movement is like bacteria, it has grown a life
> all of it's own all across this Nation. It may be advisable for all,
> to have contingence plans in place, as this is one issue that is not
> going to go away ... There is a high probability that we could see
> the flash mobs, round dances, and blockades become much less
> compliant to laws, in an attempt to get their point across. The
> escalation of violence is ever near. (ibid.: 4066)

In inflating the potential for violence, Russett warns of growing movement
support as well as the potential for more disruptive protests. Yet, Russett
also conjures representations of biopolitical management by likening Idle
No More to "bacteria" that threatens the health of the nation. In referring to
Idle No More as bacteria, he twins the healthiness of the Canadian public
with a racialized characterization of Indigenous movements as violent. A
label for Indigenous movements that resist the narrow politics of Canadian
sovereignty, the characterization of violence delegitimizes Indigenous
claims to treaty rights and self-determination, casting these movements
as illiberal enemies of progress (Coulthard 2007). As the surveillance
complex tasked with monitoring Idle No More constructs and circulates
these caricatures of the movement as hostile, violent, and illegitimate,
it both cements the need for increased surveillance and solidifies settler
colonial logic.

Some records indicate that Russett was able to get closer to Spence and
her camp on Victoria Island than any other security agent or bureaucrat.
Russett reported that he was the only law enforcement agent permitted
to enter the Aboriginal Experience enclosure for the duration of the hunger strike. In line with the divide-and-conquer colonial narrative, Russett
focuses on any potential divisions, including commentary that Idle No
More was "showing signs of internal bickering over who is responsible for
what," in relation to the December 21 Parliament Hill march and protest
(RCMP 2015-9616: 684). Russett writes,

> It must remain clear that this Rally is by no means. connected to
> Chief Spense's hunger strike, it just happens to be occurring at
> the same location and time ... Even some of the participants and
> media are confused with this issue.

Security state agents from Indian Affairs and other policing agencies
repeated Russett's narrative in their communications and fixated at a

distance on the potential divisions within and among the Idle No More grassroots, the Assembly of First Nations (AFN) structure, and the "dissident chiefs." These divisions created and perpetuated by the security state are illustrative of divide-and-conquer practices used to marginalize uncooperative elements impeding the settler colonial project.

Indigenous movements that continue to assert sovereign relations are regarded through the settler colonial lens of the security state as entities that have broken the social contract of post-colonial Canada. Through the extensive surveillance apparatus that arose with Idle No More, the security state was confronted with the challenge of having to produce knowledge on non-conventional Indigenous actors. Though the colonial bureaucracy has long aimed to control Indigenous populations, largely under the powers of the *Indian Act*, new movements like Idle No More expose the frailties of the bureaucracy when they refuse to abide by the imposed rules of the game. As a rupture in the machinery of colonial governance, bureaucrats have to produce (and sometimes reproduce) knowledge on these Indigenous actors in an effort to re-establish control. In an example of how settler authorities must engage in knowledge practices to "know the Other" (Miles 1989; Smith 2009), the GOC fusion centre produced a presentation for its security state partners under the title of "First Nations 101" (PSC 2015-345: 21–26). Despite Canadian police having a long history of producing knowledge on Indigenous communities (Smith 2009; see also Francis 1993; Monaghan 2013a, 2013b), the GOC efforts demonstrate how new movements can rupture the confidence and certainty of colonial governance and, in this case, require an organizational "101" revisiting of what-we-know-we-know about the Indigenous Other.

The "First Nations 101" presentation is highly demonstrative of a settler colonial logic aimed at categorizing actors that may conform or challenge settler colonialism's legitimacy. One presentation slide describes a list of "several distinct groupings of actors [as] emerging within the overall protest movement" (PSC 2015-345: 50). These included the original Idle No More followers, the AFN that included the "dissident chiefs," and other categories like the "neutrals," the "supporters," the "opportunists," and — not missing an opportunity to invoke the discourses of national security — the "extremists." In their presentation of the various categories of threat, the GOC emphasize that, while there is "no central leadership," a menacing form of "ideological guidance" is being provided by the founders. Though not explicit, the language of "ideology" is raised to demonstrate critical stance of the founders toward settler colonialism. In this case "ideology" acts as a fuzzword for police to delegitimize and discredit the movement without having to explicitly criminalize it. In the absence of "crime," the movement is labelled as "ideological" and therefore needing to be policed. In a further effort to discredit and dismiss the movement, the "First Nations 101" presentation concludes by claiming, "The motivations underlying most Aboriginal grievances can be traced to a *perceived* lack of Consultation, Accommodation … and increasingly, Compensation" (ibid., emphasis added). While the politics of consultation represent the crux of ongoing Indigenous–settler conflict — whether it be legislation or land use — the "First Nations 101" presentation shows how settler authorities increasingly frame Indigenous dissent around a crafted and perpetuated racist stereotype of Native greed. As a discrediting tactic, this discourse is mobilized by the security state to suggest that First Nations will co-operate if paid enough. In addition to perpetuating racist stereotypes, the circulation of such claims works to affirm the moral superiority of settler interventions as well as the legitimacy of the GOC surveillance campaigns.

In representing Idle No More through the lens of settler colonialism, the GOC's "First Nations 101" presentation is intended to teach members of the security state to identify weak or opportunistic elements of Idle No More. With the GOC acting as a fusion centre, strategies of intervention are circulated throughout the security state in hopes of using this knowledge against the movement, as well as identifying and exposing potential divisions that are deserving of further scrutiny and surveillance. This was most poignant surrounding the highly publicized January 11 meeting between Prime Minister Harper and some AFN Chiefs, which came about as a mechanism for undercutting Spence's demand for a meeting with the Crown. Frequent attention is focused on the "dissident chiefs," identified as those working outside the AFN and potentially taking "more aggressive, possibly more radical, means of motivating the Canadian government" (INAC 2016-324: 1). As a long-standing practice of colonial surveillance, these representations are efforts to legitimize some Indigenous people as "good" actors — who are worthy of meetings — and "bad" actors — who are unwilling to co-operate and then deemed illegitimate and deserving of policing responses.

An example of these divide-and-conquer rationales that are embedded in settler colonial practices can be illustrated in CSIS emails that try to rationalize the Prime Minister's meetings with "Band Council Chiefs" on

January 11. The email emphasized that "the PM is not meeting with 'Idle No More' reps as has been publicly portrayed" (CSIS 2013-185: 9). The division between legitimate and illegitimate Natives and the hostility toward media who have not properly represented the Prime Minister's division takes a personal, even hostile tone. Russett's reports portray similar animosities. Russett explained to an analyst with the RCMP's National Security Threat Assessment Section, who conveyed the information to other officers in an email, that "this meeting is NOT/NOT a meeting between the PM and 'Idle No More.' The PM is meeting with the Council Chiefs" (RCMP 2015-9616: 1362). Russett and other security state actors seized every opportunity to fixate on potential divisions, but as Palmater (2015: 6) recalls, "Idle No More was never about grassroots citizens versus their leaders — it was about everyone working together to push the colonizer back and to assert our sovereignty." Security state obsessions with pinpointing and exploiting potential divisions ignored or misunderstood the complexity of Idle No More. The broad array of voices and actors who rallied under the Idle No More banner focused their efforts on various (and sometimes multiple) aspects of the Indigenous struggle against settler colonialism (Kino-nda-niimi Collective 2014).

Viewed through the lens of trying to police a leaderless movement, we can further comprehend security state divide-and-conquer tactics. In what the Kino-nda-niimi Collective (2014: 23) describe as a grassroots rejection of "orthodox politics," the leaderless movement allowed for communities to organize autonomously under the Idle No More hashtag or moniker, which proved to be a point of consistent frustration for security state agencies accustomed to dealing with leaders and hierarchies of command. An RCMP intelligence report notes that Idle No More is a leaderless organization "that is purposefully distanced from political and corporate influence. There is no elected leader, no paid executive director, and no hierarchy that determines what any person or First Nation can and can not do" (RCMP 2015-9616: 1065). The leaderlessness of Idle No More presented a challenge to typical divide-and-conquer tactics and provoked more panicked emails about the potential continuation or spread of the movement. Expressing anxiety about the inability for settler authorities to rely on conventional mechanisms to control the movement, an RCMP daily situation report called *Aboriginal-based issues protests* notes that "the INM founders have expressed publicly their intention to 'work outside of the systems of government,' including the traditional AFN structure" (ibid.:

273). Written in the context of mounting pressure on Spence to end her hunger strike, the RCMP note with frustration that "there is no formal connection between their movement and the AFN, nor is there an association to Chief Spence's hunger strike. It is likely the INM movement will continue after the hunger strike ends" (ibid.: 256).

Throughout the policing of Idle No More, the security state was determined to identify disagreements and exploit divisions to discredit factions that challenge the settler colonial status quo. In the case of the January 11 meeting between the Prime Minister and the "Council Chiefs," those calling for a new nation-to-nation relationship were dismissed and their demands undermined. Instead, Canadian cabinet ministers opted to meet with co-operative Council Chiefs, with the ultimate goal of facilitating resource extraction and "modern treaty" reform based on extinguishment. The movement had been "undercut" in the words of Lesley Belleau (2014: 350), or "sucker punched" in the words of Alo White (2014: 161). Despite this dramatic moment that was exploited by settler authorities as a technique of sowing division, movement participants claimed that "there aren't divisions. There is intense and widespread unity across the country" (White 2014: 161). White (2014: 161) added,

> Out of the tens of thousands who marched on [January 11], 20 self-righteous [AFN Chiefs] coasted in on the wave created by the 30-day sacrifice of Chief Spence, and all the countless hours of effort by all of us and stepped on all of us as if we were dirt on their way into the meeting with the Prime Minister.

The anger was palpable, as it seemed that the movement had been undermined and co-opted by the executive branches of the Harper Government and the AFN.

To prepare the cabinet ministers who would be meeting with Harper and the select AFN Chiefs on January 11, INAC prepared a "Historic Treaties in Canada" presentation (INAC 2017-311: 14–26). The slides profoundly illustrate the settler colonial logic of elimination surrounding treaty making (Crosby 2017). According to the "Crown perspective," the INAC presentation informs the ministers that the "primary intent [of treaty making] was to secure Crown title over lands and resources," and that "rights and obligations are limited by the text of the treaties" (INAC 2017-311: 21). In presenting a very narrow — arguably unconstitutional — interpretation of treaties as "limited by the text,"[7] INAC officials acknowledge that

Indigenous communities have different interpretations of the treaties. Given the political demand for nation-to-nation sovereignty articulated by Idle No More, the bureaucrats at INAC blurred the complex legal and ethical dimensions of Canadian sovereignty claims with their own "101" version of settler sovereignty. Triumphantly, Indian Affairs officials declare that "treaties are largely fulfilled" and that consequently, through treaty making, Canada has achieved "Unfettered access for settlement and development; Full ownership of all resources and benefits; Only need to consult in cases relating to defined treaty rights" (ibid.).

INAC further suggests that the government can use negotiations with the elected Chiefs to advance the modern treaty framework by claiming that "there may be some emerging opportunities to lay modern self-government agreements on top of a historic treaty" and "there may be ways to use consultation agreements and protocols as a vehicle to further implement the Treaty Relationship" (ibid.: 26).[8] By INAC's own admittance, during the height of Idle No More — which demanded a renewal of Indigenous–settler relations based on the spirit and intent of the treaties — Canada's position is that treaty making has been and continues to be about Canadian sovereignty and settler access to Indigenous land, and the "modern treaty framework" based on extinguishing Indigenous title continues to replicate the historic approach. While the ministers with their newly obtained treaty-making knowledge met with those Chiefs who were willing to listen, the "dissident chiefs" and Indigenous grassroots remained physically on the outside, in the thousands on the streets, and subject to the vast surveillance net of the colonial bureaucracy and integrated agencies of the security state.

Large demonstrations continued to be organized in the Canadian capital throughout the surge of Idle No More protests, and the security state continued to internally discredit the strengths (as well as the demands) of the movement. In preparing logistics for a January 11 march from Victoria Island to Parliament Hill, a CSIS email debriefing the RCMP claims that about twelve hundred people had signed up to attend the protest on Facebook, adding that "The Demo unit advised that this usually means less then 1/3 will actually show up" (CSIS 2013-185: 9). Not only did thousands march through downtown Ottawa — three thousand, according to an RCMP daily situation report (RCMP 2015-9616: 287) — over two hundred solidarity rallies were held in Canada and around the world.

Though efforts to discredit Idle No More are the norm, some internal communications reveal the colonial anxieties that the security state is trying to suppress. One RCMP email circulated on January 11 notes that the protest march is growing steadily and that things in Ottawa remain "extremely unsettled" (ibid.: 1545). Another describes the situation as "fluid and volatile" amidst "immense protests" in Ottawa and other major centres across Canada, warning of the possibility of "large reactive incidents" in the following days (ibid.: 1659). A particular point of colonial unease began to emerge due to the effectiveness of the Idle No More protests to disrupt economic activities. Though no reports of violence (from protesters) are associated with Idle No More, the security state became fixated on threats to economic activity — particularly railways, ports, and borders. Much like how the RCMP became an extension of petroleum corporations in the policing of Northern Gateway, the security state utilized the theme of "critical infrastructure" to harness an array of national security resources against Idle No More.

ECONOMIC DISRUPTIONS AND THE MISNOMER OF CRITICAL INFRASTRUCTURE PROTECTION

As Idle No More mobilizations gathered support, the security state began to re-organize their representations of the movement through the national security category of critical infrastructure. Particularly after the December 10 and December 21 National Days of Action, disruptions to the economy were the focus of various policing agencies that circulated threat warnings within the security state. As Idle No More continued to gain momentum in early 2013, the RCMP highlighted that

> significant protest days occurred on January 5, 11, 16 and 28, in which economic blockades (both partial and full) were organized on ports of entry (such as ferries and international bridges), on significant major highways, on railways, and on inter-provincial bridges. (RCMP 2013-5506: 1)

Though early periods of surveillance caught the security state off guard, the organizational rubric of critical infrastructure emerged as a technique for the police to squarely locate a means of categorizing Idle No More in an area of criminality. Moreover, critical infrastructure protection became a misnomer for the real objective of protecting economic development and thwarting challenges to settler sovereignty.

As detailed in the policing of the Northern Gateway Pipelines project, critical infrastructure emerged as an institutional mechanism to fuse the national security apparatus with the energy corporations as "security peers," despite the RCMP's claim that it is an "impartial party" to "any dispute, protest or disagreement" (RCMP 2015-9616: 85). Although no government claims have associated Idle No More events with violence against civilian populations, the security state translated the movement as a national security threat due to the targeting of "key economic axes of transportation and infrastructure (ports, ferry terminals, airports, highways, railways)" (ibid.: 1366). In some instances, these non-violent disruptions were reimagined through a lens of settler colonialism and reported as "violence against critical infrastructure" (ibid.: 1066). When these instances of "violence" against the economy occur, CSIS explains, they are because "individuals or groups appeared to co-opt Aboriginal and Idle No More demonstrations, causing blockades to rail lines, bridges and highways" (CSIS 2013-185: 12). Sensitivities surrounding Idle No More's blockades and disruptions targeting "key economic axes of transportation and infrastructure" were heightened in the days approaching the January 16 National Day of Action and threat of "country-wide economic disruptions" (RCMP 2015-9616: 3216). In preparation for "total blockades of the highways and Rail lines for 24 hours, nationally on January 16, 2013" (ibid.: 107), the security state mobilized a series of high-level meetings to mitigate any potential disruption. A briefing note for the RCMP Commissioner highlights a central preoccupation with economic threats, noting that "Over the past several weeks, demonstrations have been held at shopping malls, government and public facilities, roads and highways, rail lines and FN Band Offices, but increasingly the focus of demonstrations have been targeting transportation infrastructure" (ibid.). Although the monitoring of Indigenous movements in Canada is a long-standing governance practice, the magnitude of the surveillance against Idle No More demonstrates the power of the movement in challenging settler colonial economic interests.

Thousands of pages of documents produced by the security state further reveal the extent of monitoring, which included an effort to track statements by Indigenous leaders associated with raising international pressure and economic disruption. One of the most widely circulated threats was made by Nepinak to reporters in Manitoba:

> We have had enough ... we have nothing left to lose. The Idle No

> More movement has the people, it has the people and the numbers
> that can bring the Canadian economy to its knees. It can stop [the
> Prime Minister's] resource development plan and his billion-dollar
> plan to develop resources in ancestral territories. We have the
> warriors that are standing up now that are willing to go that far.
> So we're not here to make requests. (ibid.: 1513–15)

Recirculated throughout the agencies of the security state, the statement was highlighted to underscore threats presented by Idle No More to the settler colonial economy. A GOC situation report received by INAC notes, "An unconfirmed media report indicated ... the date of 16 Jan was allegedly noted as a day to launch a campaign of indefinite economic disruptions, including railway and highway blockades" (INAC 2012-1416: 1375). INAC's "Info Desk" circulated hundreds of media articles that included various statements by Indigenous leaders and highlighted threats to "shut down Ontario's transportation corridors, Manitoba's mining industry, and the Alberta highway that leads to the heart of the oilsands sector around Fort McMurray" (ibid.: 1128). Threats by Idle No More activists to refuse industry access to land as well as other disruptions prompted the Ontario Provincial Police (OPP) Commissioner Chris Lewis to say that "First Nations have the ability to paralyze this country, by shutting down travel and trade routes" (Galloway and Moore 2013). With the escalation of Canada-wide economic disruptions, one of the tactics employed by Indigenous communities was precisely to non-violently target economic choke points to underline demands for respect and self-determination.

Despite common rhetoric within settler colonial societies to respect Indigenous rights to protest, these rights to protest are highly conditional. It is worth noting that, despite inquiries or commissions that have followed high-profile conflicts like the Ipperwash crisis, Canadian agencies have acknowledged the unique constitutional and legal rights that are associated with Indigenous protests.[9] Although authorities acknowledge limited entitlements of Indigenous protests, restraint is rarely practised by policing agencies when protests are successful at disrupting economic interests. As Indian Affairs Minister John Duncan expressed to the media during Idle No More, "As long as it's just a protest about aboriginal issues, that's one thing, but if it's a process that leads to things being shut down and so on, I would expect (law enforcement authorities) would step in" (O'Neil 2013). In other words, "Aboriginal issues" can be protested but not if they disrupt the economic exploitation of Indigenous lands and resources.

Of particular focus within critical infrastructure protection were rail blockades as well as disruptions to energy operations and border traffic. Numerous rail blockades occurred during the course of Idle No More resistance in a series of coordinated actions, although the two-week blockade of a CN line near Sarnia received the most widespread attention from the security state because of its impact on the national economy. One week into the blockade, an INAC weekly situation report on *Protests in Opposition to Bill C-45* noted that "A full blockade of a rail line in Sarnia is causing business continuity issues." The document notes,

> Protesters plan to continue the blockade until the Prime Minister meets with Attawapiskat FN Chief Spence, who is on a hunger strike. The line, known as the St. Clair spur, carries CNCSX and CSX trains to several large industries in Sarnia's Chemical Valley and St. Clair Township. The line generally accommodates four or five trains a day. The Chemical Valley is an integral part of the Canadian economy, supplying chemicals and raw materials for the automotive, agricultural, pharmaceutical and other industries. (INAC 2012-1322: 837–38)

Reported impacts from the blockade include losses of $5 million per day alongside threats of plants being closed down (Jackson 2012). The CN blockade by members of the Aamjiwnaang First Nation highlights settlers' dubious jurisdictional claims to Indigenous land and the legal measures in the form of court injunctions employed to remove Indigenous bodies that interfere with settler economies (see Scott 2013). Blockade spokesperson Ron Plain explained why these measures are illegitimate:

> The CN police came to the first site we were at and handed us an injunction to have us removed. There is several sites where these tracks cross reserve roads and there is one road in particular where there was no agreement ever made with the Indian agents over the road because the road didn't exist when the Indian agents were around. They don't have permission to cross that road so that's where we moved the blockade to on the second day and we have been there since. They can't issue an injunction to that piece of road because they don't have legal crossing on that road. (Jackson 2012)

Angered by the ongoing blockade, CN lawyers summoned Plain to court.

In a media interview, Plain explained the approach taken toward the injunction by CN:

> I produced 250 pages of government documents which show that the tracks are there illegally. This isn't a land claim issue — in a land claim there is a dispute over ownership, here there is no dispute. No permit was ever issued to cross that road, and that makes the crossing illegal. But I was not allowed to present this evidence in court. (Cox 2014: 208)

Plain's case demonstrates, as do numerous others, the selective protection of property rights within the court system and how Indigenous claims that fundamentally challenge settler economies are deligitimized. As a tool of colonial lawfare, the use of injunctions allows corporations to suppress the legitimacy of Indigenous land claims and transform the political conflict over land into a policing problem that enables the criminalization of land defenders.

Plain's resistance and refusal to acquiesce to settler authorities made him a target for security state sanctions. Acting as advocates for CN's economic interests, INAC employees conducted Facebook surveillance to try and identify Plain as the leader at the blockade. They discovered a post celebrating the blockade's success at disrupting the economy and the costs incurred by petrochemical companies. One email from INAC bureaucrat Eileen McCarthy exclaims, "He seems to be leading the charge. FYI there is talk to start blocking all tracks that run through all FN territory in the next few days/weeks" (INAC 2012-1322: 857). Another INAC bureaucrat, Ron Mavin, then concludes, "Kendra is trying to get in touch with the Sarnia Police to get some intelligence from them" (ibid.). Numerous documents obtained from agencies of the security state offer examples where non-Native bureaucrats discuss tactics of Indigenous movements constructing rail blockades, and the interconnected pressures from industry and angry settlers demanding that the federal government do something to stop Indigenous disruptions of everyday settler colonialism. The ease with which contemporary Indian agents can proclaim their expertise and their authority over Indigenous movements — with no acknowledgement of the demands and grievances of the movements — is illustrative of the powerful rationalities that make settler colonialism seem "normal" to the practitioners within settler bureaucracies. Equally, the embedded affinities to assist economic interests are illustrative of the "insider" and "outsider" character of non-Natives and Natives in settler colonialism.

As the rail blockades continued, industry backlash prompted the colonial bureaucracy and law enforcement to intensify their efforts against the protests. INAC emails further reveal that CN's Manager of Aboriginal Relations asked a senior official to intervene and request the blockade be dismantled (ibid.: 446). Like other points of confrontation between Indigenous Peoples and settlers, CN appealed to INAC to do something because they believed police agencies were not carrying out their duties as the repressive apparatus of settler colonialism (for example, see Blatchford 2011). Emails note that CN, who filed a court injunction against the blockade, was "extremely frustrated with the police who don't seem to be doing anything to negotiate with the first nations group. CN is going back to court this afternoon in Toronto to express their concerns about the police not enforcing the injunction" (INAC 2012-1322: 451). RCMP emails on December 31 reveal that CN went to court to obtain Contempt of Court orders for the Sarnia Chief of Police and some known protesters (RCMP 2015-9616: 3937).

An RCMP briefing note acknowledges that it is CN policy to seek an injunction where a railway is blocked, and lists indictable charges including "Mischief, Intimidation (obstruct roadway) and Trespass under the federal *Railway Safety Act*" (ibid.: 1938). RCMP emails from the Critical Infrastructure Intelligence Team's (CIIT) National Security Criminal Operations, who monitored Idle No More closely, outline CN's preferred approach toward Indigenous disruptions to its business: "CN have Province wide injunctions for British Columbia, Manitoba and Saskatchewan as it relates to aboriginal blockades" (ibid.: 2266). Clearly frustrated that various policing agencies were not as aggressive in their repression of the blockades, CN applied further pressure on INAC to intervene on their behalf. Demonstrating INAC's role in pacifying Indigenous communities in the service of Canadian industry, INAC officials were highly sympathetic toward CN and showed frustration about the lack of police enforcement. At one point, showing an element of discord within the security state, INAC staffers noted that CN could call in the OPP if the Sarnia Police were unwilling to break the blockade, citing the OPP raid on the Six Nations land reclamation site near Caledonia in 2006 (INAC 2012-1322: 451).

Supplementing pressure from CN, the Canadian Propane Association sent a letter to the Minister of Public Safety urging the immediate removal of the blockade "before it causes serious damage to the propane industry"

(RCMP 2015-9616: 3813). Demonstrating the influence that corporations have within the government, the RCMP received an email from the GOC asking which actions the RCMP would take in light of the Association's letter (ibid.: 3841). Though Sarnia Police were on the record saying they did not have the capacity to break the blockade, the calls from industry for an immediate intervention soon began to echo through the judiciary as a result of CN's aggressive petitions for injuctory relief. An RCMP report notes that Ontario Superior Court Justice David Brown was quoted by the media as saying, "This kind of passivity by the police leads me to doubt that a future exists in this province for the use of court injunctions in cases of public demonstrations" (ibid.: 273). Although ignored by the mainstream media, Plain was quick to point out that Brown, who initially issued the injunction against the blockade, was a former CN lawyer and former expert witness for the company (Cox 2014: 207). Plain claimed that Brown's "ties to CN are twofold and deep, and yet he failed to disclose this past relationship with CN, which he was required to do" (ibid.). For challenging Canada's economic interests and asserting Indigenous jurisdiction over lands claimed by settler corporations, Plain was criminalized with charges for contempt in violation of the injunction. CN sought $50,000 in damages against Plain but were satisfied with the $16,000 fine ordered by an Ontario judge (Robins 2013). The ruling reveals why Plain was targeted as "the visible spokesperson of a protest that openly defied a court order," as punishment for the "brief, yet flagrant, breach of a court order in a peaceful protest that caused no property damage" (*Canadian National Railway Company v. Plain 2013*).

Hesitation from police in Sarnia demonstrates the complexities for local police in suppressing Indigenous movements. It's also worth noting that their cautious, take-it-slow approach produced divisions and further resentments within the broader security state, specifically from Indian Affairs who wanted police to act more quickly. Despite the security state's fixation of economic development as critical infrastructure protection, Idle No More supporters continued to communicate the fundamental principles of resisting colonial exploitation of Indigenous land. At the dual blockade of the Trans-Canada Highway and CN rail line at Portage La Prairie, protesters dismissed the injunction, declaring it null and void and warning the Canadian Prime Minister to honour the treaties or face further blockades. "The train is basically hauling natural resources. It's hauling billions and billions of dollars worth of First nations wealth," said Terrance Nelson of Roseau River First Nation and vice-chairman of the American Indian Movement (AIM). He added, "(Canada) is subsidized by our lands and our wealth, and our natural resources, so we're stopping the natural resources from moving" (*Winnipeg Free Press* 2013).

In addition to rail blockades, the security state paid close attention to disruptions aimed at Canada's energy infrastructure, particularly demonstrations occurring in Alberta. The RCMP's Criminal Operations unit in Alberta ("K" Division) kept close tabs on protests along Highway 63 near Fort McMurray, the tar sands' primary transportation artery (RCMP 2015-9616: 71–74). RCMP documents note that "according to reports, a full blockade of Hwy 63 near Fort McMurray has been a concern by third parties [energy companies] as it is the only corridor to many of the sites associated with the Oil Sands Industry" (RCMP 2013-5506: 2). RCMP coordinated responses with municipal police to circumvent blockades of Highway 2 in January 2013 for the purpose of maintaining access to the airport. Illustrating consistent efforts to divide and conquer, a related RCMP email notes "we have assisted [Edmonton Police Service] with access and involvement of a member of the CO's aboriginal advisory committee as well as an influential Chief to attempt to influence protest organizers" (RCMP 2015-9616: 115).

RCMP tactics to demobilize blockades were also employed southeast of Edmonton at a blockade near a "tank farm" in Hardisty, Alberta. RCMP documents stressed that the tank farm presented a major "choke point" for the movement of petroleum products from Alberta to the U.S. (RCMP 2013-5506: 2). Though heavily redacted, a briefing note to the RCMP Commissioner indicates that the RCMP were acting on behalf of Enbridge and EnCana by attempting to convince a member of the group to not enact a "full blockade" and "discuss mutually beneficial locations for the protest" (RCMP 2013-1554: 78). Given the importance of the tar sands in Canada's extractive capitalist ambitions, the threat of Idle No More actions solicited attention from the highest levels of the security state. By late December, the RCMP Integrated National Security Enforcement Team (INSET) for Alberta became involved in monitoring Idle No More protests as a potential national security threat. In emails sent by the RCMP's CIIT under the subject heading "Idle No More Protests Target Alberta Petroleum Industry," RCMP officers discuss how "K INSET are aware and responding to the current situation here in Alberta with the partners" (RCMP 2015-9616: 3931). Partners are not identified, but given INSET's fusion centre model, we assume it involves multiple levels of police and security agencies. It likely includes private and industry entities as well. Another redacted email, sent on January 17 with the subject heading "Potential Threats" and addressed to email address "Aboriginal CI (Critical Infrastructure) Reporting," was referred to the Calgary INSET for further information (ibid.: 2027). Regrettably, the contents are redacted and the RCMP have not yet issued further documents related to the email address.

A final preoccupation of the critical infrastructure surveillance associated with Idle No More was aimed at disruptions to border flows. The security state considers border crossings to be "key critical infrastructure," as outlined in an intelligence report anticipating "overt nuisance activity" related to Idle No More at the Victoria ferry terminal in B.C. (ibid.: 1063–68). In the settler colonial imaginary, border regions are a particular site of contestation (A. Simpson 2014; Walia 2013). Border disruptions are framed through the lens of anti-terrorism because challenges to Canadian sovereignty and territorial integrity expose Canada's dubious claims to Indigenous lands. Indigenous territories such as Akwesasne are situated in both Canada and the United States and, as such, do not recognize the imposed border dividing their territory. Border crossings have therefore been a site of protest to contest the restriction of flows of Mohawk people and commerce, resulting in hypersensitive settler colonial policing and surveillance. Border control is a defining, albeit artificially constructed, expression of state sovereignty.

RCMP intelligence briefings warned that Indigenous protests in support of Idle No More have "called for all border crossings in Canada to be shut down on January 5, 2013" (RCMP 2015-9616: 1065). Leading up to the January 5 shutdown, where ten U.S. border crossings were anticipated to be sites of Idle No More protests (PSC 2013-160: 749–53), the RCMP organized a teleconference call with Transport Canada and other partners, including eleven representing rail and industry interests and their private security (RCMP 2015-9616: 659–62).[10] The RCMP describe the situation at the Seaway International Bridge (Akwesasne) as "murky and fragmented," with numerous Mohawk and law enforcement actors on both sides of the border (ibid.: 661). The RCMP's Criminal Intelligence branch labelled the January 5 shutdown and other economic disruptions using discourses of national security and terrorism. An *Intelligence Bulletin* from the RCMP raises the threat of potential terrorist activities associated or coinciding with Idle No More protests, saying their goal to "interrupt criminal/extremist groups or lone individual(s)" who may use the protest to threaten public safety (ibid.: 904–16).

Similar to the RCMP, the CBSA fixated on indications of potential "extremist activity," including the presence of particular flags and groups, such as the Mohawk Warrior Society and AIM (ibid.: 1101–12). Using vague labels like "extremists" to associate the protests within the broader context of the "war on terror," actors in the security state scrutinized Idle No More for any — and all — indications of potentially radical participants. At Akwesasne, CBSA bureaucrats focused on the presence of "a few known warriors" (ibid.: 1102). While even the most mundane presence of "known" radicals is used to justify more policing despite any crime, the absence of "extremism" does not stop surveillance activity. At a protest near the Fort Erie Peace Bridge, CBSA officials were looking out for extremist identifiers but, to their regret, reported "no extremist flags/banners" (ibid.: 1104). Records from protests at Sarnia's Blue Water Bridge also reported "no extremist members observed," although there exists a potential threat of a blockade of Indian Road by an unnamed "rogue group" (ibid.: 1105). Raising the spectre of potential "violence," CBSA observers confirm that they are monitoring events with CSIS and the Integrated Terrorism Assessment Centre (ITAC), along with multiple other policing partners (ibid.: 1112). Similar to the RCMP, they warn of extremists infiltrating and disrupting peaceful protests, as well as the inability to screen those crossing the border and the disruption of the flow of people and commerce as operational impacts.

What emerged from Idle No More's successful economic disruptions, spanning hundreds of localized sites, were increased efforts to integrate the responses of policing and security agencies. By targeting key economic sectors — in particular rail lines, the energy industry, and border crossings — the organizational framework of critical infrastructure reclassified the local disruptions through the lens of "extremism" and national security. To coordinate policing efforts against Idle No More, federal authorities within the security state used the nexus of critical infrastructure and national security to implement a more permanent "fusion centre" approach to Indigenous movements.

PERMANENT INTEGRATION: A "FUSION CENTRE FOR NATIVE PROBLEMS"

Idle No More's successful disruptions provoked a perceived need to mobilize surveillance and policing functions within an operational centre of the security state. Public Safety's GOC — acting as the security state's central surveillance and intelligence-sharing hub — has emerged in recent years as the entity responsible for coordinating an integrated federal policing response to domestic issues and events concerning Canada's "national interest" (PSC 2016-10: 19). A December 2012 GOC *Monthly Overview* report reveals that "a GOC Team was established to coordinate and to provide consolidated reporting and impact analysis with respect to emerging nationwide First Nations protests organized by a group called 'Idle No More,' which is critical of Bill C-45" (PSC 2013-160: 440). Localized Indigenous protests are a regular feature in GOC reporting, but Indigenous mobilizations reaching a national scope have created a perceived crisis throughout the security state.

At the secretive, high-level Assistant Deputy Ministers' National Security Operations Committee (ADM NSOPS) held on January 15, Idle No More was the first item of discussion under the agenda heading "Domestic Extremism and Government Model for Decision Making" (CSIS 2016-93: 6). Handwritten notes from ITAC participants at the meeting show how, in an effort to consolidate an integrated federal response, officials discussed creating a "central fusion centre for Native problems" (ibid.: 1). The notes show the high level of security integration, including participants from DND, Foreign Affairs, and numerous other departments. They also indicate that Craig Oldham, Director of the GOC, was directly relaying information to the Prime Minister's National Security Advisor. The rather cryptic CSIS handwritten notes show that, at the conclusion of the meeting, Ron Hallman, INAC's Senior Assistant Deputy Minister, Regional Operations Sector, indicated that Canada–Native relations were moving from tier two to tier three: "GOC//Native — moving from Tier II → Tier III" (ibid.: 3). The subsequent notes are redacted, and to our knowledge the government of Canada has no official policy statements regarding the "tiers" of protest control.

With the security state having determined a necessity for creating a "fusion centre" to deal with "Native problems," the GOC naturally fell into this role. The GOC contained the necessary bureaucratic infrastructure to network the surveillance capacities of a variety of governmental, security, and law enforcement agencies to respond to Indigenous mobilizations challenging settler colonial legitimacy. Idle No More served as a catalyst for the GOC to embrace the function as the "central fusion centre for Native problems," a role that aimed to coordinate various actors, organize key meetings, compile and disseminate presentation materials on Indigenous movements, and implement unique communications initiatives to network the security state.

During the height of Idle No More economic disruptions, one GOC function was to coordinate meetings that would strategize about how to mitigate disruptions and threats of "economic slowdown." Multi-agency, multi-departmental meetings were held frequently during the height of Idle No More economic disruptions in January 2013. The meetings ranged from the regular teleconference calls among intelligence officers to high-level strategic meetings with "subject matter experts" trying to analyze and determine the impact of nationwide Idle No More demonstrations. According to the GOC, the purpose of these meetings was to determine next steps and develop a "business cycle" regarding reporting on the "gaining popularity and momentum" of "First Nations events across the country" (RCMP 2015-9616: 651–62). RCMP documents show that the purpose of these meetings was to coordinate national security intelligence, with participants including CBSA, CSIS, RCMP, Transport Canada, and INAC.[11]

In preparing for this series of high-level meetings related to Idle No More, a GOC team was established on January 14 to "coordinate and provide consolidated updating and impact analysis" surrounding the January 16 National Day of Action (PSC 2013-160: 444). The GOC produced and circulated to its governmental and security partners a series of reports, which included one called *First Nations Protest Matrix*, to track protests on January 16. The graph organized planned protests by province and indicated the location, time, organization, source, and event type (e.g., blockade, demonstration, round dance, etc.) (ibid.: 42–46). GOC reporting emphasizes there are "real economic impacts" (ibid.: 6) from Idle No More protests, including a National Day of Action debrief that notes "interruptions to passenger and freight trains, temporary disruptions to road traffic, and delays at border crossings/ports of entry, including significant delays at the Ambassador Bridge, Canada's busiest border crossing" (INAC 2012-1537: 1120).

The bulk of the emails justifying various meetings portray a sense of urgency around protecting critical infrastructure. ITAC meeting notes from January 15 demonstrate that the security state viewed Idle No More through a lens centred on domestic "extremism." The ITAC notes further underscore the deliberate attempts to mischaracterize Idle No More economic disruptions as a violent threat to the settler colonial status quo: "Throughout the meeting ... there was general discussion on the types of events which could potentially trigger greater protest, including potential violence and criminality" (CSIS 2015-616: 5). Notes produced by the Department of Fisheries and Oceans (DFO) participants at the January 15 meeting stress the need to develop a "national contingency plan" with the aim of identifying "inventories of risk," as well as "hot spots" and "areas of concern" (DFO 2016-260: 3, 11). The DFO's participation in the ADM NSOPS is highly illustrative. Although the DFO notes refer to settler commercial fishing as it relates to Indigenous treaty rights, the language invoked surrounding "hot spots," "risk," and "Aboriginal contingency planning" demonstrates that the demands put forth by Idle No More to recognize treaty rights were framed as challenging the political economy of settler colonialism. They were coded as national security threats with broad reverberations even at the most peripheral ends of the security state.

A subsequent series of emails obtained from Public Safety reveal that the GOC requested a "Subject Matter Experts" meeting on January 17 and a follow-up meeting with the ADM NSOPS on January 24 due to "the potential for escalation"[12] (PSC 2015-332; PSC 2015-345). The January 17 GOC "Subject Matter Experts" meeting included many of the usual suspects within the security state — CBSA, CSIS, ITAC, Transport Canada, the RCMP, INAC, DFO, and PCO. INAC records from the January 17 GOC meeting provide further information on the shared attitudes toward Idle No More. The INAC notes are unique in acknowledging some underlying issues — "lack of consultation, broken treaties, resource sharing, legislative changes, nation-to-nation relationship, honour of the crown" — but demonstrate how Indigenous grievances can be callously mentioned and ignored when the list is followed by the claim that "FNs feel that they have veto over legislation or development that affects them"[13] (INAC 2012-1537: 1194–95; INAC 2016-324: 7–8). In a narrative that could have been lifted from nineteenth-century cabinet meetings (see Carter 1990; Shewell 2004), the listing of numerous legitimate grievances is entirely dismissed because the elite functionaries of the security state feel that the Idle No More movement is acting on grievances in an irrational and unreasonable manner. By expressing that Idle No More has exceeded the bounds of settler colonial reasonability, the consensus from the meetings is that the movement needs to be subject to monitoring, management, and intervention by the security state.[14] The INAC notes further underscore the blurring of political protests with criminality: "Non aboriginal movements starting to move in, ie black block, anarchists etc.... Influence is small but growing, unknown outcome" (INAC 2012-1537: 1195). The notes also indicate "Pressure from industry on the rise politically," and "if inm makes it to spring, it could gain momentum with warmer weather" (ibid.). As we detail throughout the book, industry pressure is a primary motivating factor for security state mobilization and violence directed at Indigenous groups.

Leading up to the January 24 ADM NSOPS follow-up meeting, a draft deck was circulated amongst the security state participants. With the title "GC Contingency Planning Scenario — FN Protests & Potential Escalation," the presentation casts a classic colonial narrative over Idle No More (PSC 2013-160: 415–25; PSC 2015-345: 50–54, 85–88). In an attempt to delegitimize the movement, the GOC claims Idle No More is "a movement of dissatisfaction, and has become a lightening rod for things that are perceived by FNS as going wrong ... underlying anger not going away" (PSC 2015-345: 51). The presentation also highlights the success of the Idle No More movement in raising public awareness "without violence or excessive criminality," as if to suggest that Indigenous Peoples do not know how to express themselves in any other way (ibid.: 53). The slides warn, "The lessons learned, experience and knowledge gained while garnering these successes will outlive INM, while informing future protest organizers and the success of their endeavours" (ibid.). Warning of the potential long-term success that could come about because of Idle No More, the tone conveyed in GOC documents expresses a need to suppress the movement.

To consolidate the fusion centre for "Native problems," and to respond to what the GOC claims are "things that are perceived by FNS as going wrong," the months that followed included efforts by the GOC to put the "Contingency Planning Scenario" into practice. These efforts are itemized in other presentations addressing Indigenous resistance. For example, one secret document entitled "FN Protest Activity: Spring and Summer 2013 Forecast" is similar to the deck discussed above in that potential escalation triggers are redacted. It does note, however, the call for actions associated with "Sovereignty Summer" and that "if activities escalate, provincial and federal assistance may be requested ... an escalation will result in increased monitoring, reporting and engagement by the federal community" (ibid.: 55–59). In March, the GOC prepared a draft "Presentation to DM Breakfast:

Preparedness for First Nations Issues," which posed the question: "How does the Government of Canada prepare a whole-of-government response to a significant escalation in First Nations' (FN) protests?" (PSC 2013-160: 372–83). The document outlines all federal departments and their respective roles in relation to Indigenous protests, including INAC as the "principle conduit for information on protests," CSIS as "intelligence support regarding potential extremist involvement," and ITAC as "monitoring and providing integrated and comprehensive threat assessments of potential serious violence from domestic extremism" (ibid.: 377). According to Public Safety emails, the GOC also contributed slides to an INAC deck in collaboration with the PCO related to "protest activity" (ibid.: 4–9). Within the INAC presentation, analysts categorized Idle No More "risk levels," where "low" represented "awareness activities" such as round dances or flash mobs, "medium" represented "potentially disruptive activities, such as the deliberate interruption of critical infrastructure or transportation networks," and "high" included "extremism or serious acts of politically motivated violence" (ibid.: 5).

In attempting to monitor all Indigenous groups that may be associated with Idle No More, the Canadian government advanced an increasingly fused approach to surveillance and intelligence sharing. Given the successful disruption of everyday settler colonial industry by Idle No More, a central rationale for the integrated policing platforms was to develop more efficient security intelligence coordination. An aspect of the integrated approach included a number of specific communication lists that aimed to distribute intelligence information across sectors of the security state more effectively. Emails from various departments reveal a number of specialized units and groups that emerged post–Idle No More. Tellingly, a GOC teleconference report reveals that the RCMP is "not doing a National JIG [Joint Intelligence Group]" (RCMP 2015-9616: 658) as has been the case in previous settler colonial policing efforts targeting National Days of Action (2007–09) and resistance to the 2010 Vancouver Olympics and the G8 and G20 summit in Toronto. However, a June 27, 2013 email in relation to an Intelligence Bulletin on Enbridge Line 9 pipeline protests is addressed to the "INM Intelligence Group," suggesting that while the RCMP wished to avoid the controversy and media scrutiny associated with forming an Aboriginal JIG, they organized a group with similar scope to surveil Idle No More (ibid.: 3205, 3211).

To supplement the INM Intelligence Group, the security state created additional communication tools and email groups to monitor Indigenous protests. An email in January from Timothy O'Neil of the RCMP's CIIT reveals that there is an email group specifically designated to critical infrastructure under the heading "Aboriginal CI Reporting" (ibid.: 2027). Another RCMP email from March 2013 shows that there is yet another email group, the "INM Coordination Team" (ibid.: 2856). Furthermore, another RCMP report reveals the extent of Idle No More communications coordination and protest surveillance: "An Idle No More email account was created to manage email correspondence. Since January 2013, 575 emails have been received ... Approximately 1000 events as of April 8" (ibid.: 3977). Efforts to profile Indigenous activists supplemented the techniques employed to track and catalogue Indigenous protests within the RCMP's criminal intelligence database infrastructure. As a summer of unrest drew closer, the RCMP created a specific Police Reporting and Occurrence System (PROS) file to deal with anti–shale gas protests that started to gain momentum in June 2013 and are the subject of the next chapter. Idle No More created an opportunity for the security state to consolidate a "central fusion centre for Native problems," a permanent intelligence-sharing hub with the function of coordinating a federal policing response against Indigenous protests that challenge settler society and extractive capitalism. As Idle No More morphed into Sovereignty Summer and the Mi'kmaw resistance at Elsipogtog, the fusion centre became a permanent fixture to police Indigenous dissent.

IDLE NO MORE AND SOVEREIGNTY SUMMER

Though Canadian security agencies have a long history of surveillance and disruption against social movements, few campaigns can claim to be as far-reaching as the one that targeted Idle No More. Given the new domains of digital surveillance, the security state attempted to track every event (and, by extension, every participant) associated with the movement. Additionally, the integrated intelligence functions of fusion centre techniques have allowed a rapid proliferation of information about the movement and movement participants. As researchers and activists have detailed, the power of state agencies to gather intelligence produces a myriad of ways in which these agencies can construct misinformation and mischaracterizations, disrupt inter-movement dynamics, gather information on people and groups for future purposes, and ultimately mobilize the forces of the criminal justice system to criminalize or suppress aspects of the movement.

During the height of Idle No More, the state security complex enacted a surveillance net that monitored any expression of Indigenous dissent, with a keen focus on potential disruptions to critical infrastructure. As the spring and summer months of 2013 unfolded, the security state continued to fixate on the Idle No More brand. The "ideological" influence of Idle No More — that is, the emphasis on decolonial politics surrounding Indigenous sovereignty and self-determination — served to justify surveillance regimes that now targeted any event related to Indigenous issues. Any expression of self-determination or critique of settler colonialism could be perceived as threatening the post-colonial imaginary and thus required monitoring and potential intervention. For example, under "Strategic Considerations," an RCMP briefing note calls attention to potential unrest resulting from a call for another National Day of Action on February 14, 2013, to coincide with what the RCMP refer to as "Missing and Murdered Aboriginal Women Awareness Day" (RCMP 2013-5506: 4). Unsurprisingly, reports also include the First Nations Child and Family Caring Society of Canada (FNCFCS) planning a series of peaceful walks across Ontario on June 11.[15] This type of surveillance demonstrates that even non-disruptive events demanding justice for Indigenous women and children are coded as threatening, resulting in the participants being placed under constant scrutiny from the security state. Any event that could be remotely associated with the Idle No More movement was painted by policing and colonial authorities as potentially "extremist" or violent.

An illustrative and lasting example of the security state's perception of Idle No More is their frenzied reaction to what Idle No More activists had threatened to be an upcoming "Sovereignty Summer." Under this banner, Indigenous activists and communities asserted that they

> have the right to determine the development on their traditional and treaty territories. In defending their right to say "No" to unwanted development, First Nations like Barriere Lake, KI [Kitchenuhmaykoosib Inninuwug First Nation], Grassy Narrows and many others are advancing alternatives that help us reimagine our relationship to the environment. (Idle No More and Defenders of the Land 2014: 358)

The settler state interpreted potential Sovereignty Summer actions as possible threats that would challenge Canada's illegal claims over Indigenous lands. For example, an INAC policy agenda presentation in July

2013 outlining "challenges ahead" notes the demands associated with Sovereignty Summer for a number of changes including the "repudiation of Doctrine of Discovery and enactment of UNDRIP" (INAC 2016-765: 15). These "challenges" were seen as a potential threat to settler economies by the security state. An RCMP situation report honed in on a potential season of "economic disruption" that would target "resource development projects involving pipelines, tar sands, natural gas, fisheries or mines" (RCMP 2015-9616: 548–51). A memo to the prime minister warned of "escalating action, including blockades" (PCO 2013-226: 45).

Although parts of the security state acknowledge issues such as "unresolved land-related grievances," "perceived" failure to consult and respect treaty rights, and environmental concerns based on resource development, they nonetheless frame discussions of Sovereignty Summer as an ongoing national security threat. CSIS records include an Intelligence Report produced by Transport Canada's Security Intelligence Assessment Branch on June 20, titled *Possibility of Aboriginal Demonstrations or Blockades in Summer 2013*. Transport Canada flipped the report to ITAC for any final comments or suggestions, specifically relating to "upcoming possible violence." The report anticipates blockades to transportation infrastructure — such as rails, roads, and bridges — expressing a worry that "A rail or road blockade can have a domino effect on industries waiting for just-in-time supply chain shipments" (CSIS 2013-185: 11). Given the looming threat of economic disruption, the security state directed its resources specifically against Indigenous movements that challenged settler economies, specifically the petroleum industry, which is the subject of the next chapter.

Despite the efforts of the security state, Idle No More is a movement that lives on. It has cemented alliances such as with the Defenders of the Land network, and it has sparked new creations such as the Indigenous Nationhood Movement. At its peak during the winter of 2012–13, Idle No More rose as a movement that asserted Indigenous sovereignty, rejected Canadian legislation, and challenged the economic lifelines of the settler colony. In doing so, it galvanized policing and surveillance efforts of the colonial bureaucracy and security state. Although the security state was overwhelmed by hundreds of demonstrations associated with Idle No More in those first few weeks, the intensified efforts to surveil and control Indigenous movements eventually created the "central fusion centre for Native problems" and a consolidated machinery of surveillance. As a mechanism to provide quick responses against Indigenous movements that could threaten the economic and national interests of settler society, these integrated policing efforts would soon be deployed again. As we examine in the next chapter, anti–shale gas protests in southeastern New Brunswick would prompt the security state to mobilize against Mi'kmaw resistance surrounding the Elsipogtog First Nation.

Notes

1. The Idle No More movement began as a series of online conversations and teach-ins which were promoted on social media by adopting the #IdleNoMore hashtag. Tanya Kappo (Kappo and King 2014: 68) is credited with first using the hashtag and says that social media "turned out to provide a really effective tool. The coming together through Idle No More contributed to a growing sense of community and even a resurgence in starting to think about nationhood, our identity and what happened to us, historically."

2. A separate set of emails reveals that INAC employees were caught off guard by the movement. Ian Gray asks, "What do you mean 'idle no more'? Please clarify?" (INAC 2012-1352: 843).

3. Social media surveillance is categorized under open-source intelligence, commonly known as OSINT. OSINT is a rapidly developing domain of security intelligence particularly given new big data and analytics capacities. Also worth noting is that though policing and security agencies claim that materials are "open source," a variety of digital covert tactics are used for collecting OSINT.

4. To that end, INAC leaked an audit during Spence's hunger strike and "intentionally distorted" the finances of the Attawapiskat First Nation in a move widely viewed as aiming to discredit Spence and distract from the demands of the hunger strike and the housing crisis in her community (Pasternak 2016: 318).

5. It is not our purpose or intention to weigh in on this as settlers. Our focus in this section is to show how settler bureaucracies and the security state exploit these divisions in attempts to divide and control movements like Idle No More.

6. Russett blamed other units for the bad intelligence: "We are still waiting on updates from our Policing Partners regarding approximate numbers coming in from their areas. It should be noted that a lot of Aboriginal Communities are not sharing information with the police as readily as they use too [sic] ... it appears that they are now 'holding their cards closer to their chest'" (RCMP 2015-9616: 684).

7. See Borrows (2016) for an extensive analysis of the treaty texts. The analysis from Borrows (2016) presents a categorical rebuttal to the representation of treaty texts put forward by INAC officials.

8. An additional point warned about the risks of "liberal interpretations" of treaty rights by the courts that could cause public criticism or "financial liability."

9. This was among the more prominent conclusions of the Ipperwash Inquiry (see Linden 2007).

10. Of particular note is J.D. Irving Ltd. and Irving Corp Security who feature as prominent actors in the following chapter surrounding anti–shale gas protests. In addition, the major Canada and U.S. railway companies are present.

11. While INAC's participation was redacted from the RCMP files, CSIS documents implicate the department (CSIS 2013-185).

12. Obtaining data surrounding these meetings using the *Access to Information Act* (ATIA) has proved challenging. Having compiled a comprehensive list of departmental representatives for each of the three meetings mentioned, we filed a series of requests that, for the most part, have been met with non-compliance and other obfuscations, including unsatisfactory searches.

13. References to settler colonial anxieties over Indigenous "vetoes" appear in several documents. These are highly illustrative of how unintelligible settler colonial officials find the concept of Indigenous sovereignty. Documents obtained from the GOC also reference a perceived First Nations veto in relation to the U.N. Declaration on the Rights of Indigenous Peoples, claiming it is used by "FN academics, leadership and grassroots" to demonstrate that Indigenous Peoples have the right to a veto over resource development, use of their lands, and legislation. Subsequently, GOC files minimize UNDRIP by calling it an aspirational document that has no standing in Canadian or international law (PSC 2013-160: 421).

14. Participants in the meetings seemed to deliberately ignore the legal and ethical grievances of Indigenous communities. These practices of silencing or erasing Indigenous claims have even translated into the Access to Information branch. For example, one of our requests of INAC produced a document from the meeting that says, "New relationship has all been talk only ... frustration." The sentence — one of the only mentions of Indigenous perspectives — was redacted on follow-up files obtained from INAC (2016-324).

15. FNCFCS Executive Director Cindy Blackstock made headlines in May 2013 when it was discovered that she was under extensive surveillance for her child advocacy work surrounding the organization's discrimination complaint against the government at the Canadian Human Rights Tribunal.

CHAPTER 4

THE RAID AT ELSIPOGTOG

Integrated Policing and
"Violent Aboriginal Extremists"

And we're protecting [the land and the water], just not for us, we're protecting it for everybody. The Anglophone, the Francophone, the Irish, anybody, because it says in our treaties, the peace and friendship treaties. Everybody is welcome in Canada provided you don't ruin the land and the water. (Susan Levi-Peters, former Elsipogtog First Nation Chief, quoted in Skene 2013)

This is my physical mother that I am talking about. My physical mother, if you were to say I have probes that I want to probe her with, I want to fill her full of chemicals, I want to do ultrasounds on her body because she might have something that we want, we think she does. Will you allow us probe your mother? What's our answer Michael [swn lawyer]? No, of course. You're not going to probe my mother, you're not going to fill my mother, or your mother full of chemicals. Us as children that's the way we would feel. (quoted in Lane 2013)

"CANADA'S NATURAL WEALTH IS OUR NATIONAL INHERITANCE"

An exchange unfolded at a Mi'kmaw longhouse in November 2013 between swn lawyer Michael Connors and members of the Elsipogtog First Nation and their supporters. In 2010, swn Resources Canada Inc., a subsidiary of the Texas-based fracking giant Southwestern Energy Company, had been granted licence to explore for shale gas over large portions of the province of New Brunswick. Thousands of people would oppose the development out of fear it would lead to fracking and contaminate the land and water. Despite widespread resistance, the N.B. government supported the fracking project and mobilized the resources of the security state to suppress opposition. SWN were met by fierce resistance in Kent County around Elsipogtog in the summer and fall of 2013, leading to work stoppages, blockades, and RCMP violence and arrests. At the longhouse, Connors represented the company's position and pleaded for the blockades to stop to avoid any further violence, but was drowned out by a chorus of opposition. One woman stepped forward to describe to Connors that her mother's well had been contaminated by industrial development outside of Fredericton, but that the onus was on her family to legally prove that the development had contaminated the well. She continued,

> You are standing on Mother Earth. Mother Earth is our spiritual Mother. That is where we are made from, the clay of Mother Earth as Red People. So can I allow somebody to probe my spiritual mother, to fill her full of chemicals, and to fill her full of ultrasounds because we might have something that can give us some money. We can't stand and allow that to happen. (Lane 2013)

The steadfastness of the Elsipogtog community paid off and SWN were forced to leave the province in December 2013 and have not returned.

But this story begins much earlier and is far more complex than the narrative crafted by the RCMP and mainstream media, which have depicted violent and unruly Natives who deployed unreasonable methods to halt energy projects in Canada's national interest. While the RCMP and SWN have circulated this narrative to delegitimize the Elsipogtog community, what has been excluded from dominant accounts of the conflict are its roots in the Mi'kmaw treaty relationship and the continuation of Idle No More and Indigenous resistance to settler colonialism and extractive capitalism. While treaty relations and Idle No More provided a spark for the resistance, the violent suppression of Elsipogtog land defenders was influenced by the continued integration of security and intelligence resources to police Indigenous dissent, to counter challenges to Canadian sovereignty, and to uphold the myth of Canada as a post-colonial society.

In recent decades, Mi'kmaw populations in New Brunswick have been subjected to colonial violence for asserting their rights enshrined in the Peace and Friendship Treaties. Despite the Canadian government's acknowledgement of the terms of the treaties,[1] Mi'kmaw communities continue to come under violent attack from provincial and federal police forces for asserting their land and treaty rights.[2] The treaties, a result of six wars the Mi'kmaq fought against the British over six decades until 1779 (Ward 2004), do not cede Mi'kmaw land and affirm the Mi'kmaq as an independent Nation (Richardson 1993: 44–45; Paul 2000; Battiste 2016). Despite the treaties, the Mi'kmaw land base has been continuously eroded through a series of dubious and unethical settler land acquisitions, which eventually confined the Mi'kmaq and Wolastoqiyik (Maliseet) onto small reserves mere fractions of their traditional territories (Howe 2015: 30–48).[3] Elsipogtog First Nation is the largest Mi'kmaw community in New Brunswick with around three thousand residents, located halfway between the cities of Moncton and Miramichi in southeastern New Brunswick in the Signigtog district of the Mi'kmaq Grand Council.[4] Water is the lifeblood of their culture. Threats to Mi'kmaw land and water were the basis for a protracted conflict, which exploded in 2013 on the heels of Idle No More.

Canada's relationship with Indigenous Peoples solicited growing national and international attention in 2013. In addition to the Idle No More uprising, 2013 marked the 250th anniversary of the 1763 Royal Proclamation[5] when the British Crown declared Indigenous lands as unceded unless otherwise ceded by treaty (see Hall 2003). Adding an international dimension, U.N. Special Rapporteur on the Rights of Indigenous Peoples, James Anaya, arrived on a research mission and declared that Canada faces a "crisis" situation, particularly with regards to resource extraction activities on unceded or disputed lands (Anaya 2014). A series of uncoordinated events that followed Anaya's comments epitomize Canada's settler colonial present. First, on the day after Anaya's departure, Governor General David Johnston delivered the 2013 Speech from the Throne under the auspice of "Seizing Canada's Moment." In a blatant display of colonial erasure, Johnston declared that "Canada's natural wealth is our national inheritance" (Johnston 2013). There is nothing natural about the "inheritance" of Canada's national wealth, which only exists through the dispossession and theft of Indigenous lands. Johnston's statement exemplifies how the settler state frames itself as a post-colonial entity by implying that Canada has no history of colonialism despite the lived realities of the settler colonial present.

Although Canada acknowledges the legitimacy of the Peace and Friendship treaties, at least on paper, which established Mi'kmaq presence and authority on the land, settler states like Canada still rely on racist frameworks such as *terra nullius* or the doctrine of discovery that "declared lands to be legally empty, allowing European law to control Indigenous peoples" (Borrows 2015: 702). According to Eva Mackey (2014: 241), the

> defining colonial assumption (with continued legal standing today) was based on a belief in the natural superiority of Western civilization, which gave the Crown a stronger and more legitimate sovereignty over the territory, simply through its arrival and assertion of its claim, and despite the vibrant collectives of Indigenous people living in the territory.

Canada's "natural wealth" is based on a legal fiction supposing the inferiority of the territories' original inhabitants. These settler colonial assumptions have long enabled genocidal techniques carried out by the British military against Mi'kmaq and other Indigenous populations. In 1749, Colonel Edward Cornwallis issued a scalping decree offering "ten Guineas for every Indian killed or taken prisoner,"[6] (Nova Scotia Council Minutes 1749: 581) as well as Field Marshal Jeffery Amherst who advocated "to inoculate the Indians by means of blankets, as well as to try every other method that can serve to extirpate this execrable race" (d'Errico 2010). Although extreme examples, these perpetrators of genocide continue to be held in high esteem as their names are painted over numerous waterways, towns, parks, and monuments, which the Mi'kmaq continue to vehemently protest to this day.

Then, in a second event, Johnston's post-colonial rhetoric was complemented by the brutishness of colonial practice. The morning after the Speech from the Throne, where Johnston declared "we must seize this moment, now more than ever. Our future prosperity depends on the responsible development of these resources," the RCMP launched a heavily armed raid on the anti–shale gas camp near the Elsipogtog First Nation. Underlining the role of policing entities in reproducing the not-so-natural "inheritance" of settler colonialism, the raid had many similarities with assaults against other Indigenous communities, such as those in Kanehsatà:ke (Oka), Ts'Peten (Gustafsen Lake), Aazhoodena (Ipperwash/Stoney Point), and Kanonhstaton (Caledonia). Like many sites of heavy-handed police intervention, the land defenders were protecting unceded land against settler economic interests under the protection of the security state. The raid in Elsipogtog illustrates how techniques of settler colonialism narrate the theft of land and resources as "legal" forms of development, and the violence of policing as a normal requirement, to ensure that settler colonialism in Canada prospers thanks to, as the Governor General puts it, the "national inheritance" of resource wealth. Of course, for the Indigenous groups that disrupt the post-colonial imaginary by insisting on their rights over unceded lands, settler colonial agencies in Canada attempt to eliminate this resistance through a host of techniques including violence and criminalization.

Developing Canada's petroleum industry was a key priority of the federal government and flashpoints like Elsipogtog were viewed and framed as a threat to Canada's national security and resource-based economy. Through a comprehensive analysis of the conflict at Elsipogtog, we contend that the role of the security state is to facilitate industry access to Indigenous territory for the purpose of extracting resources and wealth. Similar to policing and surveillance efforts surrounding other major economic interests that we've detailed, the efforts taken against the community in Elsipogtog offer a further demonstration of how the security state assists in normalizing the protection of "development."

The paramilitary raid, along with its preceding and subsequent events, is an important case study to demonstrate how integrated policing resources can be coordinated against Indigenous resistance to settler colonialism. In this chapter, we supplement the work of independent journalist Miles Howe (2015) who was embedded with the land defenders and covered their activities in-depth as they developed on the ground in 2013. Howe's coverage sheds light not only on the political manoeuvres employed by the government, security state, and industry, but also on the various confrontations as they unfolded, including a counter-narrative to the raid as carefully and methodically unveiled by the RCMP. We add another dimension to Howe's accounts through an analysis and narration of events as documented by the security state. Although the RCMP were the central actor in the facilitation of SWN Resources' exploratory operations, we document the resources deployed by the colonial bureaucracy and security state in the months surrounding the raid. We have obtained dozens of files comprising thousands of pages produced by the RCMP, Indian Affairs (INAC), the Department of National Defence (DND), the Privy Council Office (PCO), the Canadian Security Intelligence Service (CSIS), Public Safety Canada (PSC), as well as its provincial equivalent, the New Brunswick Department of Justice and Public Safety. Analyzing these files has allowed us to map out a narrative that documents the unique roles of the actors in confronting shale gas opponents, and how these opponents became categorized as a violent, unlawful Indigenous threat. This is not only a story of the security state serving and protecting corporate interests but also a story of Mi'kmaw resistance to colonial erasure.

SETTING THE STAGE: SURVEILLANCE OF IDLE NO MORE AND ELSIPOGTOG

The Elsipogtog First Nation was on the security state's radar before the conflict with SWN Resources over shale gas exploration. As the Idle No More mobilizations erupted in December 2012, Elsipogtog Mi'kmaq took to the roads and rails. The RCMP's "J" Division in New Brunswick actively monitored the community when they blocked a CN rail line southwest of the community in Adamsville, as well as a blockade of Highway 11 in Rexton (RCMP 2015-9616: 43–46). The RCMP report the blockades were up for multiple days and situation reports from Transport Canada express the frustration of settler agencies over the disruption of rail traffic, including the cancellation of CN train 569 (Bathurst to Moncton) and rerouting of VIA Rail train 15 (Halifax to Montreal) (ibid.: 3534). Adding to the integrated policing of Idle No More, New Brunswick's Department of Public Safety produced security event reports to monitor Elsipogtog and other Indigenous blockades in the province.

RCMP emails reveal that Andrew Easton of the New Brunswick government's Security Directorate forwarded a security event report associated with January 11 protests to Timothy O'Neil, a Senior Criminal Intelligence Research Specialist with the RCMP's Critical Infrastructure Intelligence Team (CIIT) (ibid.: 1644). Keeping the national security CIIT group appraised of events in New Brunswick, Easton notes that Indigenous protests in the province could become "unlawful or more confrontational" (ibid.). Categorizing Idle No More protests as a threat to numerous security and economic interests, Easton notes that, "due to geography Atlantic Canada [is] more vulnerable to supply chain disruptions from protests. Critical goods and services impacts, along with economic impacts, can occur if protests escalate" (ibid.). As if anticipating the nightmare that would later besiege settler colonial authorities in New Brunswick, Easton notes,

> The Idle No More protests have the potential of building support amongst aboriginal and non-aboriginal people across Atlantic

Canada and the nation. While the focus is federal at the moment, similar concerns will impact N.B. on resource development, particularly natural gas and mineral exploration along with crude oil transportation. (ibid.: 1645)

While these early blockades were spurred by Idle No More, the integrated mobilization of the security state's surveillance resources set the stage for efforts to protect the resource extractive industries aiming to exploit unceded Mi'kmaw territories.

Leading up to the Idle No More mobilizations, Indigenous communities and environmental groups came under increased scrutiny due to opposition directed against the New Brunswick government's strategy to develop a petroleum industry centred around shale gas. In 2010, the province leased one million hectares (2.5 million acres) of land to SWN Resources. The harmful effects inflicted on the environment and potable water sources from the process of hydraulic fracturing, and the company's miserable track record from fracking operations in the United States, led to a broad-based opposition movement. Comprising a first-of-its-kind coalition of Anglophone, Francophone, and Indigenous communities (see Howe 2015: 120–23), the New Brunswick Anti–Shale Gas Alliance was formed and included dozens of municipalities, community organizations, and First Nations calling for a moratorium on exploration and development of fossil fuels. Protests against SWN commenced with their exploration work in 2011, and an RCMP CIIT assessment on *Criminal Threats to the Canadian Petroleum Industry*, which we examine in further detail in the concluding chapter, notes that a "peaceful, concerted anti–shale gas movement surfaced" (RCMP 2016-1140: 76). However, in the very next sentence, the RCMP CIIT assessment offers a glimpse into what Mackey (2016) calls the "unsettling expectation" that arises in settler populations with Indigenous land claims. Highlighting Indigenous involvement in the anti–shale gas movement, the CIIT warns, "With the perceived prospect that the hydraulic fracturing process contaminates drinking water and the air, an aggressive, violent extremist anti-fracking movement was formed within New Brunswick, including within the aboriginal communities" (ibid.: 75). In what would appear to be self-contradictory assertions between a simultaneously "peaceful" and "aggressive, violent extremist" movement, the RCMP's attempts to inflate potential threats relates directly to SWN moving operations to Kent County in southeastern New Brunswick in 2013, close to the largest Indigenous community in the province, Elsipogtog First Nation.

RCMP field notes and reports show that the security state prepared for a confrontation with shale gas opponents long before SWN's exploratory seismic testing began. Recognizing the importance of Mi'kmaw land to settler economic interests, RCMP officer field notes entered into the Police Reporting and Occurrence System (PROS) database emphasize that Kent County contains the highest concentration of natural gas deposits in Atlantic Canada (RCMP 2016-8006: 11). Further RCMP documents reveal an integrated policing approach to mitigate resistance against shale gas, detailing a series of meetings held between the RCMP, SWN, the New Brunswick government, and Irving's private security force beginning in January 2013. The RCMP were central in coordinating an integrated approach, which included a number of efforts such as forming a Shale Gas Intel Group, working to develop a security plan for SWN, and providing a threat assessment workshop to other partners (ibid.: 1–26).

RCMP's "J" Division Criminal Operations team prepared briefing notes leading up to June 3, the day SWN were expected to begin exploration activities. Briefings show how the security state put in place an elaborate plan in collaboration with SWN to facilitate the company's work: "An extensive Operational Plan, covering multiple scenarios, has been prepared and approved ... for the purpose of maintaining public safety and public order as the work by SWN begins" (RCMP 2015-8404: 1). Reflecting the close relationship fostered between the security state and resource extractive industries, the RCMP disclose that "Numerous meetings have taken place between 'J' Division Criminal Operations, the Shale Gas project team as well as other Program Managers in order to ensure 'J' Division is well prepared for these events" (ibid.: 2). A final component of the briefing highlights how the media liaison unit is drafting a communications strategy, largely employing the settler governmental discourse of having to maintain public safety and order in the face of criminal Indigenous threats. In a separate briefing, the RCMP claim their goal is to "allow peaceful protesters to conduct demonstrations in a safe manner," while underlining that their ultimate objective is "to enable SWN to continue with operations" (RCMP 2013-6342: 1).

SWN ILLEGAL: THE EVICTION ORDER
AND THE INTEGRATED RESPONSE

SWN Resources moved their seismic testing equipment into Kent County for the exploration season in June 2013. Kent County is comprised of a series of small Acadian (and some Anglophone) villages as well as the Elsipogtog First Nation, all communities who rely on the land and water for sustenance. Given the character and histories of these communities, New Brunswick's petroleum ambitions encountered immediate resistance.

Leading up to SWN's 2013 seismic testing, the Mi'kmaq declared any exploration activities illegal. On May 14, the Elsipogtog First Nation passed a Band Council resolution opposing shale gas exploration, which demanded direct consultation from the Crown (Howe 2013a). In addition, the territory slated for exploration was part of the Signigtog district of the Mi'kmaq Grand Council. A letter dated May 30 from the Grand Council and addressed to SWN's Moncton representative Mike Ezell asserted Mi'kmaw ownership of all lands and resources in the Signigtog district (comprising much of southern New Brunswick and parts of northern Nova Scotia) (Howe 2013b). The letter stated that no shale gas exploration was permitted without the expressed written consent and participation of the Grand Council and the Mi'kmaq of the Signigtog district. The Mi'kmaq Grand Council followed up its May 30 letter to SWN with an eviction notice in July. Again addressed to Ezell, the Mi'kmaq declared SWN's permits and licences for land within the Signigtog district to be "VOID and illegal":

> The Migmag Grand Council are the signators of all the Migmag peace and friendship treaties and holds title to all lands in the Signigtog District. From time immemorial, the people of the Signigtog District governed by the Grand Council, have lived upon our traditional lands, governed by our own political system, language, culture, spiritual and diverse means of livelihood. We have never surrendered our sovereignty or jurisdiction over our lands. Our laws are as valid and binding today as in the time of our ancestors. New Brunswick is unceded land and subject to Migmag jurisdiction. (quoted in Howe 2013a)

In issuing their eviction notice to SWN, the Mi'kmaq made their position perfectly clear: the land was unceded and the community was going to defend the land at any cost. However, SWN and the security state continued to ignore the Mi'kmaw position and seismic testing continued.

When SWN began to test the waters, Elsipogtog Warrior Chief James Pictou describes how the community responded:

> We started slowing down SWN. We talked to the people and the best way to gain support was we had to sacrifice. There were people who were willing to get arrested, for the cause, a good cause. To save our water, stop fracking" (quoted in Skene 2013)

Facing determined Mi'kmaw opposition, the RCMP increased coordination with SWN and the New Brunswick government's Natural Gas Assistant Deputy Ministers' (ADM) Executive Committee (herein referred to as the Shale Gas Committee) — a high-level interdepartmental entity formed to oversee the government's strategy of developing a shale gas industry by integrating pro-industry and industry (we assume from the redacted participants) elements into the security state. Despite their months of preparations, RCMP briefing notes demonstrate how the security state and SWN were frustrated by immediate opposition and interference against the exploratory efforts of the company. An initial update from the RCMP notes that opposition so far had been peaceful, but focuses particular attention on the threat of Indigenous protesters. According to the RCMP, "To date, concerned citizens have been expressing their disapproval of the SWN exploration in a peaceful manner until this afternoon when a team of employees hired by SWN were confronted by a group of protesters from the Elsipogtog First Nation" (RCMP 2015-8404: 9). While settler protesters are referred to as "concerned citizens," the RCMP begin constructing the Mi'kmaq as confrontational and illegitimate. Nowhere do the RCMP acknowledge the underlying dispute over land ownership or the lack of Mi'kmaw consent; instead, briefing notes begin to focus exclusively on Indigenous threats.

With the eviction notice ignored, the Mi'kmaq and other shale gas opponents moved to disrupt SWN operations. On June 4, a group from Elsipogtog seized a truck doing work for SWN. When questioned by the media about the legality of SWN's permits and the illegality of Mi'kmaw actions, Elsipogtog War Chief John Levi stated,

> They broke the law a long time ago when they started [testing] in our territory, in our traditional hunting grounds, medicine grounds, in attempting to contaminate our waters also. They broke [our] law. What's illegal, me taking their truck or them dumping poisons in our waters?" (Forestell 2013)

One RCMP note from the following day (June 5) warns that a peaceful protest against SWN had turned into a "volatile situation" (RCMP 2015-8404: 11). In particular, the RCMP attempt to bracket any attempts to interfere with SWN operations as illegal, despite the Mi'kmaq declaring gas explorations illegal and in contravention of their treaty relationships. The RCMP use the need to protect SWN operations as a way to brand the efforts of the Mi'kmaq as criminal, warranting violent interventions and arrests. The June 5 note, for example, describes how a group of eighty people began a "peaceful protest" but then marched along Highway 126 to SWN's worksite and were "interfering with the work being performed," which led to arrests (ibid.). Discussing potential fallout from RCMP arrests, the CIIT's O'Neil circulated an email to the critical infrastructure criminal intelligence (CICI) team (which included the Idle_No_More list) for an upcoming press conference held at the Elsipogtog First Nation amid outrage in the community after two Mi'kmaw women suffered mental, emotional, and physical trauma as a result of injuries inflicted by the RCMP (RCMP 2015-9616: 3103). Dismissing the violence inflicted on Indigenous women conducting cultural ceremonies, subsequent RCMP reports fixate on the "violence" levied at SWN materials, as "vehicles and equipment belonging to the company have been targeted by protest groups intent on interrupting lawful operations" (RCMP 2015-8404: 21–22).

By June 14, the company had moved its operations to Highway 11, east of Elsipogtog First Nation, which functions as an artery between Moncton and Miramichi. With a tone of frustration, the RCMP note that SWN activities were immediately interfered with and that work was stopped numerous times throughout the day due to blockades against the trucks. Video footage shot at the scene on June 14 shows a large line of RCMP officers position themselves in front of SWN's equipment at the junction of Routes 116 and 126. To clear a lane for SWN's trucks to proceed and thus facilitate SWN's seismic testing work, the RCMP then advance and kettle off a small group of Native and non-Native peoples blocking the road. While the RCMP use crowd-control tactics against vastly outnumbered protesters, their internal communications illustrate how the police translate any iteration of Indigenous law or culture as a threat to public safety. For example, one RCMP briefing note indicates that one of the exploration lines could pass over a sacred burial site, which could "add pressure on the company and raise concerns for public safety" (ibid.: 18). Ignoring concerns about the sacred burial grounds, the RCMP interpret the claims from the Elsipogtog community only as policing or public relations problems. No concerns are expressed regarding the Mi'kmaw burial grounds; the only concerns are about SWN being able to continue their work or preparations for media attention.

With the RCMP unconditionally supporting the activities of SWN, additional resources were directed toward more systematic surveillance against the anti–shale gas movement. Although the conflict was rooted in complex local antagonisms, the policing response integrated a national array of actors and became framed under the banner of national security and critical infrastructure. Demonstrating how rapidly the security state can deploy multi-layered surveillance and reporting mechanisms, the RCMP began producing daily shale gas updates for multiple partner agencies. The reports were compiled by Carole Doiron, a Criminal Intelligence Analyst with "J" Division's National Security Enforcement Section (RCMP 2015-9616: 799–800, 805, 822–32, 3104–14). A mysterious entity called the RCMP's Shale Gas Intel Group then coordinated and distributed daily intelligence reports that integrated SWN into the security state. An email from Doiron to the Shale Gas Intel Group indicates close coordination between the national security agency and SWN, which included sharing the company's projected daily work plans and a list of "SOIS" (suspects of interest) whose names were compiled and shared in the report (although redacted in the declassified documents) (ibid.: 805, 822–26). Demonstrating intrusive surveillance techniques deployed by the security state to track and profile Indigenous dissent, Doiron outlines next steps in policing the anti–shale gas movement, which consists of creating profiles and tracking those attending protests directed at SWN operations: "There are many SOIS named in this report and it is my intention to meet with the Shale Gas Provincial Coordinator to discuss developing profiles on them as well as doing database checks" (ibid.: 805). Though it is still unclear, based on the records declassified so far, preliminary indications from Doiron's files appear to show pervasive information sharing between private actors (SWN), the provincial government's high-level Shale Gas Committee, and multiple agencies of the security state, with all parties transferring surveillance data with indiscretion.

In addition to providing local protest updates, the daily briefings from "J" Division's National Security Enforcement Section included intelligence on potential external support being provided to Elsipogtog. One briefing emphasized that the Elsipogtog First Nation put out an official "call out to all Idle No More and Defender of the Land – Sovereignty Summer to aid and defend" the resistance movement (ibid.: 827). The RCMP also claim the Kahnawake Warrior Society are "monitoring the situation and in contact with people at the protest" (ibid.: 830). Concerned that the protests would spark further Indigenous mobilizing, an RCMP National Intelligence Coordination Centre (NICC) report warned about "increased tensions with law enforcement" as a result of prolonged protests in New Brunswick and Ontario in June, focusing on the anti–shale gas and Enbridge Line 9 protests as "emergent issues" (ibid.: 818). By integrating a number of agencies within the information-sharing loop supporting SWN's explorations, the activities of the Shale Gas Intel Group demonstrate the breadth of resources that can rapidly be consolidated under the banner of national security against Indigenous-led disruptions to settler economies.

While the RCMP supported SWN by framing protests as illegal, other governmental partners mobilized to ensure industry's unfettered access to Indigenous land. The protests had become increasingly acrimonious to the provincial government, given that one of their top priorities was to develop New Brunswick's petroleum industry. A provincial security event report shared with CSIS coincides with SWN commencing operations and conveys the parameters of the integrated policing regime facilitating extractive industries in New Brunswick: "Public Safety is in regular communication with the security, intelligence, and law enforcement community, SWN, and all other affected parties," including "Coordination of public communication amongst RCMP, government and the private sector" (CSIS 2015-501: 8–9). Department of Public Safety minutes show that the Shale Gas Committee met almost daily to coincide with SWN's exploration activities and persistent opposition.

Dozens of pages of hand-written notes narrate the government's frustration with the Mi'kmaq thwarting SWN operations, and increasingly construe Mi'kmaw protests as violent and "unlawful." Some notes fixate on identifying (and distinguishing) Native and non-Native protesters. Although the protests were quite diverse, the security state focus on the Mi'kmaq, who more often than not were at the front of the blockades of SWN's equipment. On numerous occasions in the month of June, young Mi'kmaw men and women were targeted and arrested. For example, in early June, a video shows a large number of RCMP aggressively arresting a sixteen-year-old boy who followed his mother onto the road. They transported him to the Moncton detachment and charged him with assault after a police officer bumped into him. In distinguishing between Native and non-Native protesters, the security state perceived the Mi'kmaq as the primary threat to SWN's operations, profiling and policing them accordingly.

This was further evident in security event reports produced by the province's Security Directorate. One such report, dated June 5, notes the arrests and injuries of protesters of "aboriginal heritage" and describes these early arrests as a "sentinel event" that could "change the path of what happens next" in terms of potential escalation (NB-PS 2016a: 4).[7] A report from June notes that the RCMP are preparing for disruptive protests, which they "hope to be peaceful, excluding people who are planning to be violent" (NB-PS 2016b: 76). Meanwhile, the Shale Gas Committee kept tabs on those arrested, which included efforts to track court dates and release conditions that forbade those released from returning to protests. One note from July discusses an individual who was arrested and released with conditions but still had a "very visible presence at the camp," demonstrating how thoroughly the New Brunswick government monitored activists (ibid.: 92).

In addition to criminalizing land defenders and promoting a narrative of criminality associated with the protests, the security state advocated for various legal techniques to legitimize SWN's operations. In one instance, the RCMP requested information from the provincial government on the possibility of converting disputed Crown land into private property: "RCMP requests info from Government on the SWN's intention to make the areas they are working private property under the *Work Safe Act*, violation of this (protester entering the area) would be trespassing" (ibid.). By actively seeking legal grounds to criminalize land defenders, the security state was willing to ignore the legalities and history of Crown land and simply classify the public lands as the property of SWN to facilitate a crackdown. Although the proposal was not acted upon, Security Directorate emails indicate more systematic surveillance, including executive briefings for the upper echelon of the provincial government. As protests accelerated, daily consultations with security and law enforcement agencies were held alongside provincial ministerial meetings — which included the ADM Security and Emergencies Committee — to integrate intelligence on the shale gas protests.

As part of an increasingly sophisticated multi-agency response, the daily reports produced by the New Brunswick government denote an overarching fear that shale gas protests would spread within and beyond the province's border. Officials obsessed over keeping the issue localized and avoiding media coverage, especially because the Shale Gas Committee was concerned that broader media attention would raise the potential of feeding solidarity with the Mi'kmaq. Rumours of people arriving from parts of the Maritimes and a busload from Listuguj First Nation from Quebec in mid-June was viewed by the New Brunswick government as a potential threat. Worried about Indigenous solidarity and support, the Shale Gas Committee feared that "As more people increase potential for violence increases," imploring that the "RCMP must be kept in the loop as much as possible" (ibid.: 76–77). Concerns about protests spreading to the U.S. were raised in a July 5 report that warned,

> Militants in southern Maine blocked a rail line that carries crude oil to New Brunswick's Irving Oil refinery for several hours, citing concerns that the line carried tight oil derived from hydraulic fracturing, the same process used to derive natural gas from shale. (ibid.: 101)

Faced with growing protests targeting settler industry, the Shale Gas Committee warned that "There is a considerable upswell in national activity/activism associated with Idlenomore ideology" (ibid.: 18). Casting Idle No More as some unreasonable "ideological" movement clearly demonstrates how the fundamental issue of illegal land theft is erased by replacing Indigenous claims for self-determination with a caricature of unreasonable, anti-Canadian Native protesters.

The first few weeks of SWN's exploration season proved semi-disastrous for the company and New Brunswick's agenda to create a shale gas industry, as blockades and work stoppages continuously thwarted exploration efforts. Shale Gas Committee notes reveal their primary concerns as a triple threat: "Contingencies are important for this committee," including "sustained road/exploration blockade ... increased presence of warrior society ... INM driven protests [targeting] trade, energy, and borders" (ibid.: 88). Settler colonial anxieties surrounding "contingencies" would soon become a reality, beginning with the arrival of the Mi'kmaq Warrior Society. RCMP conduct and the refusal of the New Brunswick government to recognize Mi'kmaw jurisdiction on unceded lands eventually prompted the Warriors to invoke provisions under the Peace and Friendship Treaties.

THE MI'KMAQ WARRIOR SOCIETY
AND THE TREATY RELATIONSHIP

The security state response to Mi'kmaw assertions of sovereignty over their land shows the asymmetries of settler colonial power. As the conflict progressed and it became evident that the Elsipogtog community would not acquiesce to the threats and provocations of industry and the police, the involvement of the Mi'kmaq Warrior Society became a point of fixation for the colonial bureaucracy. Warrior societies have long been on the security state's radar, framed as a potential violent threat to settler colonial interests and national security.

ITAC'S 2011 *Biannual Update on the Threat from Terrorists and Extremists* notes Warrior Societies under the heading "Domestic Issue-based Extremism: An Ongoing Security Concern" (CSIS 2012-32: 16). Associating the struggle for land rights with extremism and terrorism, the security state notes that Indigenous communities "remain focused on key issues such as sovereignty and outstanding land claims," and that, "at times more radical members of Aboriginal warrior societies advocate violence as a means to resolve these issues" (ibid.). Contrary to depictions from settler authorities, warrior societies act as treaty enforcers outside of the *Indian Act* system and are called upon to defend Indigenous land and protect Indigenous communities from hostile threats and armed attacks, thus reserving the right to bear arms themselves, as happened during the "Oka crisis" (Alfred and Lowe 2005). With the anti-shale gas resistance movement in Elsipogtog, the Mi'kmaq Warrior Society invoked their responsibilities after unprovoked RCMP violence directed at non-violent protests and cultural ceremonies. The Warriors, in a meeting with the Canadian military, self-described as mediators that "only intervene when called upon to offer services which assist in mediation, alternative measures and positive results" (DND 2014-1157: 56). Warriors played an active role in the conflict by exercising and asserting Mi'kmaw sovereignty and by invoking and living historic treaties. In defending Indigenous rights against the illegal encroachments of settler colonialism, they physically confronted the seismic testing work taking place on Mi'kmaw lands.

The Warriors' involvement in the protests caught the ire of the security state, including military and civilian intelligence officers, who viewed the Warriors' defiance as an affront to Canadian sovereignty and a threat to the post-colonial order. Mi'kmaq Warrior Society activities were under constant surveillance, construed as unlawful and requiring suppression.

One heavily redacted CSIS document contains a partial heading, "Mi'kmaq Protest Activity" and notes that Maritime military bases may experience increased interactions with First Nations (CSIS 2015-501: 1). CSIS attributes rising conflict in New Brunswick to "Aboriginal and non-Aboriginal activists and militants" attempting to stop shale gas exploration, with dozens of arrests made (ibid.). At one point CSIS describes the meetings between military officials and the Mi'kmaq Warrior Society: "The (self-described representatives of the) Mi'kmaq warrior society believe that the Canadian military has a duty to protect the Mi'kmaq from 'enemies both foreign and domestic' under the Peace and Friendship treaties signed by the Mi'kmaq and the British Crown during the 1700's" (ibid.). According to the Warriors, SWN represented a foreign enemy and the RCMP represented a domestic enemy, who was not upholding its treaty role as representative of the Crown (Howe 2015: 126–28).

As the Warriors explained to the military, who meticulously documented their discussions, under the terms of the 1752 Treaty they have the right to request a negotiator from the British or Canadian military if negotiations with the federal government fail (DND 2014-1157: 9). Despite Mi'kmaw rights under the treaties, the Canadian military turned down the request. Internal documents reporting the interactions between the Warriors and Gagetown military staff reveal how DND framed the Mi'kmaq Warrior Society as illegitimate. A ministerial advisory and situation report shared throughout the command structure of the Canadian military, including the Vice Chief of the Defence Staff and Canadian Joint Operations Command, shows that DND did not recognize the authority of the Warrior Society to negotiate on behalf of the Mi'kmaq as they only recognize *Indian Act* representatives as the legitimate authority representing First Nations. The reports argued that the Warrior Chief, James Pictou, is not an elected Chief and "had no authority to represent on behalf of FN" (ibid.: 13–26). DND officials reported that the Warriors left "not happy" and declared that the military's refusal was a violation of the treaties (ibid.: 22). DND shared documentation of their version of the interaction throughout the rungs of the security state. Providing an additional account of the conflict, CSIS documents reported that: "The Mi'kmaq warrior society plans to bolster protests against the exploration work and its members say they will use 'any means necessary' to stop the shale gas exploration on their territory" (CSIS 2015-501: 1). With the inclusion of CSIS and the upper echelons of the Canadian military, agencies of the security state used their meetings with the Warrior Society to increase the level of national security resources deployed against the land defenders.

Military documents produced from a phone conversation with the representatives of the Mi'kmaq Warrior Society on July 28, as well as a meeting on September 12, include detailed situation reports, emails, a ministerial advisory, and hand-written notes documenting the interactions. The investigator's notes were compiled and submitted by Master Corporal Selena MacLeod, military police officer at Gagetown on July 28. MacLeod also conducted an interview with and compiled "complainant statements" from representatives of the Mi'kmaq Warrior Society, who contacted DND and made a formal complaint that RCMP members "have been intimidating and committing acts of violence" (DND 2014-1157: 55, 80–101). Given that the Mi'kmaq view DND as responsible for treaty rights, the Warriors demanded that DND intervene in the spirit of Crown–Indigenous relations and stop the RCMP violence. DND's report included a "summation of the allegations and their treatment by RCMP J Div, that violated the Treaty Rights of the Mi'kmaq Nation" (ibid.: 104). Included are lists of RCMP arrests throughout June and July. Importantly, the Mi'kmaq Warrior Society highlight how many of these arrests targeted traditional Indigenous practices. MacLeod notes that although the Warriors do not want to see a violent outcome, due to the actions of the RCMP, they "foresee no positive outcome unless the CAF intervenes" (ibid.: 56). The Mi'kmaq Warrior Society claimed that the RCMP's violent interventions were captured in a radio transmission interception: "FN members used a cell phone application that transmits radio frequency, at which time heard an RCMP transmit 'that they declared war' on the FN members" (ibid.: 55). A situation report warns that First Nations reinforcements were "en route to stand-off with RCMP ... indications are that FN will match the numbers of the RCMP and will not hesitate to challenge the RCMP" (ibid.: 9). DND reporting of the request shows that the Warriors foresaw the coming assault as a culmination of increasing violent escalations by the RCMP. In calling for the external mediator, the Mi'kmaq Warrior Society drew attention to how the RCMP were following a long line of racist and anti-Native practices, reflective of settler colonialism's eliminatory logic toward assertions of Indigenous rights. Yet, instead of upholding their responsibility to the treaties, DND recirculated their interactions with the Mi'kmaq Warrior Society through the security state to paint a picture of impending Native criminality.

The military denied assistance to the Mi'kmaq Warrior Society and subsequently targeted the land defenders with increased surveillance. DND's Canadian Forces National Counter-Intelligence Unit (CFNCIU) warned that the refusal to intervene in the conflict could result in backlash in the form of direct action and protests directed against military assets (DND 2016-1403: 8). In attempting to further undermine the Mi'kmaq Warrior Society, the CFNCIU suggests that "The group that attended the base could be assessed as extremists within the Mi'kmaq community" (ibid.). Although the Warriors' attempts to seek a DND negotiator prompted the military to view them with increased suspicion under the label of extremists, the phone call on July 28 is significant. According to journalist Miles Howe, on the morning of July 28 a standoff ensued between a line of Mi'kmaq Warriors and a line of RCMP. It was at that moment when Warrior Chief James Pictou phoned Gagetown, and the military then acted as a liaison between the Warriors and the RCMP. It is unclear exactly what was said or if the 1752 Treaty factored in to the conversation between the RCMP and DND, but the RCMP withdrew shortly thereafter. Not only that, SWN then withdrew all of their equipment and did not return for two months (Howe 2015: 126–28). Despite the brief retreat, the security state and SWN began to reconfigure their approach. The Mi'kmaq Warrior Society's intervention is an important turning point in how the security state postured itself in opposition to the anti-SWN protests. As the conflict progressed, the security state branded the Mi'kmaq Warrior Society, who were asserting sovereignty over the territory in question, as a source of criminality that threatened what Governor General David Johnston called the "national inheritance" of settler colonial wealth and prosperity.

"OUT OF LEFT FIELD": THE MI'KMAQ'S EVICTION NOTICE AND THE SETTLER COLONIAL RESPONSE

Despite suffering significant losses and repeated work stoppages, SWN, with the support of the RCMP and the New Brunswick government, decided to begin work around Elsipogtog once again in September 2013. Demonstrating a lack of awareness toward the mounting antagonisms by the police and the continued resistance from the Mi'kmaq, an email from the Security Directorate's Andrew Easton expressed "hope for a peaceful few weeks" (NB-PS 2016b: 142). It took only two days of SWN seismic testing for conflicts to flare up. A September 29 security event report notes that protests have restarted and a large crowd, including a "more militant First Nation group," were blocking a SWN staging facility located close to Highway 11 with calls on social media for assistance to blockade the highway (ibid.: 140). Former Elsipogtog Chief Susan Levi-Peters explained, "They made a compound in Rexton and then they put spotlights on it and then they put a gate on it and it was as if it was their trophy. They put all their [equipment] there" (quoted in Skene 2013). The SWN staging facility was an Irving-owned compound housing five "thumper trucks," around a dozen pick-up trucks, and multiple boxes of geophones and related equipment totalling several million dollars (Howe 2015: 131). Located by a scouting party from Elsipogtog, the find was described as a "bonanza strike" (ibid.). RCMP reports note that "Facebook users organized a 24-hour presence" at the SWN compound, which included twenty-nine people and eighteen vehicles blocking the entrance (RCMP 2015-8404: 38). The RCMP in turn set up a blockade to stop the movement of protesters on Route 134 and increased their presence as people continued to arrive.

Not satisfied with less passive means of suppressing the protest, RCMP began making arrests. One RCMP note suggests that "A number of males were at the blockade, apparently looking for a confrontation" (ibid.). The same note also warns of a possible convergence of anti-petroleum and Idle No More protests in the province, and that "Social Media is being monitored by the 'J' Division Criminal Intelligence Analyst to track activities of the protesters" (ibid.: 39). Worried that the land defenders were gaining momentum and numbers, the RCMP tasked other Divisions with a request for intelligence on any "potential outside influence or threat linked to the Shale Gas Exploration protest activities in New Brunswick" (ibid.: 42). As a result of the equipment blockade forcing a total work stoppage, Public Safety's Security Directorate activated the New Brunswick Security Event Management Plan and established the Security Operations and Security Executive Groups to coordinate surveillance and policing of the protests. Frustration was evident among the Shale Gas Committee members. One complained, "We need to get out in front not just reacting to protests" (NB-PS 2016b: 60). The same set of notes raises the possibility of including the Prime Minister's Office (PMO) in efforts against the Mi'kmaq, asking, "Is this being put on paper to PMO" (ibid.). In a context of increased panic, the colonial bureaucracy had to contend with mounting opposition from the Elsipogtog leadership.

The Mi'kmaq community contesting SWN intrusions on their territories had displayed considerable patience over months of facing violence and intimidation by the RCMP, while having their treaty rights and jurisdiction systematically undermined and ignored. On October 1, a large demonstration occurred at the blockaded SWN compound where Elsipogtog Chief Arren Sock read aloud a Band Council Resolution reclaiming First Nations stewardship over all unoccupied Crown land. The RCMP closely documented the events noting that 150–200 people marched and surrounded the compound, and emphasized the riskiness of the protesters by recounting that the protests caused a "temporary breach" (RCMP 2015-8404: 42). The Resolution proclaims that "we are capable of managing our lands better than other governments or corporations," that "we have lost all confidence in governments for the safekeeping of our lands held in trust by the British Crown," and that "we have been compelled to act and save our water, land and animals from ruin" (Howe 2015: 134). Elsipogtog Councillor Robert Levi then indicated that an eviction notice would be delivered to SWN demanding the equipment be removed by midnight and escorted to the Canada–U.S. border (ibid.: 134–35).[8]

The colonial bureaucracy must have viewed the declaration that Elsipogtog members were "ready to go out and stake their claims on unoccupied Crown lands for their own use and benefit" as a direct threat not only to a reserve system meant to contain Indigenous populations, but also to the sovereign integrity of the Crown (ibid.: 134). INAC's Atlantic Communications branch tracked the stewardship declaration and eviction notice to SWN (INAC 2013-1348: 26; INAC 2013-1624: 436–42). INAC emails questioned the validity of the declaration and attempted to rationalize the situation as a result of a lack of (modern) treaty progress and attempts otherwise regarding "their *claim* of stewardship over all unoccupied alleged 'Crown' land," as being "out of left field" (INAC 2013-1624: 417, emphasis added). Even more important than the legality of the declaration, INAC worried about the influence of movements asserting sovereignty: "it shows the Idle No More side of the prov–FN relationship" (ibid.: 404). Predicting the future arrests of the Elsipogtog Chief and Council on October 17, INAC noted, "Anyone can make a declaration but to act on it could lead to arrests" (ibid.). INAC viewed the Elsipogtog declaration of sovereignty as a fundamental threat to the tenuous settler colonial fictions of Canada as a post-colonial society, and went so far as to advocate for their allies in the security state to arrest individuals who advanced these claims.

Worries about the "Idle No More side" of relations with Indigenous communities suggests that the methods of pacifying Native communities under the *Indian Act*, while violating treaty relations, might not be successful. In response to these potential threats, INAC responded with strategic efforts to delegitimize the Elsipogtog leadership as extremists and radicals. INAC documents claim, "this is not being presented as a consultation/accommodation issue, but a complete veto that is being framed by Chief Sock as the re-occupation of traditional territory for the express purpose of terminating all mineral/gas exploration" (INAC 2015-989: 1). INAC's effort to present themselves as interested in "consultation" and "accommodation" dialogue is completely disingenuous and at odds with the historical (and contemporary) dealings with Elsipogtog and other communities. These rhetorical devices should not be understood exclusively as political games but instead as an aspect of governmental process to produce a feeling and identity of accommodation within the settler bureaucracy. As processes that produce an identity of INAC officials as reasonable and interested in fairness and (economic) progress, these rhetorical practices of settler colonialism coincide with the production of Indigenous identities — particularly the Warriors — as irrational and hostile. As a process that places the Mi'kmaq into a deep cultural repertoire of settler colonial racism, INAC's framing efforts rationalize the punitive and violent measures taken against Indigenous communities that assert sovereignty and resist settler colonialism.

With the equipment blockade established, SWN's fall season was in jeopardy. The company claimed economic losses of $60,000 per day (*Global News* 2013). With operations shut down indefinitely, SWN turned to the courts. As we saw in the previous chapter surrounding the Aamjiwnaang rail blockade, one tool employed by industry in collaboration with the criminal justice system is the use of an injunction to bring down Indigenous blockades. SWN injunctions played pivotal roles in the violent raid that followed and in the ensuing conflict. On October 3, RCMP Criminal Operations updated the Commissioner that SWN lawyers had informed them that an injunction order was obtained to "prohibit blockage of access to working sites" (RCMP 2015-8404: 27). RCMP notes explain that the injunction was

> directed at named and unknown protesters and will contain an enforcement provision that authorizes the RCMP to arrest persons who fail to abide by the order of the court. Operational Strategies will determine if, when and how this order will be enforced. (ibid.)

The RCMP delivered hand-written threats to those at the blockade outlining the implications of the RCMP enforcing the injunction. In bold type at the top, the RCMP claim to respect the right to demonstrate in a lawful, peaceful, and safe manner. However, they note that "this is an unlawful demonstration, as it blocks access and prevents others from doing their lawful work," which could result in a number of criminal charges, imprisonment, and a criminal record (see Skene 2013). Threatening the full extent of colonial lawfare against the peaceful blockade, the RCMP issued a warning that the criminal charge of mischief endangering life could mean life imprisonment (ibid.). The message was clear: continue to threaten settler economies and you will be punished. For their part, the Shale Gas Committee describes the injunction as a "useful tool" as it "clarifies what is legal and not legal" (NB-PS 2016b: 57). As soon as the injunction was granted by the courts, the RCMP began preparations to raid the camp in order to free SWN's equipment. As the security state drew up raid plans, the provincial government entered into talks with the Elsipogtog Band Council in an effort to negotiate an end to the blockade.

Negotiations between the Elsipogtog Chief and Council and the New Brunswick Premier were dubbed the "Alward talks." On October 8, the Shale Gas Committee expressed optimism that negotiations — described as "not public" — would provide results with a "short term focus" (to liberate the equipment) (ibid.: 61). Further notes reveal the government's negotiation tactics attempting to pinpoint and manipulate co-operating players, including "acceptance from other elders" and that the community seemed to be aligned with the Band Council. However, the Shale Gas Committee was wary of the role that the "warrior group" would play amid concern that "some may not listen" to the Band Council (ibid.). Efforts hedged on manipulating the Elsipogtog Band Council to bring down the blockade. However, the influence the colonial bureaucracy believed the *Indian Act* leadership possessed over those maintaining the blockade camp was misplaced (Howe 2015: 138–43). RCMP briefing notes in the first few days of October express frustration over the inability to negotiate a cessation to the blockade and that "other tactical options, besides road closures, are being developed" (RCMP 2013-6342: 22).

A series of fast-moving events prefaced the raid. An RCMP briefing observes that the Alward talks "did not materialize to a point of meaningful input on resolution" (ibid.: 35). The failed negotiations meant that SWN's equipment would not be freed. In conjunction with the breakdown in negotiations, the security state factored in legal manoeuvres as SWN's interlocutory order was scheduled to be challenged in court on October 18 (and was eventually overturned) (NB-PS 2016b: 55). Security state moves demonstrate the disdain held for Indigenous communities challenging resource extractive industries and Canadian sovereignty. The RCMP had threatened those at the blockade with life imprisonment if mischief charges caused "danger to life," yet hundreds of armed police took part in a dawn assault on a sleeping camp the day before the injunction had the possibility of being overturned. The security state had perpetrated a potentially very dangerous scenario with potentially devastating consequences — injury/loss of life, imprisonment — for those at the blockade, who had been painted by the security state as criminals in need of punishment. A demonstration of how the RCMP attempted to surprise and manipulate Indigenous land defenders was explained by the Mi'kmaq Warrior Society's District Chief Jason Augustine: "[The night of October 16], a Native RCMP brought us a tobacco wrapped in red felt and told us, it's peace now. So that night we all went to bed thinking it was peace" (quoted in Nicholas 2014). This dirty move by the RCMP occurred less than twelve hours before a violent raid to carry out the SWN injunction that was about to expire.

At the same time as the RCMP's duplicitous peace offering, the RCMP were amassing hundreds of officers as reinforcements, called in from across New Brunswick, as well as Quebec, Nova Scotia, and Prince Edward Island. All that was required was a public relations pretext, which materialized as a result of provocations from Irving's private security force, Industrial Security Ltd. (ISL). An RCMP account indicates that Irving guards were obstructed from making a shift change and "verbal threats have been received by employees from camouflaged protesters" (RCMP 2015-8404: 50). The document says that "plans are being developed to extract the employees and replace them with RCMP members," should another attempted shift change fail. Unmentioned in the RCMP report however, according to Howe's counter-narrative, was that the Warriors were provoked by ISL guards, who worked closely with the RCMP (Howe 2015: 149–50). A pattern of police and private security provocation ensued. For example, an agreement between the Warriors, the RCMP, and ISL stated that shift changes would occur at the back of the compound. Yet, police and Irving undermined these agreements. In one instance, ISL employee (and RCMP veteran) Gary Flieger exited the compound from the front gate facing the camp and approached the sacred fire with his weapon out, while another guard filmed the encounter. This move was unprecedented, as the entry and exit point for Irving guards (the back gate) was well established in addition to it being forbidden to carry weapons near the sacred fire. One of the Warriors escorted Flieger back through the front gate of the compound. The Warrior was later charged with assault and unlawful confinement. RCMP public relations materials presented in the aftermath of the raid claim that, "On October 16, death threats were made by some of the protesters against members of a private security firm at the compound being blocked" (PCO 2013-517: 20–24). Howe (2015: 148) suggests that this move was premeditated to bait the Warriors into a confrontation that would demonstrate an "increasingly hostile situation" in need of remediation at the blockade site.

An October 16 RCMP briefing reveals that plans to carry out the impending raid were already in motion. The briefing note explains,

> Extra resources are en route to be available at the protest scene or on stand-by status. An operational plan has been developed to deal with potential site issues and flashpoints everywhere. A Tactical intervention plan to resolve the situation is also in place. (RCMP 2015-8404: 50–51)

Simultaneously, in Ottawa, Public Safety Canada's Director General of Communications instructed his staff in an email on October 16 to "Please monitor this issue very closely over the next 24 hours" (PSC 2013-334: 1089). Notes produced by the Shale Gas Committee on October 16 further outline the "high order scenario" amid an elevated threat level (NB-PS 2016b: 55). Anticipating a successful raid, the committee discussed an alternate location for SWN's equipment, warning in a tersely written message: "Next few days dynamic" (ibid.). That same day, Governor General Johnston delivered the Speech from the Throne. It was time to "seize Canada's moment."

THE RAID: "CROWN LAND BELONGS TO THE GOVERNMENT, NOT TO FUCKING NATIVES"

As dawn broke on the morning of October 17, the Mi'kmaq Warrior Society's District Chief Jason Augustine was awake and on traffic patrol, walking in a thick fog on the road near the encampment. He was surprised to see buses around a newly established RCMP road blockade. He recounted,

> The next thing I know an RCMP jumps out from my side with guns drawn telling me to put down my gun. I told him ... it's only a flashlight and a phone ... They told me, "you gotta go." I said, "go

where?" This is my Mi'kma'ki, this is where I'm from. I can't go nowhere, this is where I live. (quoted in Nicholas 2014)

By this time, Augustine saw large formations of RCMP officers moving to surround the Warrior camp with guns drawn. An exchange was caught on videotape as the sky began to lighten in the early morning hours: "So you guys *do* work for SWN," Augustine confirms with the RCMP in the video. "I'm gonna tell my kids from the grave, that I stood up for their water. I stood up for your guys' kids' water too. All of your guys' kids," says Augustine, making a sweeping motion with his arm. Augustine further explains to the RCMP that "This is Mi'kma'ki, what we're doing here is a peaceful thing. You guys are being violent."

Hundreds of RCMP officers had amassed in various locations as they moved in on the Warrior encampment. They were heavily armed. Leading the raid was the militarized Emergency Response Team, dressed in camouflage and equipped with assault and sniper rifles. Some had dogs. As agents carrying out settler colonial policy, the RCMP seemingly took pleasure in crushing this challenge to Canadian sovereignty. Being told that the Mi'kmaq were going to reclaim Crown land affronted an ethos of Canada's "national inheritance" and offered a moment where members of the security state could express their racist attitudes. This is why it is not surprising that, during the assault, one of the camouflaged officers yelled, "Crown land belongs to the government, not to fucking Natives" (APTN 2013c). This statement underlines that the conflict was based exclusively on the land, competing jurisdictions, and the treaty rights of the Mi'kmaq. When Indigenous Peoples challenge Canadian sovereignty and assert their rights, settler society typically responds with anger and violence, all the while deflecting the underlying land issue and constructing it as something else (see Battell Lowman and Barker 2016). The first wave of officers was met by the Warriors with Molotov cocktails, which were ineffective in halting the advance. A standoff ensued before teams of police targeted individual Warriors for arrest. Suzanne Patles, a lieutenant with the Mi'kmaq Warrior Society, filmed units of RCMP moving in on the camp through the field. While in her car uploading videos and spreading word of the raid, she was surrounded. She describes an officer brandishing an assault rifle and raising it in the air to swing it down as she protected her head: "It went through the windshield and it hit the top of my head and at that moment I was pulled out of the car and hit several more times with the assault rifle in the head" (quoted in Skene 2013).

When the raid commenced, the RCMP had established two blockades on the roads surrounding the camp in an attempt to seal off any supporters or media access. As word of the unfolding raid spread quickly on social media, hundreds of people rushed to the site from the Elsipogtog reserve. They easily overwhelmed the RCMP blockades and were met by dozens of tactical officers. A standoff ensued. Mi'kmaw men, women, children — the "aggressive, violent extremists" as later characterized by the RCMP — were tear-gassed, pepper-sprayed, and shot with rubber bullets. Elsipogtog resident Amanda Polchies described how community members linked arms at the RCMP line while police tried to push them back (ibid.). At that point Elsipogtog Elder Doris Coupage was pepper-sprayed in the face at close range. An iconic image would emerge as a result of what Polchies did next:

> I had this feather and I didn't know what to do and the first thought in my mind was pray. So I kneeled down in the road and I started praying. I was praying for Doris and I was praying for the other woman that had gotten sprayed and I was praying for my people, hoping that this will end peacefully. That nobody would get hurt, that nobody would die. (ibid.)

"Canada's moment" was being seized in a display of what Pam Palmater described as "a battle of drums and feathers versus SWAT teams and assault rifles — not the rosy picture painted by Canada to the international community" (Palmater 2015: 224). Forty were arrested, including the Elsipogtog Chief and some Council members. As a result of the violent raid and mass arrests, six RCMP police cruisers were set on fire in protest. Though media and police accounts of the raid emphasized the violent nature of the camp, the raid and the arrests resulted in "no reported injuries to police resources," which numbered 285 officers (RCMP 2013-6342: 37).

As the raid unfolded, the colonial bureaucracy monitored the situation closely, carefully constructing and repeating a narrative that the RCMP were merely responding to a violent situation. Bolstered by the mainstream media,[9] the security state justified its antagonist provocations and the subsequent violent mass arrests as a necessary sequence of events in response to the burning police vehicles. Although the police cars were burnt after the raid, a carefully crafted RCMP press release claimed that

> Setting police cars on fire created a dangerous situation for everyone in the area and it was at that point that police were forced to

physically confront some in the crowd who refused to obey the law. Forty people were arrested. (PCO 2013-517: 20)

Internal RCMP briefings that chronologically replayed the day's events undermine these falsified accounts given to the media and the public. An October 17 RCMP briefing shows that the arrests preceded the alleged arsons: "Prisoner count at 11:28; 21 males, 7 females ... Total arrests at approx. 40 for by 1330 hrs ... As of 1345 hrs five (5) police vehicles have been set on fire" (RCMP 2013-6342: 37).

To consolidate the security state's efforts to manipulate the public version of events, the RCMP staged a press conference displaying various items and weapons seized at the camp to paint a picture of Native criminality, a public security threat in need of elimination. According to the RCMP, weapons seized included firearms, improvised explosive devices, ammunition, knives, and bear spray. During the press conference, the police were not queried on the legal length of the knives or the privileges afforded to Indigenous Peoples regarding the possession of ammunition, or if the ammunition matched the rifles, or if the rifles were loaded (Howe 2015: 160). A key message crafted by the RCMP notes, "The weapons and explosives we seized show that this was not a peaceful protest and there was a serious threat to public safety. We took the action necessary to eliminate that threat" (PCO 2013-517: 20). This version of events was produced and reproduced by the mainstream media, prompting this response by Leanne Simpson (2013a):

> Canadians will hear recycled propaganda as the mainstream media blindly goes about repeating the press releases sent to them by the RCMP designed to portray Mi'kmaw protesters as violent and unruly, in order to justify their own colonial violence. The only images most Canadians will see is of the three hunting rifles, a basket full of bullets and the burning police cars. Most will be happy to draw their own conclusions based on the news — that the Mi'kmaq are angry and violent, that they have no land rights, and that they deserved to be beaten, arrested, criminalized, jailed, shamed and erased. The story here, the real story, is virtually the same story in every indigenous nation: Over the past several centuries we have been violently dispossessed of most of our land to make room for settlement and resource development. The very active system of settler colonialism maintains that dispossession

and erases us from the consciousness of settler Canadians except in ways that is deemed acceptable and non-threatening to the state. We start out dissenting and registering our dissent through state sanctioned mechanisms like environmental impact assessments. Our dissent is ignored. Some of us explore Canadian legal strategies, even though the courts are stacked against us. Slowly but surely, we get backed into a corner where the only thing left to do is to put our bodies on the land. The response is always the same: intimidation, force, violence, media smear campaigns, criminalization, silence, talk, negotiation, "new relationships," promises, placated resistance and then more broken promises. Then the cycle repeats itself.

The Mi'kmaq had put their bodies on the line to protect the water for all peoples living on that land and were met with the brutal violence of the security state. The RCMP were self-proclaimed heroes and the Mi'kmaq "violent, gun-toting and car-burning Natives" (Howe 2015: 161). The RCMP purposefully constructed a narrative to justify a violent assault and eliminate the Warrior camp, misconstruing the events to serve their purpose. Outside of internal RCMP documents, nowhere was the real objective of the raid expressed: the liberation of SWN's equipment.

The security state labelled the Mi'kmaq as violent to justify further characterization of the resistance against shale gas as criminal, a national security threat. Using the label of violence to characterize the entirety of the Indigenous-led resistance, CSIS described that "militants and extremists have engaged in equipment sabotage, multiple road blockades, and the destruction of six RCMP vehicles ... resulting in over 100 arrests since June 2013" (CSIS 2015-54: 5–6). CSIS emphasized the ridiculous claim made by RCMP Assistant Commissioner Roger Brown that the existence of weapons and explosives seized at the site "were akin to a Boston Marathon–type of bombing" (ibid.). Placing an emphasis on the economic impacts of Elsipogtog's efforts to defend their traditional territories against settler economies, CSIS contends, "The cost of industrial equipment sabotage has exceeded $250,000 (excluding the estimated $300,000 to replace the six RCMP vehicles) while the additional cost to law enforcement has surpassed $4 million" (ibid.: 6). The memo warns that the conflict in Elsipogtog might serve as a precursor to more Indigenous resistance to extractive activities if the Canadian government continued to approve controversial energy projects, such as the Northern Gateway Pipelines. In addition to focusing on Native criminality and economic losses inflicted on Canada's extractive industries, CSIS also focused on the threat of solidarity protests. CSIS detailed how more than fifty solidarity protests and blockades were carried out by other activists following the raid. Demonstrating the impact that Idle No More had on the settler state's psyche, colonial authorities immediately scrambled after the raid to react against solidarity demonstrations.

SOLIDARITY PROTESTS AND THE THREAT OF AN "IDLE NO MORE–LIKE MOVEMENT"

In recent years, the effect of violent police assaults on Indigenous communities asserting treaty rights and defending their land has been to galvanize nationwide mobilizations from diverse Indigenous communities. Agencies of the security state voiced concerns that Indigenous movements could disrupt the post-colonial order by highlighting the potential of an "Idle No More–like movement" that could once again threaten the settler economy and critical infrastructure (PSC 2013-334: 978). RCMP "J" Division's Emergency Operations Centre reported "several highway blockades" in New Brunswick on the evening of the raid. Fearful of the potential mobilization of Indigenous activists, the RCMP also warned that "Aboriginal sympathizers may travel to New Brunswick to support Shale Gas protesters here" (RCMP 2015-8404: 67).

Over the years, communities and Warrior Societies have acted in solidarity by setting up blockades on their own land or mobilizing to reinforce Indigenous communities under police attack. The prospect of reinforcements bolstering an already large and determined resistance movement emanating from Elsipogtog and Kent County, and potentially establishing larger blockades and land defence camps, was immediately interpreted as a threat that could jeopardize SWN's ambitions to recommence seismic testing. Despite their earlier cheerleading of RCMP provocations, meeting notes produced by New Brunswick's Shale Gas Committee recognize the instability produced by the militaristic RCMP actions by warning that "lengthy significant consequences" in the form of solidarity protests could negatively impact industry and commerce in the province (NB-PS 2016a: 3). Elsewhere in New Brunswick, the RCMP note that a blockade in Oromocto targeted the Irving Corporation for their all-encompassing role in supporting SWN and the RCMP.[10] Faced with numerous new blockades and protests, the New Brunswick Critical Infrastructure unit mobilized amid what were described as "unlawful protests," and the security state prepared for widespread solidary actions (NB-PS 2016b: 4).

The "central fusion centre for Native problems" discussed in the previous chapter was operationalized in anticipation of backlash to the raid. As with other displays of Indigenous resurgence, the Government Operations Centre (GOC), as the security state's fusion centre, mobilized to coordinate an integrated surveillance and policing effort against the activists. The GOC created situation reports and acted as a liaison with the multiple partners and units comprising the security state. In one email, the GOC warned the PCO of the potential emergence of an "Idle No More–like movement" (PSC 2013-334: 978). The GOC coordinated meetings and intelligence products with numerous policing and security partners, as well as monitoring social media for the RCMP (ibid.: 1082). Fearful of another Idle No More uprising, a GOC report warns that "social media activity is significant on a national level" and that "all major national news networks and newspapers are covering this event as a lead story" (ibid.: 512). As the events surrounding the raid and solidarity protests made national headlines with potential international reach, the GOC began to extensively map and catalogue protests. Preparing for protests at border crossings, the GOC also reached out to its counterpart in the United States. An email to the U.S. Department of Homeland Security's National Operations Centre late on October 17 summarized a phone call alerting them to the potential spread of solidarity protests. A synopsis of the conversation warned,

> Through social media such as twitter and facebook, this incident is escalating. We suspect it could escalate to the level of Idle No More. On Oct 17, there were protests at the Canadian embassies in New York City and Washington. This movement could spread in the U.S. It is getting international media attention. We are monitoring very closely ... Conversely, if there is anything of significance in the U.S., please let us know. (ibid.: 688)

Four minutes later, at 11:44, a report shared across the "GOC-Analysis" listserv notes that "additional protests are possible affecting critical infrastructure, government offices, exploration activities or other resource development work" (ibid.: 512). With the potential of an "Idle No More–like movement" emerging to challenge settler colonial attempts to seize Canada's (post-colonial) moment, the GOC framed these types of protests — targeting the settler economy and bureaucracy — as "unlawful."

Given the federal government's oil and gas aspirations, the accelerated social media attention and nationwide scrutiny led to the direct involvement of the PCO. As the colonial bureaucracy's lead department advising the Prime Minister on emerging issues of national importance mobilized, the PCO's Director of Operations for the Security and Intelligence division, as well as the Crisis Management Cell of the department's Security Operations division, were involved in responding to and coordinating intelligence associated with solidarity blockades (PCO 2013-517). Security and intelligence officials within the PCO, including Gordon Voogd, Brigitte Diogo, and David Vigneault, shared emails summarizing the events at Elsipogtog, placing emphasis on the backlash:

> Upwards of 50 protests in support of the Elsipogtog First Nation are planned for today and over the weekend according to the Idle No More website. A handful will occur in the U.S. and include the Canadian consulates in New York and San Francisco. (ibid.: 18)

The PCO was also concerned with First Nations leaders travelling to Elsipogtog to demonstrate support, including the Assembly of Manitoba Chief's Grand Chief Derek Nepinak who issued a statement criticizing the RCMP for "unabashed violence and terrorism inflicted ... against our indigenous Mi'kmaq and non-indigenous brothers and sisters who were peacefully assembled on their ancestral lands" (ibid.: 12). Two separate emails exchanged on October 21 indicate that the Prime Minister and the National Security Advisor organized a meeting in the raid's aftermath, demonstrating the impact that the Elsipogtog resistance had on the highest offices of settler colonial order (ibid.: 6–7). Other PCO emails tracked events as they unfolded after the raid, including Premier Alward's insistence that SWN resume operations as well as a New Brunswick Anti–Shale Gas Alliance news conference calling for a public inquiry into RCMP actions and promising to raise $100,000 to litigate the province to halt shale gas development.

Military assets were also integrated into security state efforts following the raid. DND emails show how the military monitored the protests and were prepared to act if called upon. The military's Counter-Intelligence Unit monitored the multiple shutdowns of the Trans-Canada Highway in New Brunswick at Campbellton, Perth-Andover, Kingsclear, and Rexton[11] (DND 2013-1238: 57–58). DND officials were also worried that demonstrations could impact activities around Gagetown — the second largest military base in the country — in southwestern New Brunswick. Captain Kyle

Spindler sent an email on October 17 that reads, "Apparently there is a plan for the natives to block the bridge tomorrow, including the Burton bridge" (ibid.: 11). The Burton Bridge is situated over the Saint John River on the northern end of Gagetown. Further emails demonstrate the involvement of high ranking officers who were "ready to react" if necessary. Captain "RJ" Clark from Maritime Forces initiated a discussion with his commanding officers. It reads, "Sir — if you have not seen the news, the fracking protest in N.B. we discussed last week has taken a turn for the worse with RCMP and FN and other protesters in active confrontation with each other," and goes on to note that New Brunswick's Emergency Management Office and the Nova Scotia RCMP are relocating assets to assist (ibid.: 13–15). Brigadier-General Nicolas Eldaoud — Commander of the 5th Canadian Division — replied, "Indeed Sir, we are closely monitoring the situation. Even if I don't expect that this situation will escalate to an ALEA [Assistance to Law Enforcement Agencies] operation, we will be ready to react" (ibid.: 14). Rear Admiral John F. Newton also chimed in, noting that Gagetown's 5th Division "will feel the more direct and proximal pressure from this," and requested the division to be the primary relay of intelligence information (ibid.). Although Brigadier-General Eldaoud doubted that an ALEA situation would materialize, further emails show that Gagetown indeed received a request for military support from the RCMP.

Immediately following the raid, DND emails show that the RCMP requested logistical support, fusing military resources with policing efforts around Elsipogtog. As early as the afternoon of October 17, DND was informed that their assistance was required to establish a base of operations near Elsipogtog. On October 18, an email containing subject line, "Re: CJOC [Canadian Joint Operations Command] Ops Advisory — Request for Canadian Forces Assistance — RE Shale Gas Exploration in N.B. operational file" — was shared with dozens of military personnel, including the Strategic Joint Staff and Judge Advocate General (ibid.: 24). Ignoring any underlying issue of land theft, the advisory describes the conflict as an "environmental protest," linked to "ongoing First Nation dissatisfaction with resource development and extraction in Canada, as well as *general dissatisfaction embodied* in the Idle No More movement" (ibid., emphasis added). Belittling and delegitimizing the Indigenous land defenders, communications practices within DND solidify the violence of settler agencies within a historical continuum where unruly Natives are depicted as unreasonable and hostile.

Anticipating further conflict, the RCMP request from DND includes rations and quarters for sixty members, with a potential increase up to one hundred members "depending on the escalation of the operation" (ibid.: 29). The RCMP request also includes a drill hall and two staging areas for operational briefings. Aware of the potential threat level change due to the involvement of military resources, the advisory notes that "it is important that your chain up to the [Minister of National Defence] is aware of this potentially highly volatile situation where CAF is offering some logistical aid to the RCMP" (ibid.: 22). The backlash emanating from the RCMP raid provoked a fused policing approach involving multiple government departments and security agencies responding to the mobilization of an "Idle No More–like movement." Meanwhile, the "highly volatile situation" around Elsipogtog remained as SWN, the RCMP, and the New Brunswick government prepared for yet another round of seismic testing.

"RUN WITH THE HORSES WE HAVE": CRIMINALIZATION AT ELSIPOGTOG AND SWN'S FINAL PUSH

SWN's exploration operations in southeastern New Brunswick in 2013 had faltered. Forced to withdraw in late July and immediately blockaded again in late September, the company had completed only a fraction of seismic testing work on multiple lines in proximity to Elsipogtog. A determined Mi'kmaq-led resistance had been successful in tracking and confronting SWN activities. With SWN's operations described as "effectively stopped" for a period of six weeks, RCMP briefings indicate that the company will recommence seismic testing in mid-November, amid expected protests and "potential violence" (RCMP 2013-6342: 1; RCMP 2015-8404: 53).

Although the RCMP led an armed paramilitary-style assault against the Mi'kmaq, causing numerous injuries, the security state, SWN, and the media continuously reframed the Mi'kmaq as violent and unruly. This was exemplified in the visit by SWN lawyer Michael Connors to a Mi'kmaw longhouse set up on Highway 116 near Elsipogtog, leading up to the November testing. The exchange was captured on video and shared via social media networks. Connors pleaded with the group to allow for fourteen days of seismic testing work unimpeded, and even offered to drop SWN lawsuits against several community members. "I'm not asking anyone not to protest, but I am asking that we don't do anything that would lead to violence. Unfortunately, blockades lead to violence" (APTN 2013b). Community members present maintained that "blockades are not violent, police are violent" (quoted in Lane 2013). For Connors and SWN, "violence" referred to disruptions that prevented SWN from carrying out its work, whether or not physical violence occurred or not. At the same time, the use of violence by police against blockades is an always-present reality, which Connors seemed to acknowledge. Elsipogtog War Chief John Levi levelled with him: "We are going to be there ... we never ceded this land and we are going to protect it before these waters are contaminated" (APTN 2013a).

With Mi'kmaw eviction notices, the invocation of historic treaties, and their declaration of sovereignty systematically ignored and undermined, the Elsipogtog First Nation turned toward the colonial courts and filed for an emergency injunction to halt seismic testing. An RCMP briefing note details that the Elsipogtog First Nation argued, "SWN activity, and the license issued by the Government is in contravention of their treaty rights as they were not adequately consulted" (RCMP 2015-8404: 36). Notes from the Shale Gas Committee on November 13 express concern that the "injunction might challenge crown's exploration policies & the right to grant exploration licences" (NB-PS 2016b: 43–44). Elsipogtog's injunction declared SWN's operations as "illegal, unconstitutional, null and void," claiming that the exploration was a violation of Mi'kmaq title and treaty rights (*Elsipogtog v. New Brunswick 2013*). Elsipogtog also claimed "the absence of prior meaningful consultation and accommodation" and as such also named the Assembly of First Nations Chiefs in New Brunswick (AFNCNB), which INAC recognized as the legal negotiating body to fulfill duty to consult obligations (ibid.).[12] The injunction was ultimately rejected by the courts, demonstrating how settler colonial law privileges Canadian economic interests over treaty rights and the duty to consult. On the other hand, injunctions requested by industry against Indigenous protests are almost always granted. Regardless, Elsipogtog's resistance persisted.

The community's next move would trigger panic within the colonial bureaucracy. An INAC email discussing Elsipogtog's injunction notes the First Nation withdrew its membership from the AFNCNB, and was no longer represented under the draft consultation protocol (INAC 2015-989: 4–6, 63–66). In an attempt to mitigate Indigenous opposition surrounding free, prior, and informed consent, the province had drafted a duty to consult policy in 2011 and entered negotiations with the AFNCNB, representing nine New Brunswick First Nation communities including Elsipogtog. The AFNCNB was, according to INAC, empowered to "conduct procedural aspects of consultation" on behalf of New Brunswick First Nations (ibid.: 8). For INAC, having a legal entity such as the AFNCNB that was closer to government and industry was pivotal to manufacture "consent" for resource development projects, including the Energy East Pipeline proposal. However, Elsipogtog's withdrawal, which represented around 30 percent of the total population of Bands comprising the AFNCNB, served to unravel the process.

INAC noted Elsipogtog's influence on other New Brunswick First Nations as Madawaska and Woodstock also withdrew, influenced by "recent events in N.B." (ibid.: 7). Revealing bureaucratic manoeuvres to maintain control over the process, hand-written notes produced by the Shale Gas Committee meetings on November 28 note that "Oromocto [First Nation] may join the AFN, Oromocto would provide numbers" (NB-PS 2016b: 40). But the issue goes further than Elsipogtog and shale gas and links to the future of pipelines in the province. Referencing Energy East Pipeline consultations, INAC emails note that the Madawaska and Woodstock First Nations had initially consented to the AFNCNB negotiating on their behalf. However, INAC bureaucrats panicked because they had not yet obtained physical copies of the Band Council resolutions providing consent. Concerned with the "influence Elsipogtog's withdrawal may have on others," an email advises to pick a date and move forward with whoever is "in" and suggests that "maybe it's time to just run with the horses we have" (INAC 2015-989: 7). Elsipogtog manoeuvres to halt shale gas exploration threatened to unravel the existing framework coveted by the settler state to fast-track resource development projects, putting in jeopardy the future of energy projects in the province and beyond.

Attempting to salvage their exploratory operations in the final weeks of 2013, SWN and the New Brunswick government sought a series of injunctions to criminalize protests. Leading up to seismic testing, SWN advised the RCMP that they would turn to the courts for another round of injunction orders if faced with protests (RCMP 2015-8404: 53). Following the dramatic October 17 raid, injunctions were deployed as the primary tactic of colonial lawfare, denied to the Mi'kmaq yet used as a tool to legalize land theft and criminalize the land defenders. In an effort to make the Mi'kmaq illegal on their own land, SWN and the province obtained injunctions to create a "work safe zone" for shale gas exploration while the RCMP reinforced its numbers and acted as the primary enforcement mechanism for New Brunswick's petroleum agenda. Throughout, the Mi'kmaq's demand for recognition under the treaties was outright ignored, despite the RCMP acknowledging the contested legalities in a "strategic considerations" memo that states: "Elsipogtog and its leaders has been very clear that actions by SWN Resources are illegal and being conducted on disputed territory" (ibid.: 22). While making note of the contested legalities, the RCMP's actions show how they act to uphold one side of these legal disputes — that of settler law. Given the insistence of the Mi'kmaq on asserting their sovereignty, the RCMP operate on the assumption that Indigenous law must be subordinated to settler order.

Faced with determined resistance and daily work stoppages, SWN were granted an injunction prohibiting protesters from hindering or interfering with its equipment beginning November 22 (RCMP 2013-6342: 33). The RCMP immediately moved to enforce the injunction by arresting at least three people "attempting to obstruct workers near the SWN truck compound in Moncton" (ibid.). RCMP records show how they insisted on placing "appropriate [release] conditions" on protesters to "prevent their return to the work site," and detail a protocol finalized on November 27 with the Director of Public Prosecutions for "arrest and release of protesters under criminal contempt of court" (ibid.: 40). In efforts to clear out the protesters, briefing notes related to the enforcement of the SWN injunction show how RCMP had "developed, and imposed on SWN and its contractors, a clear contact protocol to ensure timely and thorough communication between exploration companies and the RCMP" (RCMP 2015-8404: 49). The RCMP-imposed protocol demonstrates a fused approach to policing Indigenous opposition that increasingly involves industry to facilitate the criminalization of the protesters who attempted to protect their legal claims to their lands.

In addition to a series of injunction measures, the criminalization of land defenders ensued. An RCMP briefing notes the formation of Project J-TRIM, an investigative team to "pursue charges ... related to the take-down of [October 17]" (RCMP 2013-6342: 38). The same briefing, dated November 6, notes that some still remained in custody and others were released on conditions. A follow-up briefing in December confirms fifty-five people charged with twenty different types of offences, totalling ninety-one *Criminal Code* charges (ibid.: 42).[13] Despite security state criminalization efforts, the RCMP noted that increasing numbers had come out to oppose SWN at two protest sites, including "a number of individuals that had not been seen at previous events" (RCMP 2015-8404: 36). In an attempt to criminalize those present, the RCMP noted that "the protest group has become increasingly more aggressive and intimidating, and have armed themselves with sticks, knives, and sprays" (ibid.). RCMP also engaged in attempts to incapacitate the protesters by forcing them into an equivalent of "free speech" pens, what the New Brunswick government euphemistically proposed as a "safety zone" (NB-PS 2016b: 113–14).

Despite police and government support for SWN, the RCMP observed that it was unlikely that the company would finish their work before the expiration of the injunction order. Given the logistical difficulties that would arise in keeping the Elsipogtog community off their own land without an injunction to legitimize the repression, the New Brunswick government authorized SWN to work at night (ibid.: 103–06). Meanwhile, SWN filed for and was granted additional injunctions, first extending to December 2 and then to December 17. With the Mi'kmaq committed to defending their lands, SWN were repeatedly met with blockades and the sabotage of its geophone equipment while the RCMP continued to support the company by making arrests. Despite the multiple injunction orders and RCMP repression, SWN packed up on December 6, having completed only 27 kilometres of exploration, less than half of their stated goal.

ELSIPOGTOG CATALYST AND "VIOLENT ABORIGINAL EXTREMISTS"

The Mi'kmaq-led resistance surrounding the Elsipogtog First Nation had succeeded in rupturing not only the goals of the New Brunswick government to develop a fracking industry, but had also successfully challenged the settler colonial status quo. SWN were forced to permanently retreat from the province despite a highly coordinated effort between government, industry, and police, with internal documents revealing that over four hundred RCMP personnel were involved in policing the shale gas protests in 2013, with a total cost calculated by the RCMP of over $12 million (RCMP 2013-7388). The Mi'kmaq-led victory also altered the political landscape, as the next provincial election was framed as a referendum on shale gas. The ruling Conservative Party was soundly defeated and an indefinite moratorium on hydraulic fracturing is now in place. Moreover, the impact of the Mi'kmaw resistance had far-reaching and long-lasting impacts on the settler state's psyche. In addition to breathing "new life into the fading [Idle No More] movement," according to an RCMP report, backlash against the raid and the botched exploration season provoked widespread fear and hostility across the security state (RCMP 2016-1140: 604). Resulting in efforts to profile and criminalize land defenders, these hostilities were anchored in settler colonial rationales that reframe assertions of Indigenous sovereignty and self-determination as irrational and hostile threats to settler common sense. Rooted in long-standing racism, the provocations of settler colonialism reveal the moral and legal hypocrisies of "post-colonial" society, yet also reproduce a security-centric desire by settler Canada to eliminate forms of Indigenous dissent.

Elsipogtog's resistance to shale gas development is a potent demonstration of the particularly hardline stance taken by settler colonial agencies in their efforts to eliminate Indigenous sovereignty assertions over land and resources. As a coordinated and extensive multi-agency effort to crackdown on organized resistance to resource development, the case study is a poignant example of how settler colonialism translates land defence into a threat to Canadian society and national security. In the aftermath of the police raid in Elsipogtog, the RCMP's Critical Infrastructure Intelligence Assessment on *Criminal Threats to the Canadian Petroleum Industry* was published shortly after SWN's disastrous exploration season. Key findings from the report, published on January 24, 2014, note that "Recent protests in New Brunswick are the most violent of the national anti-petroleum protests to date" (ibid.: 87). The RCMP describe the Mi'kmaq who resisted as "violent aboriginal extremists" who "will continue to engage in criminal activity" and "pose a realistic criminal threat to Canada's petroleum industry" (ibid.). Crafting Indigenous Peoples as adversaries to the post-colonial order and to settler ambitions to extract resources from Indigenous lands, the CIIT report notes, "The development of Canada's natural resources is amongst the primary concerns within many aboriginal communities" (ibid.: 77). Framed as being anti-progress and anti-Canadian, the underlying motives for Indigenous resistance — the destruction of their lands and subjugation of treaty rights — are ignored. Canada's response to Indigenous land defence that challenges settler economies is criminalization and punishment.

In addition to Elsipogtog efforts catalyzing the "anti-petroleum movement" fixation of the security state, the RCMP went one step further the following year. In March 2015, the NICC's National Tactical Intelligence Priority produced a report — *Project SITKA: Serious Criminality Associated to Large Public Order Events with National Implications* — which profiled 313 activists the security state associated with "serious criminality" surrounding "Aboriginal public order events" (CSIS 2016-47: 11–66). As the newest iteration of aggregating intelligence data on prominent activists, Project SITKA created protester profiles of eighty-nine of the individuals it considered to be threats to "natural resource development, particularly pipeline and shale gas expansion," regardless of actual evidence of criminality. As mentioned in our introduction to this book, over half were associated with the Mi'kmaw resistance at Elsipogtog — thirty-five from New Brunswick and ten from Nova Scotia, categorized as "disruptive or volatile," out of a total of 182 individuals uploaded into the PROS database related to "unlawful protests" in Kent County (ibid.: 31). The security state viewed the Mi'kmaq as a threat, as an affront to Canadian sovereignty, by targeting "outside influencers" who came from neighbouring provinces to support Elsipogtog. Settler colonialism facilitates the erasure of colonial history and attempts to permeate the post-colonial order through a twisted series of double standards. The Mi'kmaw Nation predates Canada and the RCMP by millennia and the Peace and Friendship Treaties by more than a century, yet Indigenous interprovincial mobilizations (where provincial boundaries were imposed on the various districts comprising Mi'kma'ki, the Mi'kmaw homeland) are framed as threatening and criminal while the RCMP's interprovincial mobilizations to attack a land defenders camp on unceded territory are framed as normal, even heroic.

Project SITKA demonstrates a totalizing surveillance effort to profile, track, and implement a web of permanent surveillance across Indigenous groups, communities, and social movements. Admittedly, the RCMP are not concerned with identifying root causes of dissent; rather, the security state's efforts are to integrate surveillance and modernize policing databases so that front line officers can respond accordingly to Indigenous land defence protests that stymie settler colonial efforts of "seizing Canada's moment." Although the security state deploys a range of police and surveillance powers in an effort to suppress opponents of extractive capitalism, the Elsipogtog case study demonstrates that social movements have the ability, using far fewer resources and facing marginalizing tactics from the mainstream media and settler society, to persevere and defeat powerful forces. Movements such as the Mi'kmaq-led resistance at Elsipogtog in 2013 serve to shatter mythical proclamations such as "Canada's natural wealth is our national inheritance" and rupture the post-colonial order. The security state understands this grassroots power, and as a result it continues to employ more covert strategies and develop policing tactics to profile, criminalize, and eliminate Indigenous dissent.

Notes

1. Under the Peace and Friendship Treaties of 1760 and 1761 in the Maritimes, the Mi'kmaq and the Wolastoqiyik (Maliseet) signatories did not surrender rights to lands or resources. Today, the Mi'kmaq and the Wolastoqiyik maintain that they continue to hold Aboriginal rights and title throughout their traditional territory. Also, the Supreme Court ruling in the Marshall decision confirmed that the Mi'kmaq and Wolastoqiyik possess a treaty right to hunt, fish, and gather for a moderate livelihood (INAC 2013).

2. See Obomsawin (1984 and 2002) for accounts of police violence directed at Mi'kmaq communities at Listuguj and Esgenoôpetitj.

3. Moreover, Miles Howe (2015) connects the familial and political linkages between early settlers who stole Mi'kmaw land and the province's contemporary elites facilitating industry expansion and resource extraction.

4. The Grand Council represents the pre-contact, traditional form of government over the lands comprising Mi'kma'ki in present-day eastern Canada.

5. See note 1 in Chapter 1.

6. Cornwallis reasoned that declaring war on the Mi'kmaq would have the effect of recognizing them as a sovereign people. Thus, the Mi'kmaq were declared "rebels" and the British military ordered to "annoy, distress & destroy the Indians every where."

7. Documents released from New Brunswick's Department of Justice and Public Safety do not contain file numbers. We have cited using year of release and a subsequent letter (a and b) to distinguish between files that were released to us.

8. The Mi'kmaq Warrior Society sent their own eviction notice to SWN's head office in Texas on October 7, vowing to do "whatever it takes" to protect the land and water and claiming that "any destruction done to our lands and waters is a threat to not only our way of life, but also as a threat to our overall survival" (Mi'kmaq Warrior Society 2013).

9. CSIS documents show that *Sun* reporter Kris Sims vetted an anti-Native article with the agency before publishing, on November 2, 2013, "Our Warrior Problem: Militant Natives are causing trouble, and they aren't going away." An email on September 17 is mainly redacted, including the sender and recipient, but is classified as secret and seems to demonstrate that the reporter was vetting a draft through CSIS, in a bizarre instance of collaboration between right-wing settler media and the security apparatus: "Here is my proposed article. Please let me know how you feel, and add/delete as necessary ... [redacted] ... in this matter, however if you think that would not be appropriate, I won't" (CSIS 2015-501: 2–3).

10. The Irving family was implicated in the conflict by providing private security and owning the compound used by SWN as a staging facility. The multi-billion dollar family conglomerate owns hundreds of private companies in the oil, gas, shipping, transportation, and retail sectors. The Irvings also monopolize media in the province, owning most of the newspapers — including all three

English-language dailies — and three radio stations (see Poitras 2015; Livesey 2016). While New Brunswick remains one of the poorest provinces, the Irvings became rich off the theft of Indigenous land and resources, including claiming ownership of 1.8 million acres of forest (in addition to holding multiple logging licences to clear-cut Crown land). The company also supports fracking and tar sands pipelines (Energy East), presumably because it also owns a refinery and shipping infrastructure in Saint John.

11. As Campbellton and Rexton are not located along or near the Trans-Canada Highway, the report indicates that the CFNCIU Halifax Detachment may not be familiar with New Brunswick geography or that their sources are not as reliable and credible as purported. The report lists three sources — A, B, and C — as "tried and trusted," with "reported reliably in the past and who can be depended upon with confidence" (ibid.).

12. INAC documents show how New Brunswick Energy Minister Craig Leonard stated publicly that he had determined that the duty to consult requirement had been met, simply by virtue of the province notifying Indigenous communities that testing is taking place (INAC 2015-989: 14).

13. The briefing indicates that thirty-eight of the fifty-five were First Nations (RCMP 2013-6342: 42). Of the thirty-eight, two Mi'kmaq warriors pled guilty to weapons-related charges and were sentenced to fifteen months each in prison. While the Crown argued for five-year sentences, defence lawyer Allison Menard argued that from an Indigenous perspective, the warriors were part of a larger movement of an independent nation protecting their land and water (Roache 2014).

POLICING THE IMAGINARY "ANTI-PETROLEUM MOVEMENT"

Throughout this book we have exposed new configurations in the "war on terror," and we have discussed how the security state is an expansion of trends in intelligence-led, fusion-centre policing. Although a central focus of national security policing in the "war on terror" is directed at the "radicalization" of Arab and Muslim segments of the population, our purpose has been to document how the dramatic reorganization of policing under the banner of national security has transcended into widespread targeting of domestic social movements. Indigenous activism is one of those prominent areas of increased scrutiny. This is evident from the 2007 CSIS presentation to energy corporations at the Canadian Association of Petroleum Producers security briefings, where CSIS agents implored industry representatives to consider the primary threats to their critical infrastructure not to be Islamic terrorism, but domestic "extremism." A recap of the meeting says, "Domestic extremists are emerging from their post 9/11 introspection," and suggests that "among aboriginal and environmental extremists, there is a rediscovered militancy" (CSIS 2012-27: 18). As the collaborations between the security state and energy corporations have illustrated, national security policing is about surveillance and intelligence-driven networks that serve as an extension of extractive capitalism. The "war on terror" has enabled the security state to redirect substantive resources and focus toward Indigenous groups and social movements that challenge dominant economic powers. Particular attention should be paid to its ambitious efforts to expand the tar sands and other industrial projects on disputed Indigenous lands while gutting environmental protections in the process.

A number of activists, researchers, and scholars have highlighted a resurgence of Indigenous movements challenging the settler colonial status quo

(Alfred 2005; Palmater 2015; Snelgrove, Dhamoon, and Corntassel 2014). Central to these Indigenous-led contestations are assertions of Indigenous self-determination and a foregrounding critique of how settler colonialism remains the constant, fundamental character of Canadian society. A key component of contemporary settler colonialism resides in how Indigenous assertions of autonomy and freedom are increasingly, if not almost exclusively, governed under the policing infrastructures of security, terrorism, and extremism. While we acknowledge that Indigenous movements have always been governed through "policing" mechanisms (we stress this includes Indian Affairs), a powerful combination of struggles that challenge the fundamental legitimacy of colonial sovereignty and the expansive bureaucracies of "security" has provoked an intensification of these policing practices. This is most clearly illustrated by the extensive surveillance of Indigenous movements and, we suggest, efforts to consolidate increasingly integrated security state capacities are still unfolding. As Indigenous and environmental movements increasingly challenge the Canadian state's ambition to become an "energy superpower" by working with the tar sands, shale gas, and extractivist industries, groups such as the Unist'ot'en and the Mi'kmaq Warrior Society have been targeted and labelled as "violent Aboriginal extremists" and "environmental criminal extremists."

Our case studies highlight that Indigenous resistance efforts have been successful in not only challenging federal and provincial claims to Indigenous land and disrupting the post-colonial imaginary, but also in halting settler resource extractive industries. In the cases of Enbridge's Northern Gateway Pipelines proposal in B.C. and SWN Resources' shale gas exploration efforts in N.B., both projects were ultimately stopped as a result of direct action to shut down work efforts. Coupled with national mobilizations like Idle No More and localized struggles such as those of the Algonquins of Barriere Lake, the reaction of the security state has been to consolidate policing and intelligence resources to focus on perceived internal threats to national security. To justify campaigns of harassment and intimidation, Indigenous communities' and movements' resistance efforts are increasingly constructed as national security threats and framed under the rubric of "domestic extremism" within the "war on terror." The response directed against Indigenous resistance to big energy projects has merged multiple agencies and departments into a policing effort that engages in widespread surveillance and conceptualizes itself as a political antagonist to what national security agencies refer to as the "anti-petroleum movement." Under the mantle of protecting critical infrastructure, the security state has rationalized a widespread surveillance program targeting opponents of destructive energy projects related to the tar sands or fracking and, to legitimize these practices, has also engaged in the construction of the anti-petroleum movement as a quasi-criminal identity.

We'd like to note that the "anti-petroleum movement" that we detail is not an actual social movement. In line with how criminological scholars have noted that police "make crime" based on the self-defined categories and expectations that they hold toward society (see Ericson 1981; Haggerty 2001), the notion of the "anti-petroleum movement" has been constructed by the security state to categorize a broad array of actors with the characteristics — irrationality, hostility toward economic development — that the police ascribe to them. These policing practices, which Ian Hacking (1995) calls making "human kinds," are self-referential processes that justify police practices. We stress that these practices say much less (if anything) about the social realities of the groups under surveillance, while saying a great deal about the relationships of power and aspirations for control that animate the policing agencies who engage in "kind making."

As a construction that emerges from the critical infrastructure assemblage of the security state, the "anti-petroleum movement" illustrates how settler colonial agencies normalize extractive capitalism while demonizing its opponents. Outlined in a 2014 report from the Critical Infrastructure Intelligence Team (CIIT), the naming of an "anti-petroleum movement" represents how the discourse and resources of national security have been shaped to target activists that challenge the corporations who have partnered with the security state through critical infrastructure programs. The report — *Criminal Threats to the Canadian Petroleum Industry* — starts by listing some "key findings." It begins, "There is a growing, highly organized and well-financed, anti-Canadian petroleum movement, that consists of peaceful activists, militants and violent extremists, who are opposed to society's reliance on fossil fuels" (RCMP 2016-1140: 87). The framing of "anti-Canadian" also borrows heavily from oil-funded lobby groups like Ethical Oil that promote Canadian tar sands oil as more ethical than imported oil from regimes like Saudi Arabia. A highly disingenuous campaign run by Ezra Levant, the Ethical Oil lobby effort offered an early display of the nationalistic xenophobia that has become Levant's trademark. While the RCMP borrow from this framing of tar sands oil, their report also used research from right-wing personalities such as Vivian Kraus that fixates on how U.S. funding has spurred a "growing" environmental movement. Typical of "moral panic" discourses (see Cohen 2002), the report demonstrates how the movements under surveillance are not simply protests, but considered by the RCMP as a threat to Canadian society.

Noting the anti-fracking movement near the Elsipogtog First Nation, the CIIT report evokes national security language in stating that "violent anti-petroleum extremists will continue to engage in criminal activity to promote their anti-petroleum ideology" (RCMP 2016-1140: 87). In a disingenuous attempt to represent the security state as objective and non-ideological, the report echoes the narratives of climate change deniers who challenge the science of anthropocentric climate change. The report claims, "Governments and petroleum companies are being encouraged, and increasingly threatened, by violent extremists to cease all actions which *the extremists believe*, contributes to greenhouse gas emissions" (ibid.: 87, emphasis added). Characterizing the science of climate change as a form of "extremist" belief, the report casts a wide net of potential security threats. "Non-governmental environmental groups such as; Greenpeace, Tides Canada, and Sierra Club Canada, to name a few," says the report, believe that "climate change is a direct consequence of elevated anthropogenic greenhouse gas emissions which, *they believe*, are directly linked to the continued use of fossil-fuels" (ibid., emphasis added). Written in 2014, the report presents a somewhat shocking — given that it is at odds with even the dominant media, who believe in consensus climate change science — display of climate change denial.

By representing a deliberately misconstrued version of climate science, the RCMP frame those that oppose tar sands development as ideologically-driven, criminal extremists. The position taken by the RCMP, a dramatic endorsement of tar sands development and itself a highly ideological rejection of consensus science, is a product of the partnerships and friendships fostered through nodes of the security state under the rubric of "critical infrastructure." The RCMP, in effect, are protecting their friends. Moreover, they are casting opponents of the tar sands as enemies of Canadian society. With nothing but anecdotal and mostly historical examples of lawbreaking — nothing remotely close to terrorism in the form of violent attacks on civilian populations — the report goes on to warn, "These violent protests are likely an indicator of what the petroleum industry, and the law enforcement community, must be *prepared to confront* as the development of Canada's petroleum resources continues and expands" (ibid.: 86, emphasis added). Underlining the confrontation with tar sands and fracking opponents, the RCMP themselves are representing a form of social conflict that misconstrues the level of crime or violence stemming from social movements, while at the same time escalating the perceived conflict on behalf of the extractive industries. The RCMP then quote Canada's Counter-Terrorism Strategy, which also targets animal rights advocates, environmentalists, and anti-capitalists, noting that these groups or individuals "could choose to adopt a more violent, terrorist strategy to achieve their desired results" (ibid.: 85). Completely decontextualizing property attacks that have taken place during volatile conflicts to defend Indigenous lands and treaty rights, the report warns: "Violent incidents, such as ... the destruction of petroleum equipment and threats to petroleum personnel in New Brunswick, clearly illustrate the nature of criminal threats confronting the Canadian petroleum industry" (ibid.).

In positioning themselves as the defenders of extractive capitalism, the RCMP have demonized opponents through discourses of criminality, and their concerns about the well-being of the tar sands extend beyond potential threats of disruptions or blockades to include the impacts of social movements on the brands and public image of tar sands development. Take, for example, the following claims from the report about the "anti-petroleum movement":

> Research and analysis done in support of ongoing RCMP criminal investigations shows those involved in the anti-Canadian petroleum movement have an interest in drawing public attention to, and in building recognition of, the perceived environmental threat from the continued use of fossil fuels. (ibid.: 86)

As a statement that clearly shows the criminalization of dissent, the RCMP security establishment have equated the mobilization of public education and pressure as a threat because it "draws public attention" toward issues of environmental justice. Yet, for the RCMP, the "perceived" notion of anthropocentric climate change is the threat they are policing. The RCMP report adds, "The publicizing of these concerns has led to significant, and often negative, media coverage surrounding the Canadian petroleum industry" (ibid.). Though concerns about negative publicity against the petroleum industry should have no bearing on the policing agenda of national security agencies, the close relationship between extractive corporations and the security state has fused their interests.

Though fused interests between extractive industries and policing institutions have long precedent as an aspect of settler colonization in Canada, the current iterations are shaped by contemporary conflicts between the desire to develop the tar sands and the opposition to these industry efforts. Yet, they retain many aspects of their settler colonial legacy. Most notably, the security state has constructed the "anti-petroleum movement" as a "new" iteration of Indigenous struggles against land theft and settler colonialism. Under the heading "Aboriginal Opposition," the RCMP write,

> Natural resource exploration and development projects — most notably on disputed aboriginal land — have historically been a contentious issue within many aboriginal communities. Due to the environmental and land use implications, some factions of the anti-petroleum movement, most notably in New Brunswick, Ontario, and British Columbia, have aligned themselves with violent aboriginal extremists. In general, members of this aboriginal extremist faction do not have support within their own communities, where traditional protest activity is often restricted to nonviolent types of actions such as site blockades. (ibid.: 85)

It is worth deconstructing this passage because the characterizations above demonstrate several important facets of how the RCMP have constructed the "anti-petroleum movement" and its relationship to settler colonialism. First is an explicit acknowledgement that at the core of extractive capitalism is the settler colonial project. Though couched in euphemistic language like "disputed" land and "land use implications," the RCMP provide a tacit acknowledgement — though simultaneously attempt to limit or even erase its implications — of the theft of unceded land and its historical injustices. With an acknowledgement of the legally and ethically dubious grounds on which extractive capitalism operates, the second acknowledgement is the threat of movement solidarity between ecological and Indigenous groups. Notably, this "alignment" is presented in itself as menacing and even inauthentic. The language of the passage presents the "alignment" as an act of opportunism — enemies colluding against a more noble cause. Casting these colluding elements as "factions" and "extremists," they are dismissed as fringe or illegitimate actors whereas the implicit non-factions and non-extremists are assumed to be supportive of extractive capitalism. As part of the larger project of demonization and delegitimization, a third aspect of this passage is its traditional divide-and-conquer approach to constructing Indigenous communities. As a potent technique of settler colonialism, those who oppose the liberal project, oppose extractive development, or express opposition to land theft are characterized as outsiders, as violent, as individuals who represent Indigeneity that must be assimilated, isolated, and eventually eliminated.

A final element of the passage above is worth highlighting for how it illuminates the practices of settler colonial policing: the characterization of blockades as non-violent. Within the thousands of contemporary documents that detail the mundane and widespread surveillance of Indigenous movements, blockades are always characterized as violent and illegal. Blockades are often strongly associated with a "traditional" resistance to settler colonialism and non-conformity with the norms of settler colonialism. In this case, blockades are presented as legitimate "traditional" practices and contrasted with "direct action" tactics like "civil disobedience, unlawful protests, break and entry, vandalism and sabotage ... [and the advocacy of] the use of arson, firearms, and improvised explosive devices" (ibid.: 86). Without any hint of irony, the only examples of violence toward civilians (i.e., terrorism) cited by the RCMP in their report are the Oklahoma City bombings in 1995 and the 2011 mass killing in Norway by Anders Breivik — both terror acts carried out by right-wing neo-fascists. In their representations, the RCMP highlight the rise in "violent rhetoric" associated with the Indigenous-led movements against extractive capitalism, and the few examples of property destruction, before the suggestion that police are tolerant of blockades as a form of Indigenous protest (ibid.: 85).

What should we make of this RCMP claim that the police respect blockades as forms of non-violent civil disobedience? As we illustrated with the Algonquins of Barriere Lake, Northern Gateway, Idle No More, and Elsipogtog, the erection of blockades against resource extraction was met with police violence and criminalization, as well as a host of punitive social and political consequences. For the RCMP to suggest that the security state is tolerant of blockades is not simply disingenuous. This statement illustrates the intellectual elasticity of settler colonialism, which can imagine a tolerance toward "traditional" Indigeneity only when contrasting these fictitious, law-respecting, imaginary protesters with immediate threats that need to be contained or eliminated. In reality, there is no tolerance for blockades or any refusal to accept the norms of settler colonialism.

Some blockades are tolerated for longer periods depending on their socio-economic impacts, yet the protesters are always constructed through a lens of settler colonialism that characterizes Indigenous protesters as violent. Moreover, Indigenous movements that take dramatic actions are not regularly but, we would contend, *always* represented by police agencies as antithetical to the Canadianizing mission, while the police are self-depicted as objective do-gooders whose aim is to surveil and eventually eliminate this threat to settler colonial progress.

Invocations of "extremism" are only the contemporary manifestation of this settler colonial process. In the concluding remarks of the anti-petroleum movement report, the RCMP make more explicit the link between disrupting economic interests and the label of "extremism." The report notes, "Anti-petroleum activists, militants and violent extremists have shifted their focus from the Oil Sands to the proposed multiple pipeline projects" (ibid.: 74). It continues, "Aside from New Brunswick, the most urgent anti-petroleum threat of violent criminal activity is in Northern British Columbia where there is a coalition of like-minded violent extremists who are planning criminal actions to prevent the construction of the pipeline" (ibid.: 51). The reference to northern B.C. specifically targets the Unist'ot'en Camp and other Indigenous communities opposed to the Northern Gateway Pipelines. In the report, the RCMP provide no evidence or examples of criminal behaviour or any evidence that could remotely live up to claims about "a coalition of like-minded violent extremists." With dramatic rhetoric, the RCMP instead suggest implicitly that the construction of a camp on unceded territory in the pipeline path, the activities there, and the invocation of Indigenous law to stop industry and RCMP trespassers, constitute a threat to settler colonialism in the form of criminality.

A separate intelligence report prepared by the CIIT — *Activities Related to Pipeline Infrastructure* — justifies the security state's ongoing surveillance of Indigenous and environmental activists. The CIIT report notes that "violent criminal actions targeting energy infrastructure *may* occur if extremists perceive peaceful actions as being ineffective" (RCMP 2015-1447-3: 132; emphasis added). Suspicious incidents reported through the Suspicious Incident Reporting (SIR) system in June and July 2014 include "acts of vandalism, equipment sabotage and theft, and signs of unauthorized access" which are "consistent with previous reporting involving the energy sector"[1] (ibid.: 132–33). Other examples of criminality include "threatening rhetoric on social media" as well as "threatening messages directed at high ranking government officials" (ibid.: 136). Yet, the latter is not attributed to northern Indigenous communities, rather a solidarity group — Settlers on Stolen Land — targeting Conservative Member of Parliament offices, including Industry Minister James Moore, in the Vancouver area with acts of civil disobedience (ibid.: 133). No evidence of violence or criminality associated with the Unist'ot'en or neighbouring communities along the pipeline path is offered. Yet, the Camp is construed and framed as the primary "criminal" threat for refusing industry access onto their unceded territories. Regardless, the RCMP use the associated widespread opposition and petty crime (e.g., theft of copper wire) to justify targeting those asserting Indigenous sovereignty and challenging settler authority.

CANADA'S INDIGENOUS "RISK FORECAST"

Indigenous mobilizations for self-determination against Canada's resource extractive industries and energy superpower ambitions produce deep anxieties within the security state. Following the release of the "anti-petroleum extremism" report and leading up to the decision to approve the Northern Gateway Pipelines proposal, the federal government feared backlash such as that emanating from the Mi'kmaq-led resistance around the Elsipogtog First Nation. One week before Gateway was formally approved, senior government officials met with CSIS in Ottawa to prepare for associated protests. CSIS agents warned that the pipeline approval "could have a distinct impact on Government-Aboriginal relations, particularly during summer and fall 2014" (CSIS 2015-54: 17). Two memos were prepared by CSIS Assistant Director of Policy and Strategic Partnerships Tom Venner to CSIS Director Michel Coulombe surrounding the June 9, 2014 Deputy Ministers' Committee on Resources and Energy meeting in Ottawa. The purpose of the high-level meeting was to prepare the security state for a "federal response to protests associated with resource and energy development in anticipation of possible events in summer 2014," with the issue being "driven by violence of the hydraulic fracturing protests in New Brunswick in 2013" (ibid.: 2). Although heavily redacted, the memo notes that "traditional Aboriginal and treaty rights issues, including land use, persist across Canada" (ibid.: 3). The report added, "Discontent related to natural resource development across Canada is largely an extension of traditional concerns. In British Columbia, this is primarily related to pipeline projects (such as Northern Gateway)" (ibid.). A recurrent theme throughout this book, "traditional concerns" or "sovereignty concerns" are framed by the security state as a threat to extractive capitalism that requires surveillance and potential repression.

Security state preparation surrounding the Deputy Ministers' Committee on Resources and Energy meeting demonstrates the increased consolidation of policing and intelligence resources directed against Indigenous movements. Enclosed with the memos were two tabs: an assessment on the *Violent Confrontation over Seismic Testing (Hydraulic Fracturing) in New Brunswick* and a GOC report titled *Government of Canada Risk Forecast — 2014 Protests and Demonstration Season* (ibid.). The GOC's "risk forecast" was prompted by the fallout from Elsipogtog as the security state determined that Aboriginal issues were the leading motivator of unrest in the country (ibid.: 11). Public Safety bureaucrats delivered this presentation at the Deputy Ministers' Committee on Resources and Energy meeting, which included an assessment of "possible medium-risk activities (characterized by disruption to critical infrastructure including transportation networks)" (ibid.: 14). Public Safety claims that the methodology for the "risk forecast" was based on a "five-year environmental scan" of past protests as well as an April 1, 2014 interdepartmental meeting with nine federal partners to share intelligence and collectively determine if any "future potential large, disruptive or geographically widespread protests or demonstrations in Canada which may rise to the level of national or federal interest" (ibid.: 9).

Clearly, Idle No More and the Indigenous protests challenging extractive capitalism had a deep impact on the security state's calculations. The GOC's primary concern was the strategic effect of such protests, including their growing frequency, impact on critical infrastructure, and required federal response. The GOC's "environmental scan" categorizes dissent into four categories, including social, political, environmental, and First Nations issues. The latter include "all protests with a First Nations nexus, including Idle No More protests, Assembly of First Nations–organized events, fishing-related protests, and treaty or resource development–related protest activities" (ibid.: 10). Although the security state is engaged in pervasive surveillance, profiling, and criminalization, using counter-terrorism resources the GOC admits that "there has rarely been 'a significant actual or potential threat to public safety'" (ibid.: 11). Instead, "large, disruptive, and geographically widespread protests and demonstrations have caused disruption to government services and critical infrastructure" (ibid.). For the security state, the targeting of government offices and economic linkages is enough to blur Indigenous dissent with criminality and terrorism.

Although the security state will go to great measures and use vast amounts of resources to suppress and eliminate Indigenous resistance against its petroleum agenda, the Elsipogtog case study and others in this book demonstrate that social movements have the ability, using far fewer resources and facing marginalizing tactics from the mainstream media and settler society, to persevere and disrupt extractive capitalism. Acknowledging the potential for grassroots social movements to engage in radical and transformative politics that can disrupt settler colonialism as well as extractive capitalism, the security state continues to fashion itself as the defender of the status quo by developing policing tactics to profile, criminalize, and eliminate Indigenous dissent.

SURVEILLANCE AND CRIMINALIZATION OF SOCIAL MOVEMENTS

As we have attempted to highlight in this book, Indigenous movements in Canada are increasingly categorized as extremist and subjected to forms of surveillance under the ambit of national security. As social movements scholars have demonstrated, categories and risks produced by security bureaucracies can determine the inclusion or exclusion of social actors and, for movements categorized as threats, surveillance practices often aim at criminalization and suppression (Boykoff 2007; Kinsman and Gentile 2010; Wood 2014). Much of this research underlines that police surveillance tends to exhibit "function creep," where the activities of security agencies expand beyond their original mandates and outpace capacities for legal or public oversight. With an ever-expanding mandate, security agencies produce categories and characteristics that rationalize further surveillance, providing a self-fulfilling rationale to justify expansive policing. The notion of an "anti-Canadian petroleum movement" is an explicit example of policing entities constructing a threat to justify expanding resources and practices of surveillance.

Research on the impacts of surveillance has argued that mass surveillance challenges the conduct of those surveilled. Knowledge of being under surveillance has been shown to have "panoptic" effects, demonstrating the legacy of Foucault's (1977) suggestions surrounding the broad powers of the gaze to structure social conduct (see Bennett et al. 2014; Lyon 2006; Wilson, Haggerty, and Smith 2011). Surveillance itself can promote a dangerous culture of suspicion and paranoia, producing cyclical patterns of (in)security. A consequence of these accelerators is that police utilize the insecurity constructions from their policing practices to rationalize increased "national security" resources, yet we stress that these practices have an additional productive impact in socializing the police and business community. By constructing the figure of a criminal and terrorist threat that is hedged against "Canadian interests," the police reproduce their own image as the virtuous agents of control and position the companies as victims (and partners) needing protecting. These caricatures are amplified when the subjects of police scrutiny are racialized, particularly when police construct these protesters as unreasonable Natives — or, as members of the RCMP have described them — members of Indigenous "sovereignty" movements.

In this book, we have pieced together the diffuse and systematic ways in which policing entities construe Indigenous movements as irrational, violent, and extremist threats, while simultaneously exalting themselves as reasonable and objective. Anchored in long-standing cultural repertoires of settler society, these processes of settler colonialism code Indigenous claims as unreasonable and produce a common, shared attitude within the security state that perceives the unrelenting scrutiny of these movements as justified. It is precisely these socializing powers of settler colonialism that have made the widespread surveillance against, and interventions within, Indigenous communities seem normal.

Adding important context to how settler colonialism reproduces a cultural norm of mass surveillance are the layers upon layers of policing and surveillance powers in the contemporary security state. Our efforts in this book are to give a general sketch of the sprawling national security bureaucracies and highlight their surveillance practices targeting Indigenous movements — yet, despite our efforts (and those of other researchers) to shed light on these bureaucracies, they remain largely opaque. National security and police agencies still regularly deny claims that they engage in systematic, regular surveillance of Canadians. And despite the obvious incompatibility of their denials and a general refusal to address a growing list of surveillance-related scandals, Canada's opaque security state has been granted increased powers and responsibilities. Nothing is more illustrative of these dynamics than powers conferred to the security state by Bill C-51, the updated *Anti-terrorism Act* (ATA).

Passed through Parliament in early 2015, along with a number of other security-related bills and amendments (see Forcese and Roach 2015), the government of Canada relied on a rehearsed exaggeration of terrorist threats to extend national security powers with the ATA. Among the

significant powers granted to the security state were information sharing provisions contained in the *Security of Canada Information Sharing Act*
(SCISA), which was embedded in C-51, and a form of speech crime related to
advocating or promoting terrorism. Although framed as targeting Islamic
militants, provisions of the ATA that criminalize speech crime have been
crafted in far broader terms, defining speech crime as to "knowingly advocate or promote the commission of terrorism offences in general"(Criminal
Code S. 83.221 (1)). With the caveat of "in general" offering a particularly
loose definition — even by the standards of "terrorist activities" — it would
be entirely plausible, certainly given our case studies, to include an array
of social movement–related activities within this language. Initial impacts
of these legislative changes are unknown — the public only finds out
when charges are laid — yet our case studies point to how agencies of the
security state consider an extremely broad range of activities to fall under
the notion of national security, extremism, and critical infrastructure, all
of which could potentially cue these new powers of criminalization. Aside
from potential prosecutions — which nonetheless remain unlikely — we
would stress that the criminalization of speech acts opens an even greater
risk of mass surveillance. Such a general definition of speech crime offers
a wide-ranging rationale to security agencies who may feel encouraged to
engage in mass surveillance against the people and groups they believe
might advocate practices deemed to be national security threats. Such
an expansive interpretation would only cement the mass surveillance of
social movements.

Even more dubious than the potential misuse of speech act criminalization are provisions of the SCISA. In a move that significantly enhances the
information sharing practices of the security state, the SCISA allows seventeen
federal agencies, including health, revenue, finance, as well as the security
and policing agencies, to share info about "activities that undermine the
security of Canada" (SCISA 2015, C. 20, S. 2). The SCISA defines an activity as
undermining the security of Canada "if it undermines the sovereignty,
security or territorial integrity of Canada or the lives or the security of the
people of Canada" (ibid.). With an emphasis on sovereignty and territorial
integrity, Indigenous movements would fit squarely within this ambit.
Analyzing some deficiencies with the SCISA, Craig Forcese and Kent Roach
(2015: 154) have detailed the expansive scope of this definition — including
in contrast to current legal definitions of "national security" — and have
warned "it risks sweeping virtually everything under the security label."

Notably, the scisa contains one exception on information sharing specifically addressing activities pertaining to "advocacy, protest, dissent and artistic expression" (scisa 2015, c. 20, s. 2, S.2 (i)). More-or-less similar to the 2001 ata that declares protests and dissent immune from surveillance powers of the security state, these exceptions have proven to have no bearing on policing practices for a very obvious reason: the pervasive intelligence collection and surveillance practices are never challenged in court. Much of the mass surveillance and collection of personal information remains stored away in databanks, retrieved when police access the pools of data for risk assessments or profiling — but rarely as evidence in court processes where activists can challenge the dubious legalities of police activity. The security state has had little difficulty criminalizing activists (particularly Indigenous people) for various public order or contempt offences, or by charging them with violent crimes after they are provoked or attacked by police — as we have shown with our case studies. Much of the intelligence collected remains in the expanding catalogues and databanks managed by the security state, often unbeknownst even to those who are charged with crimes. Surveillance data on these activists are not relied upon as evidence in trials. The practices are not challenged in courts; they remain secret.

Instead of focusing on the legal thresholds opened up by the scisa and the ata, we contend that these efforts produce new cultural thresholds within the security state. Police culture is far more powerful in the socialization of police than trainings or policy standards (Bittner 1990; Fassin 2013), and the continued trend of giving more resources and powers to policing agencies serves to reproduce cultural norms that place the security state at odds with the law. In ways that we highlight in this book, sentiments of members of the security state regard themselves as above the law, not subject to it. This is most acute with Indigenous law or treaty law. Even more pertinent for the enculturation of mass surveillance is that the scisa follows the expanded trajectory of "critical infrastructure" as a means of criminalizing opposition to extractive capitalism and the exploitation of Indigenous lands. The scisa explicitly lists "interference with critical infrastructure" among its examples of activities that trigger new information sharing capacities and, as we detail, critical infrastructure has become a convenient category for security and extractive companies to forge ties against Indigenous movements.

Moreover, because of the hurried and ambiguous language that resulted from the politicized marshalling of the ATA and the SCISA, the government of Canada — and its lawyers — have had to implement creative interpretations of vague definitions and exceptions. As revealed in background documents released with the federal Green Paper — a Liberal venture to extend elements of Bill C-51 — bureaucrats in the security state deem the SCISA's protest exemption to be inapplicable when related to undefined "violent actions" (PSC 2016: 29). As we detail, with the flexible definitions of "violence" applied by the security state to social movements, these exemptions to the exceptions will ensure that policing entities can have recourse to legal rationalizations should they need them. Given that much of the surveillance we detail in this book never goes to a courtroom, we suspect that the important elements of these manoeuvres are not the specific legal thresholds opened to the security state but a powerful signalling of *carte blanche* that enables a culture of mass surveillance.

In addition to new powers emboldening security agencies to engage in security intelligence in ways that are completely antithetical to evidence or notions of procedural fairness, we underline that the expansion of the security state is antithetical to social democratic life. The security state has empowered a myriad of agencies and officials to make decisions, monitor, and intervene in the affairs of denizens — in large part without providing acknowledgement of doing so or any ability to challenge these practices. In addition to a mass diffusion of policing powers and an inadequate "accountability" structure, a society that allows an unchecked growth of security and surveillance runs the risk of producing a mass "chilling effect" that threatens the principles of social democracy. A chilling effect refers to how surveillance and aggressive policing will reduce an individual's social participation (and communication) because of the fear of future consequences, rippling through society to produce group consequences. Mass expansion of security and policing powers in Canada has opened questions regarding the chill on protests and dissent, not only for Indigenous Peoples, but for those who hope for a less violent and more egalitarian society — a society where the security state and extractive capitalism would have far less power and control.

SETTLER COLONIALISM AND REINING IN THE SECURITY STATE

In our efforts to detail the expanded powers of the security state, we have focused on the policing of Indigenous communities as embodying a particular character of settler society. We stress that all policing is racialized, whether it be the racialization of whiteness that carries privileges and accommodations, or long-standing tropes of "gang" policing that racialize communities of colour, or the expansion of "radicalization" policing that engages in Orientalist racializations that code religious "indicators" as security threats. Policing is modelled on racial hierarchies, yet we suggest that a foundation for the racial hierarchies in Canada is shaped by settler colonialism. Though Canada exalts itself as post-colonial, Indigenous land conflicts draw out the deeply embedded colonial mentalities that settler society holds against Indigenous communities (see Mackey 2016). In this book, we detail that this explicit indicator of Canada's settler colonial character can be illustrated by how Indigenous movements shatter the myths of neutrality and objectivity that are typical of police agencies.

Policing agencies in Canada have long stylized and promoted themselves as independent and objective, yet we show how members of the security state (including Indian Affairs) hold highly normative and punitive — sometimes outright racist — attitudes toward Indigenous people. Comments like "Welcome to ABL World!" or telling an activist to "come back when he was sober" (Chapter 1) or "Crown land belongs to the government, not to fucking Natives" (Chapter 4) exemplify how these attitudes inform the policing of Indigenous communities. Most explicit in the policing of Indigenous movements are the normative beliefs that Canadian authorities have a duty to develop resources on Indigenous land, and that Indigenous Peoples are incapable of or hostile to economic development. Attempts to challenge these deeply hostile characterizations by asserting sovereignty, treaty rights, or notions of Indigenous self-determination are translated through the policing lens of public order threats, then through an enlarged domain of "national security" that considers sovereign expressions of Indigenous freedoms as threats to Canada's post-colonial order.

Through the mass expansion of security bureaucracies and resources, the "war on terror" has accelerated the policing of Indigenous communities. Yet, policing practices retain their fundamental character of settler colonialism. We believe it is useful to emphasize that these practices are rooted in a logic of elimination, a structured approach of colonial power to manage Indigenous lifeworlds with the goal of suppressing and ultimately eliminating expressions of Indigenous self-determination and sovereignty. Indigenous sovereignty remains an Achilles heel for post-colonial Canada, and policing practices reflect how the sovereign aspirations of Indigenous communities raise the dubious ethical and legal grounds in which Canada claims authorities over Indigenous life. We underline that the structured efforts to eliminate Indigenous threats to the post-colonial status quo are complex. Though some elements of these anti-Native sentiments are explicitly racist, right-wing, or neo-fascist, we focus on how far more widespread governmental powers work to naturalize the structured antagonisms against Indigenous sovereignty.

The main purpose of our research has been to document the extensive surveillance and policing apparatus that has arisen to control Indigenous movements and communities, as well as to illustrate how the security state engages in the violent repression of Indigenous movements. These practices should neither be considered as uncontested, nor are they successful in suppressing the aspirations and desires of Indigenous movements. In fact, we would stress the opposite: the machinations of the security state illustrate the fragility of settler society. What we detail in terms of the extensive mobilization of policing resources against Indigenous movements shows how powerful and inspirational contemporary Indigenous movements have become. The need for settler society to repress Indigenous movements is not new, yet the resources and technologies afforded by contrary policing agencies have amplified these policing efforts, particularly given the expansion of national security. Although the trends toward mass surveillance and more invasive policing are clearly accelerating, efforts to contest these trends have also taken root. It is not our goal to comment on or prescribe tactics for these dynamics of contention, only to provide an illustration of how the security state engages in mass surveillance and policing efforts against Indigenous movements. Forces of social transformation are incumbent upon the movements that direct them, and as settlers supportive of decolonization movements in Canada, we stress a need to rein in the security state as an important and necessary aspect of empowering the sovereignty aspirations of Indigenous communities.

Note
1. An email to O'Neil from criminal intelligence analyst Sofia Manolias with "E" Division notes that "the energy sector is directly filling in their incidents" in the SIR portal (RCMP 2013-5745: 204).

REFERENCES

ABL (Algonquins of Barriere Lake). 2016. *Mitchikanabikok Inik* (Algonquins of Barriere Lake). Newsletter from Chief and Council. Vol. 2, Issue 1 (May).

____. 2008. "Quebec judge imprisons Algonquin Chief for two months for peaceful protest: Crown asks for one year to send 'clear message' to impoverished community." Press release. Dec. 10.

____. 1992. Declaration and Petition.

____. 1989a. Letter to Sam Elkas, Québec Minister of Public Safety. Nov. 8.

____. 1989b. Letter to Albert Cote, Québec Minister of Forestry. Sept. 29.

____. 1988. Background notes, Canadian Environmental Network AGM, May 7. Ottawa, Canada.

Adams, Howard. 1995. *A Tortured People: The Politics of Colonization.* Penticton, BC: Theytus Books.

Aird, Rebecca. 1990. *Alienation of Traditional Lands through Conflicting Use.* Report prepared for the Algonquins of Barriere Lake.

Alfred, Taiaiake. 2005. *Wasase: Indigenous Pathways of Action and Freedom.* Peterborough: Broadview Press.

Alfred, Taiaiake, and Jeff Corntassel. 2005. "Being Indigenous: Resurgences against Contemporary Colonialism." *Government and Opposition,* 40: 597–614.

Alfred, Taiaiake, and Lana Lowe. 2005. "Warrior Societies in Contemporary Indigenous Communities." *Upping the Anti,* 2: 83–103.

Amoore, Louise. 2011. "Data Derivatives: On the Emergence of a Security Risk Calculus for Our Times." *Theory, Culture & Society,* 28, 6: 24–43.

Anaya, James. 2014. "Report of the Special Rapporteur on the Rights of Indigenous Peoples, James Anaya, on the Situation of Indigenous peoples in Canada." United Nations. Human Rights Council, 27th session, May.

APTN National News. 2013a. "Elsipogtog Prepares to Confront SWN's Machinery." Nov. 13. ‹http://aptnnews.ca/2013/11/13/elsipogtog-prepares-confront-swns-machinery/›.

____. 2013b. "Heavy RCMP presence accompanies SWN's return." Nov. 12. ‹aptnnews.ca/2013/11/12/heavy-rcmp-presence-accompanies-swns-return/›.

____. 2013c. "Crown Land Belongs to the Government, Not to F*cking Natives." Oct. 17. ‹aptnnews.ca/2013/10/17/crown-land-belongs-to-the-government-not-to-fcking-natives›.

Asch, Michael. 2014. *On Being Here to Stay: Treaties and Aboriginal Rights in Canada.* Toronto: University of Toronto Press.

Auditor General. 2013. *Report of the Auditor General of Canada.* "Chapter 8: Spending on the Public Security and Anti-Terrorism Initiative." Ottawa: Office of the Auditor General of Canada.

Backhouse, Constance. 1999. *Colour-Coded: A Legal History of Racism in Canada, 1900–1950.* Toronto: University of Toronto Press.

Barker, Adam. 2009. "The Contemporary Reality of Canadian Imperialism: Settler Colonialism and the Hybrid Colonial State." *The American Indian Quarterly,* 33, 3: 325–51.

Barker, Adam, Toby Rollo, and Emma Battell Lowman. 2016. "Settler Colonialism and the Consolidation of Canada in the Twentieth Century." In Edward Cavanagh and Lorenzo Veracini (eds.), *The Routledge Handbook of the History of Settler Colonialism.* Routledge.

Barrera, Jorge. 2014. "RCMP Tracked Movements of Indigenous Activist from 'Extremist' Group: Documents." *APTN,* Oct. 17. <http://aptnnews.ca/2014/10/17/rcmp-tracked-movements-indigenous-activist-extremist-group-documents/>.

Barron, Laurie. 1988. "The Indian pass system in the Canadian West, 1882-1935." *Prairie Forum,* 130: 25–42.

Battell Lowman, Emma, and Adam Barker. 2016. *Settler: Identity and Colonialism in 21st Century Canada.* Halifax: Fernwood Publishing.

Battiste, Marie. 2016. *Living Treaties: Narrating Mi'kmaw Treaty Relations.* Sydney, NS: Cape Breton University Press.

BCCLA (British Colombia Civil Liberties Association). 2014a. Letter to Shayna Stawicki, Registrar, Security Intelligence Review Committee. Feb. 6.

___. 2014b. Letter to Ian McPhail, Chair, Commission for Public Complaints Against the RCMP. Feb. 6.

Belleau, Lesley. 2014. "Pauwauwaein: Idle No More to The Indigenous Nationhood Movement." In The Kino-nda-niimi Collective (eds.), *The Winter We Danced: Voices from the Past, the Future, and the Idle No More Movement.* Winnipeg: ARP Books.

Bennett, Colin, Kevin Haggerty, David Lyon, and Valerie Steeves (eds.). 2014. *Transparent Lives: Surveillance in Canada.* Athabasca University Press.

Benvenuto, Jeff, Andrew Woolford, and Alexander Laban Hinton. 2015. "Introduction: Colonial Genocide in Indigenous North America." In *Colonial Genocide in Indigenous North America.* Durham: Duke University Press.

Bittner, Egon. 1990. *Aspects of Police Work.* Boston, MA: Northeastern University Press.

Blatchford, Christie. 2011. *Helpless: Caledonia's Nightmare of Fear and Anarchy, and How the Law Failed All of Us.* Toronto: Anchor Canada.

Boldt, Menno. 1993. *Surviving as Indians: The Challenge of Self-Government.* Toronto: Toronto University Press.

Borrows, John. 2016. *Freedom and Indigenous Constitutionalism.* Toronto: University of Toronto Press.

___. 2015. "The Durability of Terra Nullius: Tsilhqot'in Nation v. British Columbia." *UBC Law Review,* 48: 701–42.

___. 2005. "Crown and Aboriginal Occupations of Land: A History & Comparison." Research paper commissioned by the Ipperwash Inquiry, Ontario, Canada.

Bowles, Paul, and Henry Veltmeyer. 2014. *The Answer Is Still No: Voices of Pipeline Resistance.* Halifax and Winnipeg: Fernwood Publishing.

Boykoff, Jules. 2007. *Beyond Bullets: The Suppression of Dissent in the United States.* Oakland: AK Press.

Brooks, Mark. 2014. "The Cautionary Tale of Kalamazoo." *Alternatives Journal,* 40, 1.

Brownlee, Jamie, and Kevin Walby (eds.). 2015. *Access to Information and Social Justice in Canada.* Winnipeg: Arbiter Ring.

Canada. 2009a. *National Strategy for Critical Infrastructure.* Ottawa: Government of Canada.

___. 2009b. *Action Plan for Critical Infrastructure.* Ottawa: Government of Canada.

Canadian National Railway Company v Plain. 2013. ONSC 4806.

Cannon, Lawrence. 2008. "Précisions aux Algonquins." *Le Droit,* Sept. 22: 17.

Carter, Sarah. 1990. *Lost Harvests: Prairie Indian Reserve Farmers and Government Policy.* Montreal: McGill-Queen's University Press.

Cohen, Stan. 2002. *Folk Devils and Moral Panics* (third edition). New York: Routledge.

Comack, Elizabeth. 2012. *Racialized Policing: Aboriginal People's Encounters with the Police.* Halifax and Winnipeg: Fernwood Publishing.

Coulthard, Glen. 2015. "The Colonialism of the Present" (by Andrew Bard Epstein). *Jacobin Magazine,* Jan. 13.

___. 2014a. *Red Skin, White Masks: Rejecting the Colonial Politics of Recognition.* Minneapolis: University of Minnesota Press.

___. 2014b. "#IdleNoMore in Historical Context." In The Kino-nda-niimi Collective (eds.), *The Winter We Danced: Voices from the Past, the Future, and the Idle No More Movement.* Winnipeg: ARP Books.

___. 2007. "Subjects of Empire: Indigenous Peoples and the 'Politics of Recognition' in Canada." *Contemporary Political Theory,* 6, 4: 437–60.

Cox, Ethan. 2014. "Scapegoat for a Movement?" In The Kino-nda-niimi Collective (eds.), *The Winter We Danced: Voices from the Past, the Future, and the Idle No More Movement.* Winnipeg: ARP Books.

Crosby, Andrew and Jeffrey Monaghan. 2016. "Settler Colonialism and the Policing of Idle No More." *Social Justice,* 43, 2: 37–57.

___. 2012. "Settler Governmentality and the Algonquin of Barriere Lake." *Security Dialogue,* 43, 5: 420–37.

Crosby, Andy. 2017. "The Truth about Treaties: Internal Government Documents Reveal Canada's Position at the Negotiating Table." *Briarpatch Magazine,* 46, 4: 20–24.

d'Errico, Peter. 2010. *Jeffrey Amherst and Smallpox Blankets: Lord Jeffrey Amherst's Letters Discussing Germ Warfare Against American Indians.* ‹http://www.umass.edu/legal/derrico/amherst/lord_jeff.html›.

Dafnos, Tia. 2014. "Negotiating Colonial Encounters: (Un)mapping the Policing of Indigenous Peoples' Protests in Canada." PhD thesis, York University.

Dafnos, Tia, Scott Thompson, and Martin French. 2016. "Surveillance and the Colonial Dream: Canada's Surveillance of Indigenous Self-Determination." In Randy Lippert, Kevin Walby, Ian Warren, Darren Palmer (eds.), *National Security, Surveillance and Terror.* Springer International Publishing.

Deloria, Vine, and Clifford M. Lytle. 1984. *The Nations Within: The Past and Future of American Indian Sovereignty.* Austin: University of Texas Press.

Di Gangi, Peter. 2003. *Algonquins of Barriere Lake Man-Made Impacts on the Community and Fish & Wildlife, 1870–1979.* Ottawa: Sicani Research & Advisory Services.

Diabo, Russ, and Shiri Pasternak. 2011. "Canada Has Had First Nations Under Surveillance: Harper Government Has Prepared for First Nations 'Unrest.'" *First Nations Strategic Bulletin,* 9, 1–5 (January–May).

Earl, Jennifer. 2011. "Political Repression: Iron Fists, Velvet Gloves, and Diffuse Control." *Annual Review of Sociology,* 37: 261–84.

Elsipogtog v New Brunswick (Attorney General). 2013. Queen's Bench of New Brunswick. FM-54-13.

Ericson, Richard. 1982. *Reproducing Order: A Study of Police Patrol Work.* Toronto: University of Toronto Press.

___. 1981. *Making Crime: A Study of Detective Work.* Toronto: University of Toronto Press.

Fassin, Didier. 2013. *Enforcing Order: An Ethnography of Urban Policing.* London: Polity.

FNSB (First Nations Strategic Bulletin). 2011. Volume 9, Issues 1–5 (January–May).

Forcese, Craig, and Kent Roach. 2015. *False Security: The Radicalization of Canadian Anti-Terrorism.* Montreal: Irwin Law.

Forestell, Harry. 2013. "NB Newsmaker June 4." *CBC News,* June 4. <http://www.cbc.ca/player/play/2389480104>.

Foucault, Michel. 1977. *Discipline and Punish: The Birth of the Prison.* New York: Vintage.

Fountain, Tim. 2016. "What Did Justin Trudeau Say about Canada's History of Colonialism?" *CBC News online,* April 22. <www.cbc.ca/news/indigenous/trudeau-colonialism-comments-1.3549405>.

Francis, Daniel. 1993. *The Imaginary Indian: The Image of the Indian in Canadian Culture.* Vancouver: Arsenal Pulp Press.

Galloway, Gloria, and Oliver Moore. 2013. "Idle No More Protests, Blockades Spread Across Country." *Globe and Mail,* Jan. 16. <theglobeandmail.com/news/politics/idle-no-more-protests-blockades-spread-across-country/article7406990/>.

Gehl, Lynn. 2014. *The Truth that Wampum Tells: My Debwewin on the Algonquin Land Claims Process.* Halifax and Winnipeg: Fernwood Publishing.

Girard, Richard, and Tanya Roberts Davis. 2012. *Out on the Tar Sands Mainline: Mapping Enbridge's Web of Pipelines: A Corporate Profile of Pipeline Company Enbridge.* Ottawa: The Polaris Institute.

Gitxaala Nation v Canada. 2016. FCA 187.

Global News. 2013. "Judge Rules Not to Extend SWN Injunction Against Shale Gas Protesters." Oct. 21. <globalnews.ca/news/915092/judge-rules-not-to-extend-swn-injunction-against-shale-gas-protesters/>.

Graybill, Andrew. 2007. *Policing the Great Plains: Rangers, Mounties, and the North American Frontier, 1875–1910.* Lincoln: University of Nebraska Press.

Gregory, Derek. 2004. *The Colonial Present: Afghanistan, Palestine, and Iraq.* Malden, MA: Blackwell.

Groves, Tim. 2012. "Canada's Spy Groups Divulge Secret Intelligence to Energy Companies." *The Dominion,* 85: 4–5.

Gunton, Thomas, and Sean Broadbent. 2013. *A Spill Risk Assessment of the Enbridge Northern Gateway Project.* School of Resource and Environmental Management: Simon Fraser University.

Hacking, Ian. 1995. "The Looping Effects of Human Kinds." In Dan Sperber, David Premack and Ann James Premack (eds.), *Causal Cognition: A Multidisciplinary Debate.* Gloucestershire: Clarendon Press.

Haggerty, Kevin. 2001. *Making Crime Count.* Toronto: University of Toronto Press.

Hall, Anthony. 2003. *American Empire and the Fourth World: The Bowl with One Spoon.* Montreal: McGill-Queen's University Press.

Hereditary Chiefs of the Likhts'amisyu Clan. 2010. "Enbridge representatives are issued a final trespass notice by the Likhts'amisyu Clan of the Wet'suwet'en Nation." *Vancouver Media Co-op,* August 26. ‹vancouver.mediacoop.ca/newsrelease/4525›.

Hixson, Walter. 2013. *American Settler Colonialism: A History.* New York: Palgrave Macmillan.

Horn, Kahn-Tineta. 1983. *A Review of the Band Election Process Under Section 74 and the Customary Systems Now Existing on Indian Reserves.* Ottawa: Department of Indian and Northern Affairs.

Howe, Miles. 2015. *Debriefing Elsipogtog: The Anatomy of a Struggle.* Halifax and Winnipeg: Fernwood Publishing.

___. 2013a. "SWN Issued Notice of Eviction by Geptin of District Grand Council." *Dominionpaper.ca,* July 29. ‹halifax.mediacoop.ca/story/swn-issued-notice-eviction-geptin-district-grand-c/18423›.

___. 2013b. "'I Can Honestly Say I've Never Been Consulted'." *Dominionpaper.ca,* June 15. ‹halifax.mediacoop.ca/audio/i-can-honestly-say-ive-never-been-consulted/17998›.

Idle No More. n.d.a. "The Story." ‹www.idlenomore.ca/story›.

___. n.d.b. "The Vision." ‹www.idlenomore.ca/vision›.

Idle No More and Defenders of the Land. 2014. "Idle No More Solidarity Spring: A Call to Action." In The Kino-nda-niimi Collective (eds.), *The Winter We Danced: Voices from the Past, the Future, and the Idle No More Movement.* Winnipeg: ARP Books.

INAC. 2013. *Fact Sheet — Progress Report on Aboriginal and Treaty Rights Negotiations in the Maritimes and the Gaspésie.* Ottawa: Department of Indian and Northern Affairs.

Jackson, Kenneth. 2012. "Sarnia Rail Blockade Enters Fourth Day, Police Have No Intention of Shutting It Down: Mayor." *APTN National News,* Dec. 24. ‹http://aptnnews.ca/2012/12/24/sarnia-rail-blockade-enters-fourth-day-police-have-no-intention-of-shutting-it-down-mayor/›.

Jennings, John. 1986. "The North West Mounted Police and Indian Policy after the 1885 Rebellion." In Laurie Barron and James B. Waldram (eds.), *1885 and After: Native Society in Transition.* Regina: Canadian Plains Research Center, University of Regina.

Johnston, David. 2013. "Speech from the Throne to Open the Second Session Forty First Parliament of Canada." Oct. 16. <https://lop.parl.ca/ParlInfo/Documents/ThroneSpeech/41-2-e.html>.

Kappo, Tanya and Hayden King. 2014. "'Our People Were Glowing': An Interview with Tanya Kappo." In The Kino-nda-niimi Collective (eds.), *The Winter We Danced: Voices from the Past, the Future, and the Idle No More Movement.* Winnipeg: ARP Books.

The Kino-nda-niimi Collective. 2014. "Idle No More: The Winter We Danced." In The Kino-nda-niimi Collective (eds.), *The Winter We Danced: Voices from the Past, the Future, and the Idle No More Movement.* Winnipeg: ARP Books.

Kinsman, Gary, and Patrizia Gentile. 2010. *The Canadian War on Queers: National Security as Sexual Regulation.* Vancouver: UBC Press.

Kundnani, Arun. 2014. *The Muslims Are Coming! Islamophobia, Extremism, and the Domestic War on Terror.* New York: Verso Books.

Lane, James. 2013. "SWN Lawyer Meets with Warrior Chief John Levi, First Nations Elsipogtog & Anti-Fracking Activists." *YouTube*, Nov. 11. <youtube.com/watch?v=X8DaXQT-a2M>.

Larsen, Mike, and Kevin Walby (eds.). 2012. *Brokering Access: Politics, Power and Freedom of Information in Canada.* Vancouver: UBC Press.

Lawrence, Bonita. 2012. *Fractured Homeland: Federal Recognition and Algonquin Identity in Ontario.* Vancouver: UBC Press.

___. 2004. *"Real" Indians and Others: Mixed-Blood Urban Native Peoples and Indigenous Nationhood.* University of Nebraska Press.

Leese, Matthias. 2014. "The New Profiling: Algorithms, Black Boxes, and the Failure of Anti-Discriminatory Safeguards in the European Union." *Security Dialogue*, 45, 5: 494–511.

Linden, Sidney B. 2007. *Report of the Ipperwash Inquiry.* Toronto: Ipperwash Inquiry.

Livesey, Bruce. 2016. "Special Report: House of Irving." *National Observer*, July 21. <ww.nationalobserver.com/special-reports/house-irving>.

Ljunggren, David. 2009. "Every G20 Nation Wants to Be Canada, PM Insists." *Reuters*, Sept. 25. <www.reuters.com/article/2009/09/26/columns-us-g20-canada-advantages-idUSTRE58P05Z20090926>.

Lopez, Franklin. 2015. "Unist'ot'en Camp: Holding Their Ground Against Oil & Gas Pipelines." Video recording. Al Jazeera Media Network. AJplus.net.

___. 2014. "How to Stop an Oil and Gas Pipeline: The Unist'ot'en Camp Resistance." Video recording. Al Jazeera Media Network. AJplus.net.

___. 2011. "Oil Gateway: Stop the Flows Dispatch #1." Video recording. submedia.tv.

Lukacs, Martin. 2009. "Top Diplomat's Report to Minister Laid Out Strategy for Government Subversion of Algonquin Community." *ZNet*, Sept. 1. <zcomm.org/znetarticle/top-diplomat-s-report-to-minister-laid-out-strategy-for-government-subversion-of-algonquin-community-by-martin-lukacs/>.

Luscombe, Alex, and Kevin Walby. 2017. "Theorizing Freedom of Information: The Live Archive, Obfuscation, and Actor-Network." *Government Information Quarterly.* Early access: ‹http://www.sciencedirect.com/science/article/pii/S0740624X17301636›.

Lyon, David. 2006. "Surveillance, Power and Everyday Life." In Robin Mansell (ed.), *Oxford Handbook of Information and Communication Technologies.* Oxford University Press.

MacDonald, David. 2011. *The Cost of 9/11: Tracking the Creation of a National Security Establishment in Canada.* Ottawa: Rideau Institute.

Mackey, Eva. 2016. *Unsettled Expectations: Uncertainty, Land, and Settler Decolonization.* Halifax and Winnipeg: Fernwood Publishing.

___. 2014. "Unsettling Expectations: (Un)certainty, Settler States of Feeling, Law, and Decolonization." *Canadian Journal of Law and Society*, 29, 2: 235–52.

___. 2002. *The House of Difference: Cultural Politics and National Identity in Canada.* Toronto: University of Toronto Press.

Manuel, Arthur. 2015. *Unsettling Canada: A National Wake-Up Call.* Toronto: Between the Lines.

___. 2008. "Arthur Manuel's Submission to the United Nations." U.N. Economic and Social Concil Permanent Forum on Indigenous Issues, 7th Session, New York (April 21–May 2, 2008). Joint Submission by the KI and the Algonquins of Barriere Lake.

Masty, Benjamin. 2017. "The Journey of Nishiyuu." Video recording. Agoodah Pictures.

Matchewan, Jean Maurice. 1989. "Algonquins North of the Ottawa: Our Long Battle to Create a Sustainable Future." In Boyce Richardson (ed.), *Drumbeat: Anger and Renewal in Indian Country.* Toronto: Summerhill Press.

Matchewan, Norman. 2008. "Lac Barrière: Matchewan Réagit." *Le Droit*, Sept. 23. ‹http://www.barrierelakesolidarity.org/2008/10/community-response-to-cannons-le-droit.html›.

Mazowita, Benjamin, and Jacob Greenland. 2015. *Police Resources in Canada, 2015.* Ottawa: Statistics Canada. ‹http://www.statcan.gc.ca/pub/85-002-x/2016001/article/14323-eng.htm›.

McAdam, Sylvia. 2015. *Nationhood Interrupted: Revitalizing Nêhiyaw Legal Systems.* Saskatoon: Purich Publishing Limited.

McMillan, L. Jane, Janelle Young, and Molly Peters. 2013. "Commentary: The 'Idle No More' Movement in Eastern Canada." *Canadian Journal of Law and Society*, 28, 3: 429–31.

Mi'kmaq Warrior Society. 2013. Letter to Steven L. Mueller, President & Chief Executive Officer, swn Energy. Oct. 7.

Miles, Robert. 1989. *Racism.* London: Routledge.

Millar, Matthew. 2013. "Harper Government's Extensive Spying on Anti-Oilsands Groups Revealed in fois." *Vancouver Observer*, Nov. 19. ‹https://www.vancouverobserver.com/politics/harper-governments-extensive-spying-anti-oilsands-groups-revealed-fois›.

Miller, James Rodger. 1989. *Skyscrapers Hide the Heavens: A History of Indian-White*

Relations in Canada (revised edition). Toronto: University of Toronto Press.

Milloy, John S. 1983. "The Early Indian Acts: Developmental Strategy and Constitutional Change." In Ian A.L. Getty and Antoine S. Lussier (eds.), *As Long as the Sun Shines and the Water Flows: A Reader in Canadian Native Studies.* Vancouver: University of British Columbia Press.

Monaghan, Jeffrey. 2017. *Security Aid: Canada and the Development Regime of Security.* Toronto: University of Toronto Press.

___. 2014. "Security Traps and Discourses of Radicalization: Mapping the Surveillance of Muslims in Canada." *Surveillance and Society,* 12, 4: 485–501.

___. 2013a. "Mounties in the Frontier: Circulations, Anxieties, and Myths of Settler Colonial Policing in Canada." *Journal of Canadian Studies,* 47, 1: 122–48.

___. 2013b. "Settler Governmentality and Racializing Surveillance in Canada's North-West." *Canadian Journal of Sociology,* 38, 4: 487–508.

Monaghan, Jeffrey, and Adam Molnar. 2016. "Radicalisation Theories, Policing Practices, and 'the Future of Terrorism?'" *Critical Studies on Terrorism,* 9, 3: 393–413.

Monaghan, Jeffrey, and Kevin Walby. 2017. "Surveillance of Environment Movements in Canada: Critical Infrastructure Protection and the Petro-Security Apparatus." *Contemporary Justice Review,* 20, 1: 51–70.

___. 2012. "Making Up 'Terror Identities': Security Intelligence, Canada's Integrated Threat Assessment Centre, and Social Movement Suppression." *Policing and Society,* 22, 2: 133–55.

Monahan, Torin. 2010. *Surveillance in the Time of Insecurity.* Rutgers University Press.

Monahan, Torin, and Neal A. Palmer. 2009. "The Emerging Politics of DHS Fusion Centers." *Security Dialogue,* 40, 6: 617–36.

Morrison, James. 2005. *Algonquin History in the Ottawa River Watershed.* Ottawa: Sicani Research & Advisory Services.

Monture-Angus, Patricia. 1999. *Journeying Forward: Dreaming First Nations' Independence.* Halifax and Winnipeg: Fernwood Publishing.

Moore, Jen, Roch Tasse, Chris Jones, and Esperanza Moreno. 2015. *In the National Interest? Criminalization of Land Defenders in the Americas.* Ottawa: MiningWatch Canada and International Civil Liberties Monitoring Group.

Nepinak, Derek. 2014. "Transforming Unity: An Interview with Assembly of Manitoba Chiefs Grand Chief Derek Nepinak" (by Leah Gazan). In The Kinonda-niimi Collective (eds.), *The Winter We Danced: Voices from the Past, the Future, and the Idle No More Movement.* Winnipeg: ARP Books.

Nicholas, Clifton. 2014. "No Fracking Way!" Video recording. Devil Dog Productions.

Nottaway, Benjamin. 2007. Letter from Acting Chief Benjamin Nottaway to Honourable Chuck Strahl. Nov. 26.

Notzke, Claudia. 1995. *The Barriere Lake Trilateral Agreement.* A Report Prepared for the Royal Commission on Aboriginal Peoples — Land, Resource and Environment Regimes Project. Barriere Lake: Barriere Lake Indian Government.

Nova Scotia Council Minutes. 1749. Selections from the Private Documents of the Province of Nova Scotia, October 1. ‹https://archive.org/stream/

selectionsfrompuoonova#page/n370/mode/1up>.

O'Neil, Peter. 2013. "B.C. Chief Urges Halt to Economic Protests: Minister Joins in Appeal to Avoid Blockades." *Vancouver Sun*, Jan. 15.

Obomsawin, Alanis. 2002. *Is the Crown at War with Us?* Documentary. Canada: National Film Board of Canada.

___. 1984. *Incident at Restigouche.* Documentary. Canada: National Film Board of Canada.

Oliver, Joe. 2012. "An Open Letter from Natural Resources Minister Joe Oliver." *Globe and Mail*, Jan. 9. <www.theglobeandmail.com/news/politics/an-open-letter-from-natural-resources-minister-joe-oliver/article4085663/>.

Palmater, Pamela. 2015. *Indigenous Nationhood: Empowering Grassroots Citizens.* Halifax and Winnipeg: Fernwood Publishing.

___. 2014. "Why Are We Idle No More?" In The Kino-nda-niimi Collective (eds.), *The Winter We Danced: Voices from the Past, the Future, and the Idle No More Movement.* Winnipeg: ARP Books.

Paris, Max. 2013. "Energy Industry Letter Suggested Environmental Law Changes." *CBC News Online*, Jan. 9. <www.cbc.ca/news/politics/energy-industry-letter-suggested-environmental-law-changes-1.1346258>.

Park, Augustine. 2015. "Settler Colonialism and the Politics of Grief: Theorising a Decolonising Transitional Justice for Indian Residential Schools." *Human Rights Review*, 16, 3: 273–93.

Pasternak, Shiri. 2017. *Grounded Authority: The Algonquins of Barriere Lake Against the State.* University of Minnesota Press.

___. 2016. "The Fiscal Body of Sovereignty: To 'Make Live' in Indian Country." *Settler Colonial Studies*, 6,4: 317–38.

___. 2014. "Occupy(ed) Canada: The Political Economy of Indigenous Dispossession." In The Kino-nda-niimi Collective (eds.), *The Winter We Danced: Voices from the Past, the Future, and the Idle No More Movement.* Winnipeg: ARP Books.

___. 2013. "On Jurisdiction and Settler Colonialism: The Algonquins of Barriere Lake Against the Federal Land Claims Policy." PhD dissertation, University of Toronto.

Pasternak, Shiri, Sue Collis, and Tia Dafnos. 2013. "Criminalization at Tyendinaga: Securing Canada's Colonial Property Regime through Specific Land Claims." *Canadian Journal of Law and Society*, 28, 1: 65–81.

Patzer, Jeremy. 2014. "Residential School Harm and Colonial Dispossession." In Andrew Woolford, Jeff Benvenuto and Alexander Laban Hinton (eds.), *Colonial Genocide in North America.* Duke University Press.

Paul, Daniel N. 2000. *We Were Not the Savages: A Mi'kmaq Perspective on the Collision Between European and Native American Civilizations.* Halifax: Fernwood Publishing.

Pawlak, Patryk. 2009. "Network Politics in Transatlantic Homeland Security Cooperation." *Perspectives on European Politics and Society*, 10, 4: 560–81.

Poitras, Jacques. 2015. *Irving vs. Irving: Canada's Feuding Billionaires and the Stories They Won't Tell.* Toronto: Penguin Canada.

Preston, Jen. 2017. "Racial Extractivism and White Settler Colonialism: An Examination of the Canadian Tar Sands Mega-Projects." *Cultural Studies*, 31, 2–3: 353–75.

Proulx, Craig. 2014. "Colonizing Surveillance: Canada Constructs an Indigenous Terror Threat." *Anthropologica*, 56, 1: 83–100.

PSC (Public Safety Canada). 2016. *Our Security, Our Rights: National Security Green Paper Background Documents*. Ottawa: Public Safety Canada. <www.publicsafety. gc.ca/cnt/rsrcs/pblctns/ntnl-scrt-grn-ppr-2016-bckgrndr/ntnl-scrt-grn-ppr-2016-bckgrndr-en.pdf>.

Razack, Sherene. 2015. *Dying from Improvement: Inquests and Inquiries into Indigenous Deaths in Custody*. Toronto: University of Toronto Press.

RCAP (Royal Commission on Aboriginal Peoples). 1996. *Final Report of the Royal Commission on Aboriginal Peoples*. Ottawa: Canada Communications Group.

Richardson, Boyce. 1993. *People of Terra Nullius*. Vancouver: Douglas & McIntyre.

Rifkin, Mark. 2013. "Settler Common Sense." *Settler Colonial Studies*, 3, 3–4: 322–40.

Roache, Trina. 2014. "2 Mi'kmaq Warriors Sentenced to 15 Months over Elsipogtog Fracking Fight." *APTN*, July 30. <aptn.ca/news/2014/07/30/2-mikmaq-warriors-sentenced-15-months-elsipogtog-fracking-fight/>.

Robins, Geoff. 2013. "First Nations man faces $16k bill for 'Idle No More' blockade on CN railway." *The Canadian Press*, July 25. <https://beta.theglobeandmail.com/news/national/first-nations-man-faces-16k-bill-for-idle-no-more-blockade-on-cn-railway/article13444178/>.

Sangster, Joan. 2002. "'She Is Hostile to Our Ways': First Nations Girls Sentenced to the Ontario Training School for Girls, 1933–1960." *Law and History Review*, 20, 1: 59–96.

Save the Fraser Declaration. 2010. <https://savethefraser.ca/Fraser-Declaration-May2013.pdf>.

Scott, Dayna Nadine. 2013. "Commentary: The Forces That Conspire to Keep Us 'Idle'." *Canadian Journal of Law and Society*, 28, 3: 425–28.

Security of Canada Information Sharing Act (SCISA). 2015. Ottawa. Government of Canada.

Shenkier, Elise, and Thomas Meredith. 1997. "The Forests at Barriere Lake: Euro-American and Indigenous Perceptions of the Natural Environment." In Cragg Wesley, Greenbaum Allan and Alex Wellington (eds.), *Canadian Issues in Environmental Ethics*. Toronto: Broadview Press.

Shewell, Hugh. 2004. *"Enough to Keep Them Alive": Indian Welfare in Canada, 1873–1965*. Toronto: University of Toronto Press.

Sinclair, Raven. 2017. "The Indigenous Child Removal System in Canada: An Examination of Legal Decision-Making and Racial Bias." *First Peoples Child and Family Review*, 11, 2: 8–18.

Simpson, Audra. 2014. *Mohawk Interruptus: Political Life Across the Borders of Settler States*. Durham: Duke University Press.

Simpson, Leanne Betasamosake. 2014. "Fish Broth & Fasting." In The Kino-nda-niimi Collective (eds.), *The Winter We Danced: Voices from the Past, the Future, and the Idle No More Movement*. Winnipeg: ARP Books.

___. 2013a. "Another Story from Elsipogtog." *TheTyee.ca*, Oct. 21. ‹https://thetyee. ca/Opinion/2013/10/21/Elsipogtog/›.

___. 2013b. "Dancing the World into Being: A Conversation with Idle No More's Leanne Simpson" (by Naomi Klein). *Yes Magazine*, March 5. ‹http://www. yesmagazine.org/peace-justice/dancing-the-world-into-being-a-conversation-with-idle-no-more-leanne-simpson›.

Sium, Aman, Chandni Desai, and Eric Ritskes. 2012. "Towards the 'Tangible Unknown': Decolonization and the Indigenous Future." *Decolonization: Indigeneity, Education & Society*, 1, 1: I–XIII.

Skene, Mathieu. 2013. "Elsipogtog: The Fire over Water." Video recording. Fault Lines, Al Jazeera America.

Skolnick, Jerome. 1966. *Justice without Trial: Law Enforcement in Democratic Society*. Center for the Study of Law and Society: University of California, Berkeley.

Smith, Keith. 2009. *Liberalism, Surveillance, and Resistance: Indigenous Communities in Western Canada, 1877–1927*. Athabasca University Press.

Snelgrove, Corey, Rita Dhamoon, and Jeff Corntassel. 2014. "Unsettling Settler Colonialism: The Discourse and Politics of Settlers, and Solidarity with Indigenous Nations." *Decolonization: Indigeneity, Education & Society*, 3, 2: 1–32.

Stiegman, Martha (director). 2008. "Barriere Lake Anishabe Kachigwasin."

Swift, Anthony, and Nathan Lemphers, Susan Casey-Lefkowitz, Katie Terhune, and Danielle Droitsch. 2011. *Pipeline and Tanker Trouble: The Impact to British Columbia's Rivers, and Pacific Coastline from Tar Sands Oil Transport*. National Resource Defense Council.

Thobani, Sunera. 2007. *Exalted Subjects: Studies in the Making of Race and Nation in Canada*. Toronto: University of Toronto Press.

Tobias, John. 1983. "Canada's Subjugation of the Plains Cree, 1879–1885." *Canadian Historical Review*, 64, 4: 519–48.

Toledano, Michael. 2015. "In British Columbia, Indigenous Group Blocks Pipeline Development." *Aljazeera America*, Aug. 20. ‹http://america.aljazeera.com/ articles/2015/8/20/in-canada-police.html›.

Tuck, Eve. 2009. "Suspending Damage: A Letter to Communities." *Harvard Educational Review*, 79, 3: 409–28.

Turner, Dale Antony. 2006. *This Is Not a Peace Pipe: Towards a Critical Indigenous Philosophy*. Toronto: University of Toronto Press.

Uechi, Jenny. 2012. "Pushing Enbridge Pipeline Through without First Nations' Consent?" *Vancouver Observer*, June 8. ‹https://www.vancouverobserver.com/ politics/pushing-enbridge-pipeline-through-without-first-nations-consent›.

Unist'ot'en Declaration. 2015. ‹https://unistoten.camp/press-release-unistoten-clan-enacts-declaration-as-law/›.

Veltmeyer, Henry, and James Petras. 2014. *The New Extractivism: A Post-Neoliberal Development Model or Imperialism of the Twenty-First Century?* London: Zed Books.

Veracini, Lorenzo. 2015. *The Settler Colonial Present*. London: Palgrave Macmillan.

___. 2010. *Settler Colonialism: A Theoretical Overview*. London: Palgrave Macmillan.

Vizenor, Gerald Robert. 2000. *Fugitive Poses: Native American Indian Scenes of Absence and Presence*. University of Nebraska Press.

Walden, Keith. 1982. *Visions of Order: The Canadian Mounties in Symbol and Myth.* Toronto: Butterworth.

Walia, Harsha. 2013. *Border Imperialism.* Oakland: AK Press.

Walters, Mark D. 2001. "Brightening the Covenant Chain: Aboriginal Treaty Meanings in Law and History after Marshall." *Dalhousie Law Journal,* 24: 75–138.

Ward, James Sakej. 2004. "The Mi'kmaq and the Right to Self Determination." *ĐELÁNEN: A Journal of Indigenous Governance,* 1, 1.

White, Alo. 2014. "The Sucker Punch of January 11." In The Kino-nda-niimi Collective (eds.), *The Winter We Danced: Voices from the Past, the Future, and the Idle No More Movement.* Winnipeg: ARP Books.

Willow, Anna. 2016. "Indigenous ExtrACTIVISM in Boreal Canada: Colonial Legacies, Contemporary Struggles and Sovereign Futures." *Humanities,* 5, 3.

Wilson, Dean, Kevin Haggerty, and Gavin Smith. 2011. "Theorizing Surveillance in Crime Control." *Theoretical Criminology,* 15, 3: 231–37.

Winnipeg Free Press. 2013. "Protesters End CN Rail Blockade Near Portage la Prairie." Jan. 16. <winnipegfreepress.com/local/portage-area-site-of-latest-native-protest-187079591.html>.

Wolfe, Patrick. 2006. "Settler Colonialism and the Elimination of the Native." *Journal of Genocide Research,* 8, 4: 387–409.

___. 1999. *Settler Colonialism and the Transformation of Anthropology: The Politics and Poetics of an Ethnographic Event.* London: Cassell.

Wood, Lesley. 2014. *Crisis and Control: The Militarization of Protest Policing.* Toronto: Between the Lines.

Woolford, Andrew. 2015. *This Benevolent Experiment: Indigenous Boarding Schools, Genocide, and Redress in Canada and the United States.* Lincoln: University of Nebraska Press.

Yinka Dene Alliance. 2011. "Oil Sands Export Ban: B.C. First Nations Unite to Declare Province-Wide Opposition to Crude Oil Pipeline and Tanker Expansion." Dec. 1.

INTERVIEWS

Russell Diabo. April 27, 2017. Phone interview.

Norman Matchwan. December 13, 2010. Ottawa, Ontario.

Casey Ratt. January 13, 2011. Phone interview.

Camil Simard. January 12, 2011. Phone interview.

Michel Thusky. January 24, 2012. Ottawa, Ontario.

Tony Wawatie. January 13, 2011. Phone interview.

ATIPs Cited

CSIS 2016-93
CSIS 2016-47
CSIS 2015-616
CSIS 2015-501
CSIS 2015-54
CSIS 2013-185
CSIS 2012-222
CSIS 2012-32
CSIS 2012-27
DND 2016-1403
DND 2014-1157
DND 2013-1238
DND 2013-679
DFO 2016-260
INAC A0240846
INAC 2017-311
INAC 2016-847
INAC 2016-765
INAC 2016-448
INAC 2016-324
INAC 2015-1603
INAC 2015-1438
INAC 2015-1265
INAC 2015-1156
INAC 2015-989
INAC 2014-1546
INAC 2013-1624
INAC 2013-1348
INAC 2013-719
INAC 2013-361
INAC 2012-1537
INAC 2012-1416
INAC 2012-1391
INAC 2012-1322
INAC 2012-88

INAC 2011-1703
INAC 2011-1387
INAC 2010-2705
INAC 2010-1809
NB-PS 2016a
NB-PS 2016b
NRCan 7040-13-094
NRCan 7040-12-214
PCO 2012-678
PCO 2013-898
PCO 2013-517
PCO 2013-226
PSC 2016-10
PSC 2015-345
PSC 2015-332
PSC 2015-104
PSC 2013-334
PSC 2013-160
RCMP 2016-8006
RCMP 2016-1140
RCMP 2015-9616
RCMP 2015-9455
RCMP 2015-8404
RCMP 2015-1447-3
RCMP 2013-07388
RCMP 2013-6936
RCMP 2013-6342
RCMP 2013-5745
RCMP 2013-5595
RCMP 2013-5506
RCMP 2013-1554
RCMP 2012-7489
RCMP 2012-7309
RCMP A008499

INDEX